The Voices and Rooms of European Bioethics

This book reflects on the many contributions made in, to and by European bioethics to date, from various disciplinary perspectives and in various locations. In so doing, the book advances understanding of the academic and social status of European bioethics as it is being supported and practised by disciplines such as philosophy, law, medicine and the social sciences. The European focus offers a valuable counterbalance to an often prominent US understanding of bioethics.

The volume is split into four parts. The first contains reflection on bioethics in the past, present and future, and also considers how comparison between countries and disciplines can enrich bioethical discourse. The second part looks at bioethics in particular locations and contexts, including the courtroom, the arts and society at large, while the third part explores the translation of the theories and concepts of bioethics into the clinical setting. The fourth and final section focuses on academic expressions of bioethics, as it is theorised in various disciplines and also as it is taught, whether in classrooms or at the patient's bedside.

As an interdisciplinary overview of the state of research in European bioethics, this book will be of great use and interest to scholars and students of bioethics, health law, medicine and human rights.

Richard Huxtable is Professor of Medical Ethics and Law and Deputy Director of the Centre for Ethics in Medicine, School of Social and Community Medicine, University of Bristol.

Ruud ter Meulen is Professor of Ethics in Medicine and Director of the Centre for Ethics in Medicine, School of Social and Community Medicine, University of Bristol.

Biomedical Law and Ethics Library
Series Editor: Sheila A. M. McLean

Scientific and clinical advances, social and political developments and the impact of healthcare on our lives raise profound ethical and legal questions. Medical law and ethics have become central to our understanding of these problems, and are important tools for the analysis and resolution of problems – real or imagined.

In this series, scholars at the forefront of biomedical law and ethics contribute to the debates in this area, with accessible, thought-provoking, and sometimes controversial, ideas. Each book in the series develops an independent hypothesis and argues cogently for a particular position. One of the major contributions of this series is the extent to which both law and ethics are utilised in the content of the books, and the shape of the series itself.

The books in this series are analytical, with a key target audience of lawyers, doctors, nurses, and the intelligent lay public.

Available titles:

Human Fertilisation and Embryology
Reproducing regulation
Kirsty Horsey & Hazel Biggs

Intention and Causation in Medical Non-killing
The impact of criminal law concepts on euthanasia and assisted suicide
Glenys Williams

Impairment and Disability
Law and Ethics at the Beginning and End of Life
Sheila McLean & Laura Williamson

Bioethics and the Humanities
Attitudes and Perceptions
Robin Downie & Jane Macnaughton

Defending the Genetic Supermarket
The law and ethics of selection the next generation
Colin Gavaghan

The Harm Paradox
Tort law and the unwanted child in an era of choice
Nicolette Priaulx

Assisted Dying
Reflections on the Need for Law Reform
Sheila McLean

Medicine, Malpractice and Misapprehensions
V.H. Harpwood

Euthanasia, Ethics and the Law
From the conflict to compromise
Richard Huxtable

The Best Interests of the Child in Healthcare
Sarah Elliston

Values in Medicine
What are we really doing to patients?
Donald Evans

Autonomy, Consent and the Law
Sheila A.M McLean

Healthcare Research Ethics and Law
Regulation, review and responsibility
Hazel Biggs

The Body in Bioethics
Alastair V. Campbell

Genomic Negligence
An interest in autonomy as the basis for novel negligence claims generated by genetic technology
Victoria Chico

Health Professionals and Trust
The cure for healthcare law and policy
Mark Henaghan

Medical Ethics in China
A transcultural interpretation
Jing-Bao Nie

Law, Ethics and Compromise at the Limits of Life
To treat or not to treat?
Richard Huxtable

Regulating Pre-Implantation Genetic Diagnosis
A comparative and theoretical analysis
Sheila A.M McLean & Sarah Elliston

Bioethics
Methods, theories, domains
Marcus Düwell

Human Population Genetic Research in Developing Countries
The Issue of Group Protection
Yue Wang

Coercive Care
Rights, law and policy
Bernadette McSherry & Ian Freckelton

Saviour Siblings
A relational approach to the welfare of the child in selective reproduction
Michelle Taylor-Sands

Stem Cell Research and the Collaborative Regulation of Innovation
Sarah Devaney

Forthcoming titles include:

The Jurisprudence of Pregnancy
Concepts of conflict, persons and property
Mary Neal

Regulating Risk
Values in health research governance
Shawn Harmon

The Umbilical Cord Blood Controversies in Medical Law
Karen Devine

The Legitimacy of Medical Treatment
What Role for the Medical Exception?
Sara Fovargue and Alexandra Mullock

Revisiting Landmark Cases in Medical Law
Shaun D. Pattinson

Revisiting the Regulation of Human Fertilisation and Embryology
Kirsty Horsey

The Ethical and Legal Consequences of Posthumous Reproduction
Lewis Browne

Pioneering Healthcare Law
Essays in Honour of Margaret Brazier
Catherine Stanton, Sarah Devaney, Anne-Marree Farrell and Alexandra Mullock

End of Life Decision Making for Critically Impaired Infants
Resource Allocation and Difficult Decisions
Neera Bhatia

Birth, Harm and the Role of Distributive Justice
Burdens, Blessings, Need and Desert
Alasdair Maclean

About the Series Editor

Professor Sheila McLean is International Bar Association Professor of Law and Ethics in Medicine and Director of the Institute of Law and Ethics in Medicine at the University of Glasgow.

The Voices and Rooms of European Bioethics

Edited by Richard Huxtable
and Ruud ter Meulen

LONDON AND NEW YORK

First published 2015
by Routledge
2 Park Square, Milton Park, Abingdon, Oxfordshire OX14 4RN

and by Routledge
711 Third Avenue, New York, NY 10017

First issued in paperback 2016

Routledge is an imprint of the Taylor & Francis Group, an informa business

© 2015 Selection and editorial matter, Richard Huxtable and Ruud ter Meulen; individual chapters, the contributors.

The right of Richard Huxtable and Ruud ter Meulen to be identified as editors of this work has been asserted by them in accordance with sections 77 and 78 of the Copyright, Designs and Patents Act 1988.

With the exception of Chapter 10, no part of this book may be reprinted or reproduced or utilised in any form or by any electronic, mechanical, or other means, now known or hereafter invented, including photocopying and recording, or in any information storage or retrieval system, without permission in writing from the publishers.

Chapter 10 of this book is available for free in PDF format as Open Access at www.tandfebooks.com. It has been made available under a Creative Commons Attribution-Non Commercial-No Derivatives 3.0 license.

Trademark notice: Product or corporate names may be trademarks or registered trademarks, and are used only for identification and explanation without intent to infringe.

British Library Cataloguing in Publication Data
A catalogue record for this book is available from the British Library

Library of Congress Cataloging-in-Publication Data
The voices and rooms of European bioethics / edited by Richard Huxtable, Ruud ter Meulen.
　　pages cm. — (Biomedical law and ethics library)
　Includes bibliographical references and index.
　1. Medical care—Law and legislation—Europe.　2. Medical care—Law and legislation—United States.　3. Medical genetics—Law and legislation—Europe.　4. Medical genetics—Law and legislation—United States.
5. Medical ethics—Europe.　6. Medical ethics—United States.
7. Bioethics—Europe.　8. Bioethics—United States.　I. Huxtable, Richard, editor.　II. Meulen, R. H. J. ter (Ruud H. J.), 1952– editor.
　KJC6206.V65 2015
　174.2094—dc23
　2014042332

ISBN 13: 978-1-138-70198-4 (pbk)
ISBN 13: 978-0-415-73719-7 (hbk)

Typeset in Garamond
by Apex CoVantage, LLC

Contents

Contributors	ix
Acknowledgements	xvii
Foreword by Renzo Pegoraro	xix

1 Introduction: all of the future exists in the past?   1
   RICHARD HUXTABLE

PART I
The voices and rooms of European bioethics, then and now   9

2 Medical ethics, then and now: a 40-year perspective   11
   ALASTAIR V. CAMPBELL

3 Bioethics past, present and future: a personal and narrative
   perspective from the European continent   17
   PAUL SCHOTSMANS

4 'Getting ethics': voices in harmony in bioethics   31
   RUTH CHADWICK

PART II
European bioethics in social rooms   41

5 Personalised medicine: priority setting and opportunity costs
   in European public health care systems   43
   JOCHEN VOLLMANN

6 Phage-ethics: a 'depth' bioethical reading of Sinclair Lewis's
   science novel *Arrowsmith*   53
   HUB ZWART

7 Voices carry? The voice of bioethics in the courtroom and
   the voice of law in bioethics   73
   RICHARD HUXTABLE AND SUZANNE OST

8 A (social) room with a view (to the future): advance decisions
   and the problem of personhood   87
   TOM HAYES

PART III
European bioethics in clinical rooms   103

9 Physicians' perspectives on patient preferences and advance
   directives in England and France: other countries,
   other requirements?   105
   RUTH HORN

10 'You don't need proof when you've got instinct!': gut feelings
   and some limits to parental authority   120
   GILES BIRCHLEY

11 Beyond listening or telling: moral case deliberation as a
   hermeneutic approach to clinical ethics support   136
   SUZANNE METSELAAR, MARGREET STOLPER AND
   GUY WIDDERSHOVEN

12 Authority, markets and society: three possible foundations for
   European bioethics   148
   ANGUS DAWSON

PART IV
European bioethics in academic rooms   157

13 Medical ethics in medical classrooms: from theory to practice 159
   WING MAY KONG

14 Teaching medical students: more room for an ethical
   'differential analysis', please?   180
   ROUVEN PORZ AND ANDREAS E. STUCK

15 Bioethics in academic rooms: hearing other voices, living in
   other rooms   192
   RAYMOND G. DE VRIES

Index   207

Contributors

Giles Birchley qualified as a specialist children's nurse in 2000 and spent almost a decade working in children's intensive care. He completed his master's degree in Health Care Ethics and Law in 2010, and was joint winner of the Philosophy of Nursing Postgraduate Essay Prize the same year. He began a doctorate in medical ethics at the University of Bristol in 2012, having won a prestigious Wellcome Trust fellowship in biomedical ethics for clinicians. He is involved in teaching ethics to doctors and nurses, as well as in clinical ethics consultation. His past research has examined the role of nurses in end-of-life care and the place of conscience in medical practice. His current research interest is in the ethical and legal aspects of children's medical care and the role of the family.

Alastair V. Campbell is the Chen Su Lan Centennial Professor of Medical Ethics and Director of the Centre for Biomedical Ethics in the Yong Loo Lin School of Medicine, National University of Singapore. Previously he was Professor of Ethics in Medicine, University of Bristol, UK. He is a former President of the International Association of Bioethics (IAB), a recipient of the HK Beecher Award, elected Fellow of the Hastings Center, elected Corresponding Fellow of the Royal Society of Edinburgh and Honorary Vice-President of the Institute of Medical Ethics (IME) in the UK. His recent books include *Medical Ethics* (with Jones and Gillett, 3rd edition, 2005, Oxford University Press), *The Body in Bioethics* (2009, Routledge) and *Bioethics: The Basics* (2013, Routledge). He was formerly chair of the Ethics and Governance Council of UK Biobank and Vice-Chair of the UK Retained Organs Commission. Professor Campbell is currently a member of the Bioethics Advisory Committee to the Singapore Government and of Singapore's National Medical Ethics Committee of the Ministry of Health.

Ruth Chadwick is Professor of Bioethics at the University of Manchester. From 2002–2013 she directed the ESRC Centre for Economic and Social Aspects of Genomics (Cesagen). She co-edits *Bioethics* and *Life Sciences, Society and Policy* and has served on the Council of the Human Genome Organisation, the Panel of Eminent Ethical Experts of the Food and Agriculture

Organisation of the United Nations (FAO) and the UK Advisory Committee on Novel Foods and Processes (ACNFP). She is a Fellow of the Academy of Social Sciences, of the Hastings Center, New York; of the Learned Society of Wales; of the Royal Society of Arts; and of the Society of Biology. In 2005 she won the World Technology Network Award for Ethics.

Angus Dawson is Professor of Public Health Ethics and Head of Medicine, Ethics, Society and History (MESH) at the University of Birmingham, UK. His background is in philosophy, but he has specialised in teaching ethics to health care professionals and medical students. His main research interests are in public health ethics (particularly vaccinations and issues related to lifestyle choices) and the use of empirical evidence in moral arguments (particularly in relation to problems in gaining informed consent in clinical trials). He is joint Editor-in-Chief of the journal *Public Health Ethics* and joint Coordinator of the International Association of Bioethics' Public Health Ethics Network (InterPHEN). He has been involved in research projects funded by the Centers for Disease and Control and Prevention, World Health Organisation, European Union, Wellcome Trust and the Public Health Agency of Canada on a range of issues mainly related to public health ethics. He has been editor or co-editor of four collections of original papers mainly on topics in public health ethics, including (with Marcel Verweij) *Prevention, Ethics, & Public Health* (2007, Oxford University Press) and *Public Health Ethics: Key Concepts and Issues in Policy and Practice* (2011, Cambridge University Press).

Raymond G. de Vries is Professor, Center for Bioethics and Social Sciences in Medicine, the Department of Obstetrics and Gynecology, the Department of Medical Education and the Department of Sociology at the University of Michigan, Ann Arbor. He is also Professor at University of Maastricht (in affiliation with the Academie Verloskunde Maastricht/Hogeschool Zuyd). He is the author of *A Pleasing Birth: Midwifery and Maternity Care in the Netherlands* (2005, Temple University Press), and co-editor of *The View from Here: Bioethics and the Social Sciences* (2007, Blackwell) and *Qualitative Methods in Health Research* (2010, Sage). In 2013, he co-edited a special issue of *Social Science and Medicine* that examined how bioethics is shaped by social and cultural forces. He is currently working on a critical social history of bioethics. He is also involved in research on: the regulation of science; international research ethics; the difficulties of informed consent; bioethics and the problem of suffering; and the social, ethical and policy issues associated with childbirth, including the use of electronic foetal monitoring and women's choice of place of birth.

Tom Hayes is a Lecturer in the School of Law and Politics in Cardiff University. His forthcoming doctoral thesis examines the development of the advance decisions to refuse medical treatment (sometimes referred to as 'living wills') using Michel Foucault's work on governmentality. He has published work on advance decisions to refuse medical treatment and on organ transplantation law. In 2013, Tom went on a DAAD-funded research visit to the Institut für Soziologie in the Goethe-Universität Frankfurt, where he conducted research into the relationship between advance decisions to refuse treatment and the ageing population. Earlier in 2013, Tom was selected to participate in a workshop on the organ donor shortage in the Ludwig-Maximilians-Universität in Munich. Tom has presented his work in the UK, Europe and the USA. He teaches medical law and criminal law.

Ruth Horn is an Ethics and Society Wellcome Trust Fellow based at the ETHOX Centre, University of Oxford. Ruth is currently carrying out comparative research on advance directives in England, France and Germany. Prior to her work at ETHOX, Ruth worked at the Centre for Ethics in Medicine, University of Bristol, on a project comparing advance directives (in legal theory and clinical practice) in England and France; that study was funded by the Marie Curie IEF Fellowship Programme of the European Commission. Ruth has studied Sociology in Germany (BA, University Ludwig-Maximilian, Munich) and France (MA, University Paris Diderot; MA Res and PhD, Ecole des Hautes Etudes en Sciences Sociales, Paris). Her PhD, which examined the euthanasia debate in France and Germany was published as: *Le Droit de Mourir: Choisir sa fin de vie en France et en Allemagne* (2013, Presses Universitaires de Rennes).

Richard Huxtable is Professor of Medical Ethics and Law and Deputy Director of the Centre for Ethics in Medicine at the University of Bristol, UK. Qualified in law and socio-legal studies, his research primarily concerns end-of-life decision-making, surgical ethics and clinical ethics, and he has published widely in legal, bioethical and medical journals. Richard is the author of *Euthanasia, Ethics and the Law: From Conflict to Compromise* (2007, Routledge), *Law, Ethics and Compromise at the Limits of Life: To Treat or Not to Treat?* (2012, Routledge) and *All That Matters: Euthanasia* (2013, Hodder); he is also co-author, with Dickenson and Parker, of *The Cambridge Medical Ethics Workbook* (2010, Cambridge University Press). Richard edits the Ethics in Clinical Practice section of *BMC Medical Ethics*. A longstanding participant in clinical ethics support, Richard is a Trustee of the UK Clinical Ethics Network, as well as a Trustee of the National Council for Palliative Care, whose Ethics Forum he chairs.

Wing May Kong is a Consultant Physician in Endocrinology and Diabetes at Central Middlesex Hospital, London and the Vertical Theme Head for Ethics, Professionalism and Leadership in the Faculty of Medicine, Imperial College London, UK. In 2002, following a PhD in neurobiology, she completed the MA in Medical Ethics and Law at King's College London. At Imperial College she has developed a vertical learning programme in medical ethics and law that progressively builds on early undergraduate learning and its integration into everyday clinical practice. She is also currently Chair of the Institute of Medical Ethics, a charitable organisation whose aim is to promote education, research and dialogue in medical ethics and its application to clinical practice. Between 2000 and 2011, she was on the editorial board of the *Drugs and Therapeutics Bulletin*, a monthly journal which reviews the evidence base for medical and surgical interventions in the UK. As a consultant endocrinologist, she has a special interest in the diabetic foot.

Suzanne Metselaar studied philosophy and literary theory at the Vrije Universiteit Amsterdam and at University College London. Her PhD examined ancient and medieval philosophy and her publications include a book on the philosophy of science. She works at the Centre for Society and the Life Sciences at VU University Medical Centre Amsterdam.

Suzanne Ost is Professor of Law at Lancaster University, UK. Her research lies within the fields of health care law and ethics (with a focus on the end of life) and criminal law (with a particular focus on assisted dying and child pornography and sexual grooming). She has published widely in legal journals such as *Legal Studies*, the *Medical Law Review* and the *Journal of Law and Society*, and has written book chapters for Cambridge University Press and Oxford University Press. Her second monograph, *Child Pornography and Sexual Grooming: Legal and Societal Responses*, was published by Cambridge University Press in 2009. Her third, co-authored monograph is *Medicine and Bioethics in the 'Theatre' of the Criminal Process* (2013, Cambridge University Press), with Margaret Brazier. She was co-investigator for the Arts and Humanities Research Council funded project, *The Impact of the Criminal Process on Health Care Ethics and Practice* (2008–2011), which provided a comprehensive analysis of the role of the criminal justice system in regulating health care practice and ethics in the UK. She is the Editor in Chief of the *Medical Law Review*.

Renzo Pegoraro studied medicine at the University of Padua, graduating with an MD. He thereafter studied philosophy and Catholic theology in Padua, Rome and Georgetown University in Washington DC. He is now Professor of Bioethics at the Medical Faculty of the University of Padua and the Faculty of Theology of North-East of Italy, as well as Scientific Director of Fondazione Lanza, a centre for studies in ethics, bioethics and environmental ethics. In 2006, he was appointed Chairman of the Ethics Committee of the Venetian Institute of Oncology. Since 1998, he has been President of the Committee for Ethics in Research at the Medical Faculty of the University of Padua. From 2000 to 2002, he was a member of the National Council on Health Services. He was President of the European Society for Philosophy of Medicine and Health Care (ESPMH) and the former President of the European Association of Centres of Medical Ethics (EACME). He is now Chancellor of the Pontifical Academy for Life. His research interests encompass biomedical ethics, particularly regarding religion and bioethics, human experimentation, clinical ethics, organ transplantation and care for older people.

Rouven Porz is Head of the Ethics Unit in the University Hospital in Bern, Switzerland. He is the General Secretary of EACME (European Association of Centres of Medical Ethics), a board member of the Swiss Society of Biomedical Ethics, and Senior Lecturer at the University of Applied Sciences in Bern. He trained as a biologist with additional studies in philosophy and educational theory at the University of Saarbrücken, Germany. He has held visiting scholarships in Maastricht (The Netherlands), Newcastle upon Tyne (UK), Geneva (Brocher Foundation, Switzerland) and Amsterdam (The Netherlands). Rouven has conducted empirical and conceptual research in the field of bioethics, focusing mainly on patients' perspectives in the fields of genetic testing, reproductive medicine and stem cell research. His current research focuses on methodological issues in clinical ethics, especially in ethics consultancy.

Paul Schotsmans is Professor of Medical Ethics at the Faculty of Medicine, KU Leuven, Belgium. Paul was appointed Director of the new Centre for Biomedical Ethics and Law in 1986. From 1996–2005, he presided over the Department of Public Health. From 2005 until 2011, he was Vice-Dean of the Faculty of Medicine. He is a former President of the European Association of Centres of Medical Ethics (EACME), for which he was previously treasurer and secretary-general. He was a board member of the International Association of Bioethics (IAB), President of the Ethics Committee of Eurotransplant, as well as a member of several local and international ethics committees. He is currently Vice-President of the Belgian Advisory Committee on Bioethics, a member of the Belgian Council for Transplantation and the Belgian Council for Deep Brain Stimulation, and programme director of the Erasmus Mundus Master in Bioethics. Paul's research interest is mainly in the application of 'personalism' as an ethical model for the ethical integration of reproductive technologies, preimplantation and prenatal diagnosis, clinical genetics, stem cell research, organ transplantation and end-of-life decision-making. He is the author and co-editor of several books on bioethics and papers in leading journals.

Margreet Stolper is a researcher in clinical ethics at the Department of Medical Humanities and the EMGO+ Institute for Health and Care Research, VU University Medical Centre (VUmc) in Amsterdam. After a bachelor degree in psycho motoric therapy, she studied health science. Her PhD is about the theory and practice of moral case deliberation. Her main interests are the practice and methodology of moral case deliberation, teaching ethics, ethics support, training facilitators and empirical ethics research.

Andreas E. Stuck is Professor of Geriatrics at the University of Bern, Switzerland, and medical director of the University Department of Geriatrics at the University Hospital Bern and the Spital Netz Bern. After his clinical studies, he undertook additional training in epidemiology and statistics at the University of California, Los Angeles, and completed his habilitation on methods of geriatric assessment at the University of Bern. He was principal investigator of long-term, multi-site randomized controlled studies on preventive home visits and health risk appraisal in elderly persons, funded by the Swiss National Foundation and the European Union. As a member of the editorial board of the *Journals of Gerontology – Medical Sciences*, a member of the epidemiology of aging section of the Gerontological Society of America and an author in Pathy's *Principles and Practice of Geriatric Medicine*, he is an international leader in the field of geriatric assessment methodology and related health service research. He is actively involved in undergraduate teaching, and implemented a new curriculum for medical students related to medicine in old age, including a focus on clinical ethics.

Ruud ter Meulen is Professor of Ethics in Medicine and Director of the Centre for Ethics in Medicine at the University of Bristol, UK. He was previously Professor of Philosophy and Medical Ethics and Director of the Institute for Bioethics at the University of Maastricht (The Netherlands). Ruud has worked on a broad range of issues in medical ethics, particularly justice, health care reform and health policy, research, evidence based medicine and long-term care. He has directed several international projects and was the principal co-ordinator of a range of European projects.

Jochen Vollmann is Professor and Director of the Institute for Medical Ethics and History of Medicine and Chair of the Centre for Medical Ethics, Ruhr-University Bochum, Germany. His research interests include informed consent and capacity assessment, ethics and psychiatry, end-of-life decision-making, advance directives, medical professionalism, empirical ethics, personalised medicine, clinical ethics committees and clinical ethics consultation.

Guy Widdershoven is Professor of Philosophy and Ethics of Medicine and head of the Department of Medical Humanities at VU University Medical Center in Amsterdam, the Netherlands. He obtained his PhD at the University of Amsterdam. He was Scientific Director of the School of Public Health and Primary Care (CAPHRI) in Maastricht (2004–2009) and Scientific Director of the Netherlands School of Primary Care Research (CaRe) (2005–2012). He is a former President of the European Association of Centers for Medical Ethics (EACME). He has also been a visiting professor at ETHOX (Oxford University, UK). His research spans various national and international projects on empirical ethics and psychiatric ethics, and theory and practice of clinical ethics support. Together with colleagues, he developed the 'moral case deliberation' model for clinical ethics support in health care institutions.

Hub Zwart is Professor of Philosophy at the Faculty of Science (Radboud University Nijmegen) and Scientific Director of the Centre for Society and the Life Sciences (CSG). He studied philosophy (cum laude) and psychology (cum laude) at Radboud University Nijmegen, worked as Research Associate at the Centre for Bioethics (IGE, Maastricht, 1988–1992) and defended his thesis on consensus formation in a pluralistic society in 1993 (cum laude). He was appointed as Research Director of the Centre for Ethics (Radboud University Nijmegen, 1992–2000) and in 2000 he became full Professor/Chair of the Department of Philosophy at the Faculty of Science. He was European lead of the EU Canada exchange programme *Coastal Values* (1999–2003) and in 2004 he became Director of CSG, funded by the Netherlands Genomics Initiative and established at his department. Together with Ruth Chadwick, he is Editor-in-Chief of the journal *Life Sciences, Society and Policy* (Springer Open Access). He also is Director of Education of the *Institute for Science, Innovation and Society* (ISIS). The focus of his research is on philosophical and ethical issues in the emerging life sciences from a 'continental' perspective (dialectics, phenomenology, psychoanalysis) and with a focus on genomics and postgenomics fields: synthetic biology, nanomedicine (RNA programme) and brain research (Neuro-Enhancement: Responsible Research and Innovation (NERRI) project). Special attention is given to the use of genres of the imagination (novels, plays, poetry) in research and education.

Acknowledgements

The editors would like to express their heartfelt thanks to everyone who contributed to the 2012 EACME meeting, especially those who worked tirelessly on the organising and scientific committees, and in particular Keira McGarva for her immense contributions to ensuring that the event was such a success. We also thank Wills Hall for its hospitality and the panel who judged the student art competition which accompanied the event – we extend our congratulations to the worthy winner, Egho Ireo, and runner-up, Joe Hutton. We are grateful to the Wellcome Trust for providing funding for the conference.

The first editor would also like to thank Genevieve Liveley for her love and support, as well as Alastair, Gordon, Karen, Petra, and Richard for first introducing him to some of the voices and rooms of European bioethics. The second editor wants to thank the colleagues from many disciplines and countries for their contributions to the European bioethics projects he has coordinated and has otherwise been involved with: they have definitely shaped his thinking about what it means to be a European bioethicist. He also wants to thank Angelique Heijnen for her outstanding work as the secretary of EACME, her support of the Board and Bureau and her coordination of the EACME News and Newsletter.

Major parts of Chapter 5 were previously published in German: Vollmann, J. (2013) 'Persönlicher – besser – kostengünstiger? Kritische medizinethische Anfragen an die "personalisierte Medizin"', *Ethik in der Medizin*, 25: 233–241. The material is reproduced with kind permission of Springer Science + Business Media. This study was conducted in the research network "Personalised Medicine in Oncology: An Interdisciplinary Study on Ethical, Medical, Economical and Legal Aspects" (Grant project number: 01 GP 1001A), which is supported by the German Federal Ministry of Education and Research (BMBF).

Parts of Chapter 7 have drawn upon extracts from Chapters 1 and 7 from M. Brazier and S. Ost, *Bioethics, Medicine and the Criminal Law, Volume 3, Medicine and Bioethics in the Theatre of the Criminal Process* © M. Brazier and S. Ost (2013, Cambridge University Press). Reproduced with permission. Thanks to Margot Brazier for laying down the foundational work for the arguments presented in the 'Drama and the doctor in the dock' section of this chapter.

The author of Chapter 8 expresses his gratitude to the audience members at the 2012 EACME Conference for their comments and questions and also thanks the editors for their thoughtful observations. He takes responsibility for any errors and bequeaths this responsibility to his future selves.

Chapter 9 was previously published as R. Horn (2014) '"I don't need my patients' opinion to withdraw treatment": Patient preferences at the end-of-life and physician attitudes towards advance directives in England and France', *Medicine, Health Care, and Philosophy* (doi: 10.1007/s11019-014-9558-9). This research was supported by EU Marie Curie Actions (ADVANCED – FP7-PEOPLE-2009-IEF-254825); the Caroline Miles Visiting Fellowship, Ethox Centre, Oxford; and the Wellcome Trust (Ethics and Society Research Fellowship).

Chapter 10 was kindly supported by a Wellcome Trust fellowship in Society and Ethics: Judging Best Interests in Paediatric Intensive Care (BIPIC) (grant number WT097725FR).

The authors of Chapter 14 thank the Bern medical students for their willingness to participate in the new ethics teaching. Particular thanks go to Andrea Ernst, Jenny Amsler, Serena Wyss and Sandra Schlup. They are grateful to Stephan Born for his input into the development of the teaching. They also wish to thank Monica Buckland for language revision, Jackie Leach Scully for helpful suggestions and – last but not least – Michael Stettler for his commitment to implementing clinical ethics support services in the Inselspital Bern and the Spital Netz Bern AG.

Foreword

Twenty-five years of the European Association of Centres of Medical Ethics (EACME): a European contribution to research and education in bioethics

Renzo Pegoraro

1. Birth and development of EACME

The European Association of Centres of Medical Ethics (EACME) was founded in 1986 as a Network of Centres with the aim of promoting research, education and consultation in the field of biomedical ethics, through facilitating information exchange, support of students, teachers and researchers, and the organisation of annual conferences. Inspired by bioethics' longstanding efforts to form 'bridges' (between, for example, disciplines and people), the Association has promoted meetings and collaboration among academic and non-academic institutions involved in the field of bioethics and medical ethics throughout Europe.

EACME is currently represented by 48 full members and 12 associated members, from all around the Continent. If it is to thrive beyond any initial enthusiasm, an association needs the confidence of all of its members and, in turn, their diligent and active contributions. EACME, specifically, requires its members to exchange their experiences, perspectives, and diverse philosophical and religious opinions, without preconception, fear, or inappropriate self-interest. Twenty five years on from the birth of EACME, a great many things have changed, including the geographical and political European scene, bioethics' increasing 'institutionalisation', and the expansion in European and national laws and regulations in relation to biomedicine. Of particular recent importance, of course, has been the severe economic crisis, which has limited financial and human resources worldwide, and had an inevitable impact on health care, academic institutions, and others; the crisis appears, in turn, to have led to further differentiation within the European Union. EACME has also, inevitably, witnessed changes throughout its history, including in its personnel: several of the 'founding fathers' of the organisation, who we remember with gratitude, have since retired and some have sadly passed away.

In order to navigate these developments, both good and ill, I believe EACME could again draw on its initial (bridging) inspiration. The recent 'mission statement' should also help the association to pursue a path to success, by ensuring that younger contributors to the field are helped to cultivate a keen collaborative spirit in bioethics' broad field.

EACME's 'mission statement' developed through engagement with personal and institutional contacts, as well as discussions at the annual conferences. The key elements of the statement are as follows. First, EACME aims to promote and reinforce debate on moral values and ethical theory in relation to health care practice, biomedical research and healthcare systems, from an individual, social and legal point of view. This includes the development of methods and concepts to implement ethical deliberation in daily medical and health care practice. Secondly, EACME strongly endorses cooperation with other societies and associations in the fields of bioethics, philosophy of medicine and social medicine, both at a national and international level, particularly in regard to ethical deliberation and policy-making. Thirdly, EACME places particular emphasis on supporting and promoting young talent and junior researchers in the field of (bio)medical ethics, for example, by having special meetings of postgraduate students at the annual conference and by small grants for international exchange. Finally, EACME focuses on the development of the debate about, and in, institutional forms of (bio)medical ethics, especially in Eastern and Southern Europe.

To achieve these aims, EACME has promoted three endeavours in particular. First, EACME promotes a continuing exchange and sharing of information regarding conferences, courses, research projects and job opportunities, at European and international levels, through two instruments: *EACME News*, which is issued by email every week; and the *EACME Newsletter*, which is published three times a year, and includes articles, comments and book reviews.

Secondly, EACME promotes and provides support for young researchers through the *Visiting Scholarship Exchange Program*, which helps junior researchers to broaden their personal and scientific horizons and to enrich their academic vision. And, finally, EACME supports *Annual Conferences*, which are open to everybody and which prove to be precious occasions, that enable those involved in bioethics to come together to exchange opinions and discuss their work. The conference, in particular, offers added value to our personal quests for richer and more sensitive bioethical reflection.

Recent annual conferences held in Oslo, Istanbul, Bristol, Bochum and Lille reveal the vitality of European bioethics, captured in the respective conference themes: empirical ethics; bioethics from a cross-cultural perspective; other voices, other rooms; personalised medicine – medicine for the person?; and frailty, vulnerability and social participation. As these themes demonstrate, EACME continues to explore (and evolve) its motivations and goals, accepting the challenges coming from medicine, healthcare, and biomedical ethics, with its work supported by a Board of Directors and an Executive Office.

2. Perspectives and challenges

Recalling the sharp and stirring observations made by Paul Schotsmans (2012) in an EACME newsletter, I will allow myself to mention a few of the challenges that appear to be particularly important as EACME goes forward.

First, the multicultural and multi-religious scene which is developing in Europe needs to expand its languages, concepts, and methodologies. We should be open to an authentic dialogue, by which we can interact with the universal and with the particular in bioethics, and we should also be open to the different contributions available from different cultures and religions.

Secondly, we should be aware of the emerging differences between a 'general bioethics' and a 'specialised bioethics': some bioethicists are devoted to reflections on fundamental aspects and different, general, themes; other bioethicists appear to be more specialised within a well-defined field (for example, devoted to a particular area of science or law). Such developments may be fruitful but there is a risk of fragmentation in the development of various 'sectional bioethics', which may not easily communicate with one another.

Thirdly, bioethics must continue to make contact with real clinical life, and with the real problems arising in the clinical setting, which are lived by doctors, nurses, and other health care professionals. Such engagement should prevent bioethics from becoming too abstract, and from 'indulging in virtuosity' – such tendencies will not be useful to practitioners in healthcare, who are increasingly stressed by economic pressures and by organisational difficulties, and who may feel that bioethical reflections are distant from the real situations in which they usually live. Clinical bioethics is, therefore, fundamental to bioethics.

Fourthly, of course, we must remember the recipients of health care. As medicine becomes increasingly technological and standardised, it may become depersonalised. We must remember to focus on people, on their experiences of suffering and hope, and on their fundamental need for care. To paraphrase Toulmin's (1982) famous article, 'How medicine saved the life of ethics', today we might consider 'How ethics could save the life of medicine'.

At the same time, fifthly, we must acknowledge the risk that bioethics might become merely one more academic subject, which will lose its characteristic capacity for creating 'bridges' between different fields of knowledge and action, and between the academic-scientific world and society. Indeed, bioethics must retain its 'prophetic', critical and stimulating voice, which it can direct towards medicine and society itself.

Related to this last challenge, finally, is one of bioethics' most enduring challenges: the need to attend to the weakest, most vulnerable people, and retain a passion for justice, for rightful healthcare systems, which can appropriately meet the needs and interests of each generation, including the most impoverished.

3. Conclusions

Emerging social phenomena, the severe problem of environmental crisis, the globalisation of information, and economic dynamics exhort us to elaborate conceptual instruments and guidelines, which can create an ethics that is capable of tackling various, complex phenomena. As a meeting place for people involved in bioethics – for, indeed, bioethicists – EACME hopes to make a modest, but precious, contribution, which can build concrete 'bridges to the future'. EACME should, therefore, continue to make distinctive European contributions to research and education in bioethics, in the quest to create a real ethics for life, for everybody.

References

EACME 'Mission Statement EACME'. Available HTTP: <www.eacmeweb.com> (accessed 11 June 2014).

Schotsmans, P. (2012) 'Bioethics: Past, Present and Future: A European Perspective', *EACME Newsletter*, September 2012; 31: 2–4. Available HTTP: <http://www.eacmeweb.com/newsletters.html> (accessed 5 June 2014).

Toulmin, S. (1982) 'How Medicine Saved the Life of Ethics', *Perspectives in Biology and Medicine*, 25(4): 736–750.

1 Introduction: all of the future exists in the past?

Richard Huxtable

> Have you never heard what the wise men say: all of the future exists in the past.
> Truman Capote, *Other Voices, Other Rooms* (Capote, 2004: 70)

The 25th anniversary of the European Association of Centres for Medical Ethics (EACME) was celebrated at the 2012 annual conference of the association, which was hosted by the Centre for Ethics in Medicine at the University of Bristol, in the splendid surroundings of Wills Hall (Huxtable, 2012). The conference provided an opportunity not only to look back, but also to look forward, and thus to explore how European bioethics has evolved in the lifetime of EACME and how it might develop in the future.

Inspired by Truman Capote's celebrated novel, the conference theme was *Other Voices, Other Rooms: Bioethics, Then and Now*. Capote's novel provided a fitting metaphor, as its themes have particular resonance in and for European bioethics: coming of age; embracing one's identity; understanding others; caring and being cared for; and searching for oneself and for those to whom one is relationally bound. Yet, the choice might still seem remarkable: a work by an American author, casting a shadow over a distinctively European gathering. This, however, makes the choice particularly fitting: as will become clear from numerous contributions to this collection, US bioethics might appear to cast a long shadow, but European scholars and practitioners are more than capable of stepping out into the light and casting shadows of their own.

The chapters in this volume accordingly emerged from a selection of presentations at the 2012 conference. In keeping with both the conference theme and the ethos of EACME, the selections range across countries, cultures and disciplines, and space is afforded to established leaders in the field, as well as to emerging scholars. We will therefore hear a variety of bioethics' voices and we will be invited to look into many of bioethics' rooms.

The volume, like the conference, is divided into four parts. The first part reflects on European bioethics in the past, present and future, and in so doing considers how comparison between countries and disciplines can enrich bioethical discourse. The second part examines bioethics in social rooms: here the locations include the courtroom, an author's desk and even society (or societies) at large. Clinical rooms form the focus of the third tranche of chapters, in which we encounter a variety of dilemmas arising (at least initially) in the professional-patient encounter. The final section then considers European bioethics in academic rooms, be these classrooms, offices or even (again) the clinic itself.

Alastair Campbell, a Scottish philosopher and theologian, opens the first part of the collection, providing a personal – and characteristically candid and insightful – narrative, in which he recounts his continent-spanning journey through bioethics. Nowadays based in Singapore,[1] Alastair has previously directed ethics centres in New Zealand and the UK (indeed, in Bristol), and he was the founding editor of the renowned *Journal of Medical Ethics*, the gestation and flourishing of which he traces. Reflecting on bioethics as a field, Alastair recognises its strengths in inclusivity and inter-disciplinarity, whilst also questioning the occasional dominance of US voices. Alastair's target is, in part, the 'principlist' framework offered by Tom Beauchamp and Jim Childress (2013), in which four principles – respect for autonomy, beneficence, non-maleficence and justice – purport to capture biomedical ethics. Rather than rely on respect for autonomy (or, indeed, a principlist framework at all), Alastair calls for future enquiries in European bioethics to take a wider view, one which is alert to socio-political dimensions, including the presence of market forces and the risks of injustice.

We hear another personal voice in Paul Schotsmans' story, which he specifically locates in continental European bioethics. A Belgian theologian and bioethicist, Paul initially traces some major developments in the European bioethical scene, including the history of EACME, from its origins, right up to the 2012 conference, which was presided over by Renzo Pegoraro (who kindly supplied the Foreword to this collection). After outlining such developments, Paul points to that which he considers to be distinctive to bioethics in the continental context: concepts like personhood, as well as approaches that express the importance of relationships, solidarity and human dignity. Rather like Alastair, Paul believes that these elements can offer a vital corrective to US-led principlist thinking – although, more controversially, he sees these as distinctively tethered to continental Europe, since he suggests that there may be little to distinguish Australian, Asian and British bioethics from American bioethics.

We next hear from a leading British bioethicist, Ruth Chadwick, whose chapter implies that she would not necessarily share Paul's judgement. Mindful of various challenges to bioethics, which indicate that some people do not 'get' ethics, Ruth's main interest is in looking forward. Ruth sees the future success of bioethics as contingent on it being both diverse and harmonious. The various voices of bioethics might not always sing in unison, but discord need not be the result; sometimes quietened voices will be heard once more, just like musical themes might be taken up by different instruments in a string quartet. Provided that bioethics continues to alert people to the ethical dimensions of the situations it appraises, it will not only enable people to 'get' ethics, but also ensure that something is done about matters of concern.

Having heard from some of the different voices of European bioethics in Part 1, we next turn to bioethics' rooms and, in Part 2, to some of the social rooms into which bioethics enters. Jochen Vollman, a German physician and bioethicist, opens this part with a timely chapter, which examines the advent of personalised medicine. Jochen provides a powerful critique of this emergent science, which appears not only to be more hype than hope, but also less 'personal' (in bioethics' terms) than it might otherwise appear. The chapter therefore indicates some of the tensions that exist between regard for the individual – who appears to be at the heart of 'personalised' medicine – and the wider society. The forces occupying the broad social 'room' give Jochen particular cause for concern: like Alastair and Ruth, he notes the lurking presence of 'big pharma' and a need to attend to the difficult questions associated with distributive justice.

Hub Zwart, a Dutch philosopher and psychologist, thereafter leads us into a different room, which might be more often associated with medical humanities: the author's writing space. Whilst Jochen looked to the future and to science, Hub looks to the past and to the arts, as he provides a bioethical and psychoanalytical reading of Lewis' 1925 biomedical science novel *Arrowsmith*. Hub's close reading of the text reveals a tension at the heart of biomedicine: the desire to contribute to patients' well-being, whilst also controlling life. He hopes that, by bringing this sort of tension into the open, science novels like *Arrowsmith* might help to widen bioethics' scope.

The analysis offered by Richard Huxtable and Suzanne Ost (who are medical lawyers and bioethicists, who come from Wales and England respectively) also owes something to the arts. However, Richard and Suzanne take us into a quite different social room: the courtroom – and the English courtroom specifically. In their discussion, the courtroom – like the surgery – is depicted as a theatre, in which different dramatic stories are told and heard. Bioethics' voice is sometimes audible in this space, and so too can bioethics occasionally be heard in the law. Yet, according to Richard and Suzanne, each speaks with its own voice (or, indeed, voices) and will tell its own story; mishearing might well occur but, they argue, a dialogue between law and bioethics can be opened up and their different voices can carry.

Tom Hayes, an English medical lawyer working in Wales, captures one such discussion between law and (philosophical) bioethics, when he appraises the law's provision for advance decision-making in light of bioethics' concerns with notions of personhood and identity. Tom's title continues the artistic theme, in conjuring E.M. Forster's celebrated book *A Room with a View*, and, like Richard and Suzanne, he ponders what law can do for bioethics and vice versa. Some bioethicists detect a problem with previously autonomous individuals binding the futures of the non-autonomous individuals that they appear to have become. Tom unpicks the different philosophical accounts but suggests that the law should continue to support advance decision-making, since consistency might otherwise entail some unsatisfactory knock-on effects in the law and, by extension, society.

As Tom indicates, the law operates not in the abstract, but in the real world. The subject of his chapter, advance decision-making, is one which has international relevance, although legal provisions and clinical practices undoubtedly differ between jurisdictions. Ruth Horn, a German social scientist who also works in France and England, illustrates some of the differences in her comparison of the attitudes of French and English clinicians towards advance decision-making. Here, Ruth draws on interviews which she conducted in both countries and her chapter therefore opens the third part of the volume, in which we move into clinical rooms. Bearing out some of Paul's earlier observations, Ruth finds French physicians to be most concerned with solidarity with (and thus the welfare of) their vulnerable patients, whilst their English counterparts appear more alert to the authenticity (or not) of the apparently autonomous wishes that have been set down by their patients.

In combining empirical data with ethical reflection, Ruth's chapter provides one example of empirical bioethics research, which (as Ruth Chadwick earlier noted) has proven to be a fruitful development in contemporary bioethics. Giles Birchley, a former children's nurse who is now working in bioethics in the UK, provides another illustration of empirical bioethics in action, and his research leads us onto another ward: the paediatric intensive care unit. Giles' study therefore focuses on critically ill infants, who, unlike those patients with which Ruth and Tom were concerned, could never articulate their wishes as to their care. In many countries, decisions about such infants are made on the basis of their 'best interests'. Reflecting on his interviews with the various individuals involved in these decisions, Giles suggests that clinical authority might be considered to rest on 'objective' medical facts, but he queries the basis – and legitimate scope – of parental authority. Giles is particularly interested in the role that intuition appears to play in parents' decisions about their offspring. Giles argues that, whilst parents should be heard whenever difficult decisions must be made, there are nevertheless some limits to parental authority.

Sometimes an outside view will be sought on the dilemmas discussed by Giles, Tom and Ruth: this might involve referral to a court for a decision or a request for advice from a clinical ethicist or a clinical ethics committee. The nature and levels of such ethics support varies across Europe (and, indeed, the world) but Suzanne Metselaar, Margreet Stolper and Guy Widdershoven provide some insights into the distinctive 'moral case deliberation' method that they deploy in the Netherlands. The authors – who have expertise in philosophical bioethics and the health sciences – explain that the model involves the clinical ethicist neither passively listening to the referrers, nor actively telling them what to do, but rather facilitating a reflective dialogue, in which experiences and values are shared.

Sharing, and the communality this implies, is also a central theme of the final chapter of this part of the collection. Angus Dawson, a British philosophical bioethicist, draws examples from the clinic, which involve the individual interactions of patients and professionals, but his thoughtful analysis soon widens in scope – as, indeed, he recommends bioethics must do. Like other contributors, Angus initially questions the rewards that have been reaped by a bioethics that is autonomy-orientated: choice might appear to be a good thing, but there are risks too, not least of marketisation and abandonment. Angus therefore issues a plea for a reorientation towards social relations, and thus towards values like solidarity and community. For Angus, this reorientation will require a greater emphasis on the ethical issues arising in public health, as well as a renewed focus on the work of feminist, republican and communitarian scholars.

As the expansive scope of his chapter implies, Angus provides us with a bridge from the clinic as a treatment setting to the clinic as one of bioethics' academic rooms. These rooms – which include other classrooms – form the focus of the final part of the collection. Wing May Kong, an endocrinologist who teaches medical ethics in the UK, surveys the opportunities and the challenges in teaching ethics to medical students. She combines her thorough review of the educational literature with insightful reflections on practices in her own institution. Given its associations with reason and judgement, Wing May considers ethics to be compatible with both the science and the art of medicine. Translating theories into practice can be challenging, however, especially when there are gaps between the formal and the 'hidden' curricula. Given the pressures on these curricula, creative thinking will also be needed, but Wing May is ultimately optimistic that ways can be found to enable tomorrow's doctors to develop their moral identities.

From London we next travel to Bern in Switzerland, where we see students' first-hand accounts of how their teaching has enabled them to become more ethically attuned. Rouven Porz and Andreas Stuck – a bioethicist with a teaching background and a geriatrician, respectively – introduce us to a method they have developed, which invites the learners to view dilemmas through different ethical 'lenses'. As Wing May had pointed out, ethical skills can align with clinical skills, and Rouven and Andreas note how their method resembles the differential diagnoses that doctors must also learn to provide.

Amongst the different 'lenses' offered by Rouven and Andreas are the ethics of care and narrative ethics. These approaches promise to offer richer, more relational accounts of the moral life than that which is typically provided by the principlism that was the target of our early chapters. Principlism – and specifically the principle of respect for autonomy – then returns in our final chapter. Here, Ray de Vries offers an elegant and sustained attack on autonomy, whilst also entering a plea for the more neglected aspect of this principle, that of respect. Ray surveys the field from a good vantage point, since he is both Dutch and American and, indeed, he continues to work as a bioethicist in both the Netherlands and the US.

In sum, we hope that the volume enables the reader to hear from many of the voices in European bioethics and to enter into many of the rooms that bioethics penetrates. We are not unaware that some voices are quieter than others. Although such volumes do exist, it would require a different – and even more ambitious – collection to capture the voices of global bioethics, which could hear (for example) from those in Asia, Africa and Latin America, amongst others. We are also mindful that some of the voices of European bioethics could have been louder, not least those of scholars working in feminist ethics, in nursing ethics, on methodology in bioethics (and particularly on empirical bioethics) and on bioethics beyond the boundaries of medical ethics (and thus on issues pertaining to animals, the environment and other biosciences). Whilst the volume, like the preceding conference, achieves a broadly European scope, we are nevertheless aware that some regions are not represented and that British voices are particularly audible (but perhaps inevitably so, given the location of the conference and the publisher). Equally, there are other rooms into which we might have ventured, amongst them the surgeon's theatre, the veterinary practice and the boardrooms of policy-makers and businesses, as well as the various studios – real and virtual – in which bioethics is depicted.

We do, however, hope that the reader will agree that a broad range of views and viewpoints have been captured. Notably, despite the diversity, some striking themes have emerged. In closing, we will note the four themes that appeared most strongly to us. First, it seems that *no single discipline dominates* European bioethics. Although this might be considered a truism of bioethics wherever it is theorised, taught or practised, it is instructive to note that the same holds in Europe. As Ruth (Chadwick) observed, there are live questions about what bioethics is – is it a discipline or a collection of disciplines collaborating in a 'field of study'? If (for present purposes) we take the latter view, then, as Wing May, Rouven and Andreas convey, healthcare professionals' voices will matter in the field. However, as Alastair, Richard and Suzanne add, neither bioethics nor medical ethics (more narrowly) should be expected to hear only from these professionals. Various chapters reveal that philosophers' voices remain dominant but, as Alastair again suggests, bioethics is also not entirely their preserve, to which Paul adds that neither is it (nor indeed is EACME itself) a 'club of clerics'. Tom, Richard and Suzanne then show how law can play its part, while Giles and Ruth (Horn) reveal the important influence of the social sciences, not least in enabling bioethics to hear directly from those most affected by dilemmas emerging in the 'real' world.

Bioethics therefore hears a multitude of voices and, turning to our second theme, *bioethics needs dialogue* to occur between the different speakers. Cross-disciplinary dialogue emerges as particularly important to the enrichment (maybe even the survival) of this field of study. Ruth (Chadwick) points out that each contributing discipline might 'frame' the discussion in its own way but, whilst mindful that misunderstandings can occur, she enters a plea for open dialogue. The idea that narrative matters and that there are many ways of telling stories emerges clearly from the contributions of Hub, Ray,

Richard and Suzanne and Rouven and Andreas. Suzanne, Margreet and Guy then join the latter authors in suggesting that, in turn, there are many ways of hearing – and interpreting – stories. We see these observations in action in the chapters by Giles, Tom and Ruth (Horn), in which we are shown how different disciplinary approaches – such as those offered by law, philosophy and the social sciences – can illuminate different features of the 'story'.

From such multiplicity emerges a third theme, which is that there is *no single European bioethics*. Paul identifies a degree of homogeneity, at least in continental European approaches, but more often the point is made – and explicitly so by Rouven and Andreas – that European bioethics is distinctive by virtue of its plurality. As we will see again, this is not the pluralism of principlism, since European bioethics often chooses to look through different 'lenses'. The plurality is vividly depicted in Ruth Horn's comparison of attitudes in France and England. As Ruth Chadwick and Ray de Vries suggest, we should doubt that there is a 'common morality', which can be truly considered to be common across Europe.

From here, the question inevitably arises: are there any moral messages which are in some measure distinctive to European bioethics? And do these messages emanate from what might be called *European* bioethics or instead from bioethics *in Europe* (or, at least, parts thereof)? Our final theme suggests that there are some *distinctive values, concepts and approaches* that can be detected, although we leave it to the reader to judge whether these capture 'European bioethics' or 'bioethics in Europe'. The observation can first be made in negative terms: there appears to be, at least on the evidence provided here, little enthusiasm for principlism or for respect for autonomy in particular. Certainly, Angus reminds us that autonomy has secured some important victories, with Ruth (Chadwick) adding that we should not overlook the nuances of principlism as presented by its pioneers. However, Angus – along with Alastair and Ray (in particular) – evinces resistance to principlism, and especially to the reductionism of allowing bioethics' gaze to extend only so far as autonomy allows. As Giles' chapter demonstrates, such an impoverished view will inevitably miss those (like infants) who have yet to meet the preconditions for autonomous living.

More positively, however, we have also encountered various values which appear to come through especially strongly in the European context. Whilst there are doubtless more, three such values seem to be particularly prominent. First, as Wing May, Rouven and Andreas suggest, room is afforded to character and thus to virtue ethics. Secondly, as illustrated by Alastair, Paul, Jochen and Ruth (Chadwick), there appears to be a great deal of concern about questions of justice, along with associated issues of power and powerlessness. Finally, as Jochen, Paul and also Angus suggest, solidarity has a special place. If, then, we combine these reflections, we might come to see – as both Angus and Ruth (Chadwick) indicated – that European bioethics will often encourage an orientation away from the individual (and concerns with his or her autonomy), and towards the community at large.

There is, therefore, ample food for thought contained in the following pages. My co-editor and I hope that you will enjoy the collection as much as we have enjoyed reading the contributions and participating in the preceding conference. Hopefully, as Truman Capote indicated, by looking to our present and to our past in the ways that the authors suggest, we might best prepare ourselves for our (shared) future.

Note

1. It was in Singapore that the first editor took the photograph, which appears on the cover of this volume. In addition to capturing the metaphorical 'voices' and 'rooms', the image also speaks to the theme of crossing boundaries, since the sculpture in the foreground – Salvador Dali's *Surrealist Piano* – was part of a travelling exhibition of this important European artist's work.

References

Beauchamp, T. and Childress, J. (2013) *Principles of Biomedical Ethics*, 7th edition. New York: Oxford University Press.

Capote, T. (2004 [1948]) *Other Voices, Other Rooms*, Modern Classics edition. London: Penguin Books.

Huxtable, R. (2012) 'The EACME 25th Anniversary Conference in Bristol', *EACME Newsletter* 32 (Dec.): 2–3.

Part I

The voices and rooms of European bioethics, then and now

2 Medical ethics, then and now: a 40-year perspective

Alastair V. Campbell

2.1 A personal prologue

I got into medical ethics by accident. Back in 1964, when I returned to Scotland from postgraduate study in the States to take up a job as Assistant Chaplain to Edinburgh University, I was asked if I would also take on a part time job at the Royal College of Nursing. It was to teach a course on ethics to senior nurses who were studying for a qualification to enable them to become nurse managers. (It was known flippantly as 'morals for matrons', though this was inaccurate as many members of the class were male nurses!) Whoever designed that course (I never found out who it was) was clearly sadistic. These unfortunate nurses were required to study the theories of Kant, Bentham, Mill *and* Spinoza! What is more they had to pass a written exam at the end of the course. I don't know who were/was more terrified – they or I.

After several years of struggling to get these moral theories across and relate them to real clinical situations, I realized that what was needed was a text book that guided a clinically trained reader through the philosophical swamplands. Thus *Moral Dilemmas in Medicine* (Campbell, 1972) was born, and, thanks to advice from the medical publisher of the book, it became a course book for both nurses and doctors (though it was from my nurse students that I got the real life clinical dilemmas). The book was published in 1972 and (despite my publisher's prediction that they would be doing this, not for money, but just for reputation) it went to three editions. Thus I became an accidental medical ethicist, and so, when in 1974 the Society for the Study of Medical Ethics decided to launch the *Journal of Medical Ethics (JME)*, they eventually turned to me to become editor, having looked in vain for a doctor who knew anything about the subject. Watching this 'baby' of mine grow into the high impact international journal it has become today has been one of the great satisfactions of my life (and most of the credit for this has to go to Raanan Gillon, the second, and by far the longest serving, editor of the journal). So now, as the founding editor of the *JME*, I became an 'expert' in the field.

From the 1980s onwards (with an increasing number of invitations to lecture abroad on medical ethics), it became obvious that my two academic careers, in pastoral care (still at that time my academic home was in the Faculty of Divinity in Edinburgh University) and in medical ethics could not be sustained. I had to choose between them. Medicine eventually won, and so for the past 24 years I have been a professor of medical ethics and a director of a bioethics centre in three different medical schools, in three different countries.

I fear these personal reminiscences may seem rather self-indulgent, but I hope they may help to set a context for the general points I wish to make in the rest of this chapter. They are as follows: first, the subject area is essentially interdisciplinary, and, over the 40 plus years I have been involved in it, this aspect has grown in both strength and depth; secondly, medical ethics/bioethics narrowly escaped from American capture, a threat coming from the sheer extent of the subject in the USA, and it has become truly global, though risks of Western dominance remain; and, finally, there continues to be an uneasy tension between its origins in professional standards of practice (*of* doctors, *for* doctors and *by* doctors) and a genuine socio-political critique, both of the profession and of the wider issues of the ethics of health care. This tension remains, and probably can never be fully resolved.

2.2 Interdisciplinarity

The setting up of the *JME* entailed a commitment to interdisciplinarity from the outset. With an editor trained in both philosophy and theology and two senior medical figures as consulting editors, the journal could not be seen as narrowly medical, yet still remained very closely in touch with, and focused on, medicine. The same was true of the inaugural Editorial Board, which had doctors, nurses, lawyers, philosophers, theologians and social scientists, all very senior in their disciplines, to steer the journal's development as a major scholarly resource for both practitioners and academics. Since those early days, the sheer range and volume of research and publication in medical ethics has been quite astounding. But, as important as quantity, is the quality of interaction between disciplines. No single perspective seems to have dominated for long, though the philosophers do seem to jostle for first place a great deal!

Of the many ways in which the disciplines have come together on a common cause, I would pick out two aspects. First, there is the rise of 'empirical ethics', with the social scientists playing a key role in devising appropriate empirical methods for enriching the factual side of medical ethics, but – more than this – challenging the 'is-ought' distinction, forcing a rethink of the philosophical fear of a naturalistic fallacy (defined by the *Encyclopaedia Brittanica* as the fallacy 'of treating the term "good" (or any equivalent term) as if it were the name of a natural property'). This 'fallacy' was first identified by David Hume but became best known in philosophy after it was elaborated by G. E. Moore (Moore, 1903). Related to this is an enrichment of qualitative research in the field, giving much greater prominence to the perspectives of patients in assessing the ethical issues.

Secondly, there is the contribution of legal scholars in making the discipline go beyond narrowly clinical questions (the 'sacred dyad' of the doctor-patient relationship) to the policy dimensions of ethical quandaries in medicine and the life sciences. Here the work of the UK Nuffield Council on Bioethics has been especially prominent, a notable recent example being its work on the use and retention of DNA samples by the police (Nuffield Council on Bioethics, 2007). We should also note the huge range of European Commission funded research over the years, which has produced many insights into European and international policy matters. But these are just two examples, and one need only attend a conference of the European Association of Centres of Medical Ethics (EACME) or the World Congresses of the International Association of Bioethics (IAB) to see the exciting mix of scholars involved at the present time. Especially heartening is the large number of young scholars from many different disciplines who are keen to enter this field.

2.3 Globalization

Some years back (2000) I wrote a highly critical review of Al Jonsen's book, *The Birth of Bioethics* (Jonsen 1998), which I published in the European journal, *Medicine, Healthcare and Philosophy* (Campbell, 2000). I entitled it '"My Country 'tis of Thee" – the Myopia of American Bioethics'. Al Jonsen was a friend of mine (still is, I hope . . .), but his book was a shocking revelation of the insularity of American bioethics. His account of the 'birth' made it look as though everything had started in the States and that the concerns about American health research and health care were all that mattered ethically. What's more, his chapter on 'other countries' was downright insulting in both its brevity and its inaccuracy. When we think of the independent flourishing of the European scene, with the many centres evident in the EACME cluster and initiatives like the Erasmus Mundus Masters degree, one wonders what our American friends see in their frequent overseas trips – just the tourist sights? Yet this history was written by a well-intentioned and open-minded scholar, who still could not see past the shores of his own nation.

This risk of American colonization of the field has become much greater over the years through the amazing success of Beauchamp and Childress's *Principles of Biomedical Ethics* (2013). You find the 'Georgetown mantra' everywhere in the world, especially when doctors and other health care professionals have had crash courses in bioethics, often run by American academics. Of course, the authors themselves intended the book to be trans-cultural or perhaps 'supra-cultural', since they see the principles as capturing some fundamental human features of morality which transcend cultural difference. But, on the ground, this approach assumes a distinctively American twist, whatever the authors intended. 'Autonomy' triumphs – this in the highly individualistic form so disapproved of by Onora O'Neill (2002) – and justice remains an afterthought.

Fortunately, other forces in the field seem to have prevented this kind of 'MacBurger' approach to medical ethics. First has been the vision of Peter Singer and Daniel Wikler, when they took the initiative in 1992 to inaugurate the IAB. The IAB Constitution pays no heed to numbers of scholars in any given country. Instead a strict allocation formula for electable places on the Board prevents (at least to some extent) both national and gender dominance. We get a snapshot of this from the gender and nationality of the 10 presidents of the Association elected since 1992: 7 male, 3 female; 3 from the USA, 2 from the UK, 1 from Australia, 1 from South Africa, 1 from Finland, 1 from Germany, 1 from Argentina. This is far from perfect equity in gender and nationality, but the WASP (White Anglo-Saxon Protestant) dominance has at least been moderated.

However, even more powerful forces ensuring internationalization and inclusivity have come from the sheer diversity of theory in medical ethics and the wide geographical spread of scholars. Principlism cannot maintain any real dominance now that there are powerful advocates for culturally sensitive ethical approaches, a lively debate about 'East versus West' in ethics and the increased vitality of rival approaches, such as virtue ethics, care ethics and feminist approaches to bioethics. It is true that there are still few scholarly institutions in some regions (and Africa is especially challenged here), but still there is clear emergence of regional identities, especially in Asia – and here I must put in a plug for the journal founded by my centre in Singapore, the *Asian Bioethics Review*, a young journal still, but with a wonderful range of regional scholarship that has worldwide significance.

2.4 Socio-political critique

Let me begin this final section with a very rude comment made to me when I first met Ivan Illich (the author of *Medical Nemesis* (Ilich, 1974)). He was speaking at a London Medical Group conference at London shortly after I had been appointed editor of *JME*. When he heard the title of the journal and my position as editor he remarked, '"Medical Ethics"? – I would call it "Medical Masturbation"!' Of course this was quite consistent with Illich's negative view of modern medicine as a force driven by professional arrogance, and allied to industrialist ambitions, largely destructive of health. Later, Ian Kennedy was to raise similar doubts in his Gifford Lectures (Kennedy, 1981), drawing on Illich's observation that the main gains in health in the twentieth century had come, not from medical breakthroughs, but from a rise in living standards.

These negative accounts of medicine's achievements may appear extreme. They were to some extent the product of that heady time in the 1960s and 1970s, when *everything* was under radical questioning. I still remember the student revolutionary movements, when Edinburgh, among many universities, was occupied by students demanding greater academic power. How changed things are now, when most students just hope to get some sort of job at the end of their studies, and the more radical of the academic disciplines (in humanities and social science) are clearly out of favour with governments, looking merely for economic outcomes.

But, we cannot dismiss these criticisms of medicine as merely the intellectual fashion of a bygone academic era. In so many ways, things are *worse* now than they were in the 1970s. The gap between rich and poor, healthy and diseased has increased massively throughout the world in the post-1980s era of triumphant capitalism; and the pervasive economic influence of big pharma is to be seen everywhere, most notably in the 10/90 gap (a mere 10 per cent of research funding goes to the health problems of 90 per cent of the world's population (see Campbell, 2013: Chapter 5)). Moreover, both research integrity and research ethics are under increasing threat, as the rich world outsources the bulk of its clinical research to poor nations, who can never afford the products of the research, and when the ever mounting pressure to publish and to patent everything possible has led to both secrecy and outright fraud. Increasingly we hear from bioethicists in India and Africa of the bribery and corruption behind research and the inadequacy of ethical review. Another worrying sign of the times is the 'regulatory capture' by those with a commercial stake in research of the Food and Drug Administration (FDA) and the other drug and device regulators. A strong indication of this is the constant controversy over revisions of the Declaration of Helsinki to make research more just and socially responsible.

Where has medical ethics been in all this? Well, of course, there have been outspoken critics of the current injustices, obvious examples being Thomas Pogge and Peter Singer, but for many in the field too much time has been taken up with questions of no relevance to the most urgent problems of our day. Indeed, the optimistic predictions of many libertarian and consequentialist writers about human progress and their (unfounded) predictions of so called 'human enhancement' (even moral enhancement!) seem to me to feed into the very socio-political influences that medical ethics should be combatting. The promotion of progress and liberty has been transmuted into the ever increasing commodification of everything we prize as humans; and free market ideology seems to be everywhere, despite all the evidence that it causes immense injustice! I would like to suggest that for all of us Michael Sandel's recent publication, *What Money Can't Buy: The Moral Limits of Markets* (2012), becomes essential reading.

So I think we have moved on from castigating the medical profession for being self-indulgent and self-aggrandizing; indeed, we can see that profession itself as the victim of those very same forces that create and perpetuate injustice. But we have not escaped from the tension in medical ethics between getting the clinical encounter ethically right, and seeing that, more destructive than any failures of the profession, there is the socio-political context within which medicine seeks to promote and preserve human values to which we should also be alert. In a well-known phrase, we must surely watch out that we are not merely re-arranging the deck chairs on board the *Titanic* even as the vessel sinks.

References

Campbell, A. V. (1972) *Moral Dilemmas in Medicine*, Edinburgh: Churchill-Livingstone.
—— (2000) '"My country 'tis of thee" – the myopia of American bioethics, *Medicine, Healthcare and Philosophy*, 3: 195–198.
—— (2013) *Bioethics: The Basics*, Abingdon: Routledge.
Beauchamp, T. L. and Childress J. F. (2013) *Principles of Biomedical Ethics*, 7th edn, New York: Oxford University Press.
Illich, I. (1974) *Medical Nemesis*, London: Calder Boyars.
Jonsen, A. R. (1998) *The Birth of Bioethics*, New York: Oxford University Press.
Kennedy, I. (1981) *The Unmasking of Medicine*, London: Allen and Unwin.
Moore, G. E. (1903) *Principia Ethica.* Cambridge: Cambridge University Press.
Nuffield Council on Bioethics (2007) *The Forensic Use of Bioinformation: Ethical Issues*, London: Nuffield Council on Bioethics.
O'Neill, O. (2002) *Autonomy and Trust in Bioethics*, Cambridge: Cambridge University Press.
Sandel, M. (2012) *What Money Can't Buy: The Moral Limits of Markets*, London: Allen Lane.

3 Bioethics past, present and future: a personal and narrative perspective from the European continent

Paul Schotsmans

Living in the centre of Europe (in Leuven and Brussels, Belgium) and having had the privilege of participating in the evolving practice of European bioethics (e.g. as Treasurer, Secretary General and President of the European Association of Centres of Medical Ethics (EACME), and also as a participant in many European research projects), I take the opportunity here to share some of my personal reflections on the theoretical mainstreams of bioethics, as it is practised in the majority of European centres. Conventional wisdom has it that bioethics began in the USA, and the temptation is therefore to address European-American differences. I have regularly made this mistake, for example in my opening speech at the bi-annual conference of the International Association of Bioethics in London, in 2000. Yet, I admit that this is a simplification: some bioethicists in the USA (such as Pellegrino, Reich, Thomasma, and Walter, amongst others) had and still have strong links with European philosophers and theologians. Some of them, like Reich and Walter, were even trained in Europe. On the European continent, Francesc Abel of Barcelona, one of the pioneers of bioethics in Europe, obtained his bioethical training from André Hellegers at the Georgetown University Kennedy Center in Washington. The early beginnings of bioethics in Europe are closely linked to what happened in the USA, especially in the Kennedy Center and in New York's Hastings Center. However, in 1975, ten years prior to the birth of EACME, the British Society for the Study of Medical Ethics started the *Journal of Medical Ethics*, 'a forum for the reasoned discussion of moral issues arising from the provision of medical care' (Boyd, 2013: 661). The editor and publishers of this journal were, for a long period, defenders of 'principlism' (which I explore below), an ethical methodology which was imported from the USA to Europe. Similarly, in the Institute for Bioethics in Maastricht, principlism was regularly used as a framework for tackling bioethical problems in a pluralist society.

Besides providing some historical information about the European bioethics scene, this chapter aims to offer some personal reflections on the theoretical mainstreams of the practice of bioethics in European centres. This narrative presentation is indeed personal and therefore subjective. Another limitation is that I focus on bioethics on the European continent; indeed, it is my humble opinion that the bioethics scene in the UK occupies the mainstream of bioethics, as it is understood and practised in American, Australian and Asian bioethics centres.

3.1 Historical evolutions

Let me start with the early beginnings of EACME. In 1984–1985, some academics who were involved in the new discipline of bioethics in Europe came together in Lyon. Their intention was to create a network among European bioethics centres. EACME – or EACEM in French, as the Association's meetings were initially bilingual – was born. The Association was officially created on 2 December 1986. Present from the beginning were representatives from Spain (Barcelona: Abel), France (Lyon: Léry; Paris: Verspieren), the Netherlands (Maastricht: de Wachter), the UK (London: Nicholson and Peacock), Belgium (Brussels: Malherbe and Boné). At a preparatory meeting of EACME in January 1986 Lefèvre from Lille, Spinsanti from Rome and I from Leuven requested to join the group. Describing bioethics in Europe is impossible without honouring these 'founding fathers'. As is the case with every organization, one person takes care of continuity and practical support, which in this case was undoubtedly the Belgian Jesuit, Father Edouard Boné (formerly a palaeontologist). Father Boné took care of administration and organization and enjoyed a strong working relationship with Francesc Abel, also a Jesuit father. Abel was not only a theologian but also a practising gynaecologist in Barcelona and, significantly, he was trained in bioethics by André Hellegers, the founding father of the Kennedy Institute. As Abel (1999) commented, on the occasion of his election as a full member of the Royal Academy of Medicine of Catalonia,

> I arrived at the Kennedy Institute at the beginning of 1972.... The Kennedy Institute, the Hastings Center, Barcelona's Institut Borja and Montreal's Institute of Bioethics were the four leading institutes in the earliest days of bioethics, and the Hospital de Sant Joan de Déu's Committee for Health Care Ethics was the first in Spain and probably, all of Europe.

The presence of so many clergymen on the original Board was probably the reason why they wanted to stress the pluralist dimension of their initiative, by electing a Professor of Forensic Medicine, Nicole Léry, as the first president. Léry was not religiously linked and regularly made clear that the Association should not be 'a club of clerics'. Three centres took the lead, thanks to the generous support they received from external sponsors: the French-speaking Brussels centre (with Jean-François Malherbe), the Institute for Bioethics in Maastricht (with Maurice de Wachter) and the San Cujat De Valles centre in Barcelona (under Abel).

Frequent meetings enabled this new European association to bring together experts in bioethics. The Barcelona Institute developed an international research and communication network, arranging intercontinental meetings in Barcelona, which were supported by a generous sponsor. North-American bioethicists (such as Engelhardt, Harvey, and Pellegrino) took the opportunity to meet with European scholars. These European scholars came from far and wide: in EACME, 'European' was and is used in the broad sense of the term, i.e. from the Atlantic to the Urals. The Association aimed – and still aims – at promoting critical attention to the ethical issues arising in the development and deployment of biomedical sciences in our communities. Unsurprisingly, as a young network, the Association endured some bad times, but also enjoyed good times.

One fortunate development was that, around the time EACME began, the European Union started to sponsor research projects on bioethics, on condition that several European countries were included. The Association's membership list and the contacts made during the yearly meetings created the ideal opportunity for members to work out common research projects and to start internationally oriented cooperation in Europe. I was a partner in several of these research consortia and benefitted from the intensive exchange of ideas and influences that they provided. Mainly also due to these links with the European Union, the Association evolved into a professionally directed community. Crucially important was a radical change in the structure of the meetings: starting from some central themes, opportunities for young scholars in bioethics to present their work were created. At present, more than 60 centres from all over Europe participate in the network.

One of the advantages of the European network is that it was and is neither narrowly focused on one culture, nor dominated by one ethical approach. Centres from Southern, Eastern, Middle and Western Europe found one another, and learned about their different philosophical and ethical backgrounds. This was and is unique in the sense that elsewhere it seems that principlism remained the only methodology which can (or should be) used in bioethics. Romanic, Germanic and Eastern European cultures were and still are developing a health care ethics which is – even yet in the social construction of their health care systems – radically different from the dominant Anglo-American mainstream.

Spanish and French bioethicists had a great influence on medico-legal initiatives, such as the abortion debate which occurred in Spain and the struggle against therapeutic obsessiveness in France. There was also a continuous link with fundamental moral philosophy and theology. The impact of one of the greatest moral philosophers of the twentieth century, Paul Ricoeur, did not remain limited to France, but spread all over continental Europe. It is also amazing to observe how one of the best experts in medieval philosophy, Ludger Honnefelder (Bonn), became one of the leading ethical advisors on European health law at the Council of Europe. Equally, Dietmar Mieth, a world-renowned expert in moral theology and ecclesiology, enabled the Tübingen centre to participate in several research projects sponsored by the European Union, whilst also working with German politicians on their plans for health care law (indeed, at an airport, I once observed him comment upon and correct German political parties' election manifestos).

Unfortunately, the influence of such thinkers on the intercontinental scene remained rather weak. This weakness is mainly due to the differences in language and also to the fact that the leading bioethics journals are published in English. It is, however, regrettable that it took so long before a distinctive type of European bioethics entered onto the intercontinental scene. Indeed, the meeting of the Association with the representatives of the International Association of Bioethics in London (2000) had limited, if any, success. I observe (albeit maybe wrongly) that it was only when the turn to empirical bioethics and to care (and also to nursing) ethics was made that distinctively European bioethics developed.

Although EACME was and is an association of centres, there were regular discussions about opening membership to individual – and specifically promising junior – scholars. Whilst this did not happen, the annual meetings now provide space for young scholars to present their research to a broad, international audience. However, another European association, namely the European Society for Philosophy of Medicine and Healthcare (ESPMH), did invite individual membership. ESPMH was founded in August 1987, under the direction of Henk ten Have of the University of Maastricht; ten Have thereafter became Professor of Medical Ethics at the University of Nijmegen, the Director of the Bioethics Institute of UNESCO and, nowadays, Director of the Center for Healthcare Ethics at Duquesne University. The first conference of ESPMH was held in Maastricht, the Netherlands, with 'The Growth of Medical Knowledge' as its main topic. The ESPMH was instituted by an international group of philosophers, physicians, ethicists and other interested professionals in the field, with a view to the growing need for critical reflection on the role of medicine and health care in our society. They described the background of this network as follows:

> The Goals of the ESPMH are threefold: to stimulate and promote the development and methodology in the field of philosophy of medicine and health care; to be a centre of contact for European scholars in this field; to promote international contact between members of the various countries in and outside Europe.
>
> (www.espmh.org)

Those involved took the exciting initiative to launch a European journal, *Medicine, Health Care and Philosophy: A European Journal*. This was a great decision, as the Journal provided continental bioethicists with the opportunity to disseminate their research. The Journal may therefore be considered a 'bridge' between continental Europe and the rest of the world. Of course, the editorial boards of the *Journal of Medical Ethics* and *Bioethics*, amongst others, also came to open their doors to continental European scholars.

Such openness to collaboration was further evidenced and reinforced in some very important meetings. In August 2005, for the first time in their existence, ESPMH and EACME met together in a co-sponsored annual conference in Barcelona, Spain. Thanks to Inez de Beaufort, the meeting of the International Association of Bioethics in Rotterdam in 2012 also advanced the cause of mutual openness and understanding.

Finally, internationalization was also advanced on the teaching front, when the European Commission began sponsoring Erasmus Mundus educational programmes. The Commission's support for such programmes on bioethics and health care ethics was an important development. But even more important is that the Commission also sponsors initiatives for developing countries. As such, hundreds of young scholars from Africa, Asia and South America have been trained in European approaches to bioethics and health care ethics. By such efforts, we can look forward to an open future of mutual understanding and collaboration on a global level.

3.2 Regulatory initiatives in bioethics in Europe

The two most important developments on the regulatory level are undoubtedly the creation of an advisory committee to the European Commission and the publication of the Convention on Human Rights and Biomedicine of the Council of Europe (Council of Europe, 1997). While the first initiative emphasizes the role of the ethics advisory committee, the second initiative is more important for the future of the European Union and for so-called bio-law in Europe: it links bioethical insights and principles to the European Declaration on the Protection of Human Rights (which is itself linked with the Universal Declaration of Human Rights). In so doing, this Convention introduces ethical reflection into a legal framework. I will give a short description of these two bodies, before embarking upon a more content-oriented analysis of bioethics in European centres.

The European Group on Ethics (EGE) in Science and New Technologies is an independent, pluralist and multidisciplinary body which advises the European Commission on the ethical aspects of science and new technologies in connection with the preparation and implementation of Community legislation or policies. In December 1997, the European Commission set up this Group to succeed the Group of Advisers on the Ethical Implications of Biotechnology. During its first mandate, the EGE provided opinions on subjects as diverse as human tissue banking, human embryo research, personal health data in the information society, doping in sport and human stem cell research. At the specific request of the President of the Commission, Romano Prodi, the Group also wrote a report on the Charter on Fundamental Rights related to technological innovation. The current Group (whose mandate spans 2011–2016) has 15 members: they are nominated *ad personam*, but the composition of the EGE illustrates the diversity of cultures in Europe. In May 2014, the EGE delivered its 28th Opinion on the Ethics of Security and Surveillance

Technologies to the President of the European Commission, José Manuel Barroso (European Group on Ethics in Science and New Technologies, 2014).

The Council of Europe, which has 47 member states, wished to secure respect for human rights in biomedical research and to harmonize various regulations on bioethics in Europe. This initiative was at the origin of the creation of the very first international Convention on Bioethics. In June 1996 the Steering Committee on Bioethics (CDBI) approved the final form of the draft Convention on Human Rights and Bioethics, which was – somewhat unexpectedly – approved by the Parliamentary Assembly, and adopted by the Committee of Ministers in November 1996 (de Wachter, 1997), as the '*Convention for the Protection of Human Rights and Dignity of the Human Being with regard to the Application of Biology and Medicine: Convention on Human Rights and Biomedicine*'.

While the EGE is fully interdisciplinary and pluralist (the current Chair is the British South African professor Julian Kinderlerer), some commentators criticize the European Convention for being too strongly written from a Kantian interpretation of 'human dignity' (Hottois, 2000). Indeed, the Convention illustrates the strong connection with philosophical traditions in continental Europe, like Kantian deontology, existentialism and personalism. Examples are the prohibition of the creation of human embryos for research purposes (article 18) and the highly important article 21, which provides that it is not permissible for the human body or its parts as such to give rise to financial gain. This principle is based on the need to protect human dignity. Explicitly declared as a foundational principle in international rights instruments, human dignity is described as an inherent attribute that everyone has simply by virtue of being human. It may be stressed that hereby this concept corrects the weight given to human autonomy (highly typical for Anglo-American approaches), but it is at the same time clear that other notions of human dignity are possible. Therefore, the Convention made a philosophically oriented choice, about which debate was – and is – under way.

3.3 Bioethics in the European tradition

In my view, two concepts have guided the majority of continental European approaches to bioethics: the concept of personhood as an integrative concept and the strong belief in the value of solidarity as the basis for a just health care system. It is my belief that the majority of continental Europe still adheres to this integrative concept of personhood. I am well aware of more exclusively autonomy-oriented approaches in European bioethics, but they are in my view one-sidedly presented and too strongly linked with a misinterpretation of American principlism (indeed, the principle of respect for autonomy is only one of the four principles). The relational approach is splendidly presented in a 2000 report of a research project under the Biomed II Programme of the European Commission.

Abel and Terribas (of the Institut Borja de Bioètica) stated, in the introductory remarks:

> The objective was to establish a consensus on the formulation of basic ethical principles in bioethics and biolaw. The task has not been easy, but under the leadership of Professor Peter Kemp, Centre for Ethics and Law in Nature and Society, Copenhagen, we believe it has been successful.
>
> (Rendtorff and Kemp, 2000)

This report may help us to clarify the mainstreams of the European bioethics tradition.

3.3.1 The concept of personhood

One of the most important differences between American principlism and the majority of bioethical approaches on the European continent is connected with the interpretation of the concept of personhood: 'Our European vision of personhood goes further than a minimalist concept of the person, by not only focusing on autonomy but also looking at the concepts of integrity, dignity and vulnerability' (Rendtorff and Kemp, 2000: 23). It is important to notice that the protection of the free development of the human person is highly significant in this philosophy. The anthropological foundation has many philosophical mainstreams, including: Husserl for phenomenology; Heidegger, Scheler, Bergson, Sartre, Merleau-Ponty and Camus (amongst many others) for existentialism; Buber and Levinas for relational philosophy; the Frankfurt School for Communicative Ethics. These different theories and themes have come together to form a specific approach to medical ethics, linked to personalism, an approach which is typical of the ethical tradition in which I work (Schotsmans, 1999). Personalism in medical ethics starts from the affirmation of the relational foundation of the physician-patient relationship and strives to function as an ethical framework to promote the human person in all his or her dimensions and relationships. Crucially important for personalism is the tendency to present a dynamic and historical view on the human person.

3.3.2 The physician-patient relationship

The physician-patient relationship is typically seen as providing a structural and foundational basis for bioethics. This connection is probably linked to the strong traditions of professional ethics in countries like France, Spain, Germany and Belgium. It is my impression that continental European bioethics has always been mindful of this basic ethical culture of the medical profession. Indeed, European philosophers such as Buber (born in Vienna), Levinas (born in Lithuania) and Ricoeur (France) have advanced our understanding of the basic foundational structure of the medical profession: it is a fully relational profession, which exhibits commitment to the patient. In the aforementioned Biomed Report, after having acknowledged how paternalism has given way to respect for the will and wishes of the patient as an independent moral agent, the authors conclude: 'This means that a "friendship model" based on close encounters and prudential relationships between health care personnel and patients precedes the "contractual rights model" of biolaw' (Rendtorff and Kemp, 2000: 70). This affirmation of trust and friendship leads to a fully relational interpretation of medical practice. It is really a 'relationship': the patient does not merely decide, and the doctor does not merely execute the patient's decision. Although I acknowledge that this relational commitment is not accepted by everyone, it may explain why nursing ethics and care ethics are, in recent decades, becoming more prominent in bioethics in Europe.

3.3.3 Solidarity as the founding value of European health care systems

By stressing the value of solidarity, European bioethics has accompanied a socialized model for the delivery of health care. It is important to notice that the idea of European civilization is founded on the ideal of a movement towards social justice, where everyone is respected in his or her humanity. This ideal is premised upon a vision of a collective history, in which solidarity and fraternity mark out the creation of a civilized society, in which every citizen is protected by the rule of the law. In this context, the authors of the Biomed Report use strong words, which are probably more idealistic than realistic:

> We can even say that the welfare state has changed the contractual liberalist understanding of law, based on the social contract. Civil law has changed into social law, leading to a broader conception of state responsibility towards members of society.
>
> (Rendtorff and Kemp, 2000: 60)

Hereby they refuse to accept the liberal credo of personal liberty, instead replacing it with 'state responsibility for the destiny of a citizen'.

This approach has been responsible for the creation of a solidarity-based health care system in Europe, mostly constructed on the idea of collective responsibility. Solidarity implies that the social network is developed in such a way that not only the rich and privileged, but also the poor and the unemployed might have equal access to health care institutions and standard medical treatments. Ruud ter Meulen (1994) refers to the notion of 'humanitarian solidarity': this kind of solidarity, which is based on the dignity of the human person, protects those whose existence is threatened by circumstances beyond their own control, particularly natural fate or unfair social structures. Humanitarian solidarity should be the starting point for defining necessary care. According to such an approach, persons who are unable to care for themselves – for example, due to psychological disability arising from Alzheimer's disease or psychiatric disorder – should have priority of access to caring services. Defined in this way, the basic package should be equally accessible to all, regardless of financial constraints or the need (for example) to make co-payments. A two-tier system based on the principle of humanitarian solidarity puts care, not cure, at the centre of its efforts to provide an adequate level of health care for all (Meulen, 1994).

This solidarity-based approach is difficult to understand from a liberal perspective, and therefore, as I have frequently observed, almost impossible to accept by Anglo-American observers. Many European bioethicists apply this approach, however, and resist an overly market-oriented health care provision, which emphasizes purely free choice and individual financial responsibility. Certainly, the enormous costs of the welfare state create their own problems; however, the ways in which scarce resources are allocated differ radically, depending on whether one adopts a solidarity-based or a market-driven approach.

3.3.4 The concept of human dignity

Probably one of the most foundational European concepts is that of human dignity. Although not shared by everyone (see, for example, the critique of Gilbert Hottois on the concept and the way it is used in the European Convention), the anthropological mainstream, with strong Germanic and Romanic influences, has succeeded in preserving this concept in European bio-law:

> the issue of dignity is fundamentally one of recognizing the 'abstract nudity of humanity' in every human being. Even bodily decay cannot abolish the appeal to treat everybody as ends-in-themselves with equal dignity. It is this conception of human dignity that has become the foundation of human rights as the legal instruments to protect the human person.
>
> (Rendtorff and Kemp, 2000: 37)

Crucial debates (and accompanying legislation) on respect for the human embryo and for new-borns with severe disabilities, the prohibition on organ sales in Europe, as well as respect for the frail elderly and the dying are illustrative of this fundamental orientation.

The ethical contours of the concept of human dignity are nevertheless strongly debated in Europe. It is therefore interesting to see how the Biomed Report sought to synthesize different notions. It is worth quoting the Report at some length; indeed, I consider it crucially important to understand what was meant to be a synthesis between different options:

> Although we must admit that there are great disagreements concerning the adequate understanding of human dignity, a substantial content of the concept can be summed up in the following steps:
>
> 1   Human dignity emerges as a virtue of recognition of the other in an intersubjective relationship. This recognition is based on social

construction. As a social concept human dignity constitutes a capacity that the person has because of his or her social position.
2 Dignity is universalized and indicates the intrinsic value and moral responsibility of every human being.
3 The person must, as a result of the intersubjective understanding of dignity, be considered as without a price. Therefore, human beings cannot be objects for trade or commercial transaction.
4 Dignity is based on self-other relations of shame and proudness, e.g. in degradation and self-esteem.
5 Dignity defines certain "taboo" situations and emotions as the limits of civilized behavior. This means that there are certain things that a society should just not do.
6 In this way dignity emerges in the process of human civilization.
7 Finally, dignity includes the individual's openness to the metaphysical dimensions of life, referring to dignified behavior at the limit-situations of existence such as birth, suffering, death of a beloved other, one's own death etc.

(Rendtorff and Kemp, 2000: 35)

In concluding this section, I must admit that the work of Abel, Kemp and Rendtorff, Kemp and Abel did not really replace American principlism. The Report clearly illustrates, however, how we must understand the differences. Values such as vulnerability, dignity and personhood are central for many European ethicists working in health care institutions. To complement this content-oriented analysis, let us also look at how bioethics functions in Europe.

3.4 The functioning of bioethics: the European contribution

When Beauchamp and Childress (2013) first published their textbook *Principles of Biomedical Ethics* in 1979, they probably did not anticipate the enormous impact their work would have. At the moment, we are at the seventh edition and many medical doctors, nurses and health care personnel have been trained in the application of this ethical methodology. Its success is even symbolized in the label 'principlism'. This has led to an approach which is more or less procedural. One of its weaknesses is clearly that it may be possible to develop a line of principlist reasoning in which fundamental concepts of 'good' and 'bad' remain undefined (Clouser and Gert, 1990). In contrast, many European bioethicists are much more 'teleological' in their methodology. This implies that ethical decision-making and acting is linked to the realization of the humanly desirable (*le meilleur humain désirable* as the 'telos' or goal of our actions), a qualification which the French philosopher Paul Ricoeur would add. Ricoeur was well aware that the ideal is virtually unattainable, so he added the caveat that we should strive for the 'most humanly possible' (*le meilleur humain possible*) (Ricoeur, 1975).

This implies once again that the concept of personhood functions as a clarification of the humanly desirable: the promotion of the human person in all his dimensions and relationships is indeed the dynamic factor in the development of ethical reasoning and acting. This personalist self-understanding of some European bioethicists at the same time explains the importance of the concept of human dignity, responsibility and solidarity, all basic dimensions of the humanly desirable. Ethical reasoning and acting is therefore fundamentally normative and remains challenged by the clarification and realization of the fundamental values of being a person. Ricoeur underlines the importance of the values of identity, relationship and solidarity. These values are present in the consensus of the Biomed Report and were also the guiding orientations for ethical reflection in many continental centres of bioethics in Europe.

In developing such an approach, continental European bioethicists offer a radical critique of those who work with the principlist framework. Indeed, as Clouser and Gert made clear in their landmark 1990 article, principlism lacks a sound ethical basis on which consistent ethical decision-making can be grounded. This is not something new: European medical ethicists, especially those working in Germany and France, have always been reluctant to integrate principlism in their ethical reflections. For the majority of continental European bioethicists, bioethics needs a more anthropological foundation. Fundamental values such as personhood, responsibility and solidarity should always guide ethical evaluations and actions.

These inspirational traditions make bioethics much more than a method for medical decision-making. They help to promote an ethical culture in medicine because they situate bioethics where it really belongs: in the heart and the middle of the relationship between the physician and the vulnerable patient. This implies a revival of the importance of trust and commitment in the interactions between patients and physicians (and other health care personnel). Thanks to the impact of relational philosophy, there is no room for medical paternalism, nor room for radicalized patient autonomy. Medicine is indeed a relational profession: ethical reflection and ethical guidance should respect this fully and contribute to the well-being of patients and vulnerable human beings in the medical context. This ethical approach seeks to serve the 'culture of medicine' and should therefore have a much more influential place in the intercontinental dialogue than it has enjoyed to date. Indeed, medical ethics is more than purely decision-making and 'cold' procedural analysis.

3.5 And the future? Threats and promises

It may be unwise for an 'old man in the sea of bioethics' (to paraphrase Ernest Hemingway's wonderful book) to offer advice for the future. The only thing I can present here is some humble observations. I see promising developments, but also threats. The most important threat, in my view, is the translation of the principle of respect for the autonomy of the patient into a principle which supports the self-disposal of life and body (Schotsmans and Meulenbergs, 2005). Since the early stages of bioethics in the 1970s, the scope and the meaning of the principle of respect for autonomy has shifted away from a relational account of autonomy to an uncompromising veneration of personal freedom to choose. The human person is thus depicted as completely detached from his or her social situation and cannot be determined by his or her intersubjectivity. Thus, every human person finds himself or herself disconnected from others and from his or her own nature. I am very anxious that this notion of autonomy will take the lead in delicate ethical debates, like those on organ sale and euthanasia. In my view, this does not respect the medical culture as a fully relational endeavour.

This becomes clear, for example, in discussions about care for the dying patient. There is, in the autonomy-as-freedom-to-choose approach, no sound reason for prohibiting a person, who is freed from all social or ontological bindings, to decide that he or she wants to die. If human persons are fundamentally detached from each other, people should not consider their relational responsibilities when, for example, an individual opts for euthanasia or assisted dying. The sheer fact that it is the person's own choice is considered the sole right-making characteristic of this choice. The risk of the specific nature of the physician-patient relationship being disturbed or misunderstood because of a too individualistic and contractual approach clearly exists. This affects both the patient and the medical care that he or she receives. An absolute defence of the principle of autonomy entails therefore a number of undesirable consequences. The fading of public encounters, in which one can meet to discuss ideas and to confront personal considerations, is certainly one of them. I share the growing awareness that extending the claims of autonomy can undermine the social (e.g. families and civic institutions) and mental (e.g. processes of socialization and moral development) infrastructure upon which social order, and hence the conditions for autonomy itself, rests (Gaylin, 1996).

Linked to this evolution is a steadily growing commercialization of medicine (organ trafficking, self-tests, direct-to-consumer tests, abuses of plastic surgery, and also profit-oriented evolutions by health care providers and institutions). This is certainly one of the main challenges for humanitarian solidarity in health care. These trends, which are strongly linked to the aforementioned radicalization of personal choice, undermine an ethical culture of care and support.

It is also remarkable that the kind of bioethicist who tries to develop a comprehensive or integrated approach disappears. The *uomo universalis*, who has an integrated view on developments in medicine and health care, is no longer present. More and more – and mainly due to the technicality of medical evolutions – bioethicists are becoming experts in highly specified fields (like bio-banking, patenting, genetic screening and genetic tests, organ transplantation, end-of-life care, etc.). This is also linked to the so-called 'empirical turn in bioethics', which has as a positive side-effect an extended collaboration with the social sciences (Borry, Schotsman and Dierickx, 2005). Dissatisfaction with a foundational interpretation of applied ethics created a stimulus to incorporate empirical research in bioethics. However, this move also represents a loss of confidence in the typical normative and analytic methods of bioethics (Goldenberg, 2005). This trend to specialization in ethical expertise creates a risk that we will overlook more fundamental questions and options.

Yet, the future does not only suggest peril, it also suggests promise. The most promising evolution, which links bioethics with more fundamental ethical theories, is the ongoing interest in care ethics (Gastmans, Leget and Verkerk, 2011). It is remarkable that Gastmans continuously pleads for an explicit anthropological basis – a view of mankind that underlies care. I refer to the third section of this contribution and agree with him that this explicit anthropological basis can help us to clarify concepts closely related to care ethics such as vulnerability, interdependence, care, responsibility, relational autonomy, dignity and personhood.

Another promise is the turn to social ethics: bioethicists have too long neglected the duty to situate highly personalized responsibilities and challenges in the context of national and international health care systems and health care policies (Denier, Gastmans and Vandevelde, 2013). At this point in time, we cannot avoid the need to integrate the societal and generational environments. I am convinced that this is the future of bioethics. Without socializing the debates (even on seemingly purely private choices), we are acting as if we are supernatural human beings. Putting our choices and responsibilities into context makes them real and 'incarnates' the fundamental theories to which we are attached.

3.6 Conclusion

I have here attempted to present a kind of historical review of my perception of the evolution of bioethics on the European continent. After more than 30 years of participation in meetings and research projects, I consider this my duty, being well aware that this is a subjective narrative. It is, however, not only that: the European Convention on Bioethics illustrates that foundational concepts like human dignity, personhood and solidarity help to organize our society and our health care practices. Of course, there are and there will always be different interpretations. It remains for me nevertheless important that bioethicists should not forget their links with anthropological presuppositions. These should be clarified and synthesized. Whilst urging all bioethicists in the world to strive to meet these goals, I can only consider myself (and therefore also this contribution) as one of the little stones in the river of an unending story of care and responsibility. I, therefore, express a sincere hope that bioethics may always and everywhere integrate these many-sided approaches to medicine and health care.

References

Abel, F. (1999) *Bioethical Dialogue in the Perspective of the Third Millennium*, Barcelona: Institut Borja.
Beauchamp, T. L. and Childress, J. F. (2013) *Principles of Biomedical Ethics*, 7th edn, New York: Oxford University Press.
Borry, P., Schotsmans, P., Dierickx, K. (2005). The birth of the empirical turn in bioethics. *Bioethics*, 19 (1), 49–71.
Boyd, K. (2013) 'The Making of Medical Ethics', *Journal of Medical Ethics* 39: 661.
Buber, M. (1923) *Ich und Du*, Leipzig: Im Insel-Verlag.
Campbell, A. V., Gillon R. and Savulescu, J. et al. (2013) 'The Journal of Medical Ethics and Medical Humanities: Offsprings of the London Medical Group', *Journal of Medical Ethics* 39: 667–668.
Clouser, K. D. and Gert, B. (1990) 'A Critique of Principlism', *The Journal of Medicine and Philosophy* 15: 219–236.
Council of Europe (1997) *Convention for the Protection of Human Rights and Dignity of the Human Being with regard to the Application of Biology and Medicine: Convention on Human Rights and Biomedicine* (Oviedo Declaration), Strasbourg: Council of Europe.
Denier, Y., Gastmans, C. and Vandevelde, A. (Eds.) (2013) *Justice, Luck and Responsibility in Health Care. Philosophical Background and Ethical Implications for End-of-Life Care*, Dordrecht: Springer.
de Wachter, M. A. M. (1997) 'The European Convention on Bioethics', *Hastings Center Report*, 27: 13–23.
European Group on Ethics in Science and New Technologies (2014) Available HTTP: <ec.europe.eu/bepa/European-group-ethics> (accessed 21 October 2014).
Gastmans, C., Leget, C. and Verkerk, M. (Eds.) (2011) *Care, Compassion and Recognition. An Ethical Discussion*, Leuven: Peeters.
Gaylin, W. (1996) 'Worshiping Autonomy', *Hastings Center Report*, 26: 45.
Goldenberg, M. J. (2005) 'Evidence-based Ethics? On Evidence-based Practice and the 'Empirical Turn' from Normative Bioethics', *BMC Medical Ethics*, 6: 11.
Hottois, G. (2000) 'A Philosophical and Critical Analysis of the European Convention on Bioethics', *Journal of Medicine and Philosophy*, 25: 133–146.
Levinas, E. (1974) *Autrement qu'être ou au-dela de l'essence*, Den Haag: Kluwer.
Rendtorff, D. J. and Kemp, P. (Eds.) (2000) *Basic Ethical Principles in European Bioethics and Biolaw. Vol. I. Autonomy, Dignity, Integrity and Vulnerability. Vol.II. Partners' Research. Report to the European Commission of the Biomed II Project: Basic Ethical Principles in Bioethics and Biolaw 1995–1998*, Copenhagen and Barcelona: Centre for Ethics and Law and Institut Borja de Bioetica.
Ricoeur, P. (1975) 'Le problème du fondement de la morale', *Sapienza*, 28: 313–337.
Schotsmans, P. (1999) 'Personalism in Medical Ethics', *Ethical Perspectives*, 6: 10–19.
Schotsmans, P. and Meulenbergs, T. (2005) *Euthanasia and Palliative Care in the Low Countries*, Leuven: Peeters.

4 'Getting ethics': voices in harmony in bioethics

Ruth Chadwick

> Collective performance, as in singing the same text to different but interdependent vocal lines, can be regarded as the musical correlate of civilized democracy.
>
> (Whittall, 2002: 561)

4.1 Introduction

It has become normal to describe the process of submitting research for ethical review and approval as 'getting ethics'. I want to suggest, however, that in another sense it is becoming increasingly common that people fail to 'get' ethics in the sense of appreciating what is involved – not in ethical review of research *per se*, but more widely, and in bioethics in particular. This is the case in society at large, where in the past few years we have witnessed a number of scandals, in the United Kingdom at least, affecting many of our institutions, including Parliament, the financial sector, the Church, the BBC and the press. What has been interesting, if dispiriting, about these scandals has been the ways in which the participants involved apparently did not get, or overlooked, the ethical aspects involved in, for example, phone hacking and expense fiddling, and yet they seemed obvious to outraged members of the electorate. Some Members of Parliament who were involved in the expenses scandal said they were 'obeying the rules' as if that was the end of the ethical discussion. In bioethics, however, we have seen a different phenomenon. There may be very widespread appreciation of the fact that issues such as euthanasia, genetic manipulation, stem cell research and others regarded as 'matters of life and death' have ethical dimensions. What has been controversial is the nature and value of the academic field, which has come under criticism from a number of different directions.

In this chapter I will argue that many of the criticisms of bioethics have arisen from a failure to give sufficient recognition to the different voices within it, and I shall suggest that the future of bioethics rests on possibilities of harmony between different voices, as opposed to either unison on the one hand, or discord on the other.

At the time of writing it is ten years since an article in the *Lancet* (Cooter, 2004: 1749) made the following assertion:

> Hardly wet behind the ears, bioethics seems destined for a short lifespan. Conspiring against it is exposure of the funding of some of its US centres by pharmaceutical companies, exclusion of alternative perspectives from the social sciences; retention of narrow analytical notions of ethics in the face of popular expression and academic respect for the place of emotions; divisions within the discipline (including over its origin and meaning); and collusion with, and appropriation by, clinical medicine. To many, its embrace of everything bearing on human life renders it, paradoxically, bankrupt.

It is fair to say that some at least of the issues touched upon in this passage have continued to be debated over the decade since its publication, although there have been many developments in, for example, empirical bioethics, which may appear to make the quotation out of date. The issues of the role and future of bioethics, however, are still live. The passage incorporates a variety of potential criticisms; beginning with the suggestion in the above passage that the lifetime of bioethics will be short, I shall proceed to examine different issues about the field, in the hope of finding what can be learned from this.

4.2 Will bioethics disappear?

What does the forecast of a short lifespan mean? It is difficult to believe that the questions covered by the field will disappear. To say this, however, immediately invites the question of what those questions are – perhaps it is this which is in dispute. I shall presume, however, for the time being, that issues such as the desirability and implementation of assisted dying, and the development and implementation of new technologies, are two examples of the types of issue included in the domain of bioethics.

One possible interpretation of the idea that bioethics will disappear is that we might reach a time when we know the answers to such questions. Although it might be tempting to suppose this, however, it is normally thought to be in the nature of ethical questions that they are re-asked and re-interpreted along with social change. And yet it may be suggested that some ethical questions have been answered to the extent that it is no longer possible to query them, for example, concerning the need for informed consent on the part of research participants. This in itself has been subject to reinterpretation in the context of biobank research, with debates about broad versus narrow consent, and open and dynamic versions of consent.

Where emerging technologies are concerned, as for example happened in the early days of nanotechnology debates, it may be suspected that the ethical issues associated with them simply represent a revisiting of the issues of the long and ongoing genomics debates. Hence discussions tend to focus on whether there is anything different about the particular emerging technology. If there is not, then that might lend credence to the suggestion that bioethics might disappear. In every time and place, however, questions will continue to arise about what we should do and how we should live, whether in relation to (new) technology or in relation to health care and the life sciences more broadly conceived.

What Cooter had in mind, however, does not appear to correspond to either of these possibilities. The claim seems to be not that the *issues* will cease to arise, but that it should not be 'bioethics' which is involved in answering them. Again it is necessary to ask exactly what is meant by this claim. If the questions *constitute* the domain of bioethics then what can it possibly mean to say that it should not be 'bioethics' that is involved in answering them? To say that these questions constitute the domain of bioethics might be construed as a political act – an act of grabbing academic territory. Why should they belong to bioethics rather than arising in the social sciences, law or philosophy?

This takes us to the heart of the question: what exactly is bioethics? Is it a field of study or a professional grouping? Cooter's objection might be to the claim that there is some specific expertise which a group self-designated as 'bioethicists' has, which puts it in a position to address bioethical questions. Cooter himself argued that one of the problems consisted precisely in 'divisions within the discipline', including over its origins and meaning. Before addressing the issue of 'divisions', it may be useful to discuss Cooter's use of the term 'discipline' here, as whether or not bioethics is a discipline is one of the points at issue.

There seem to be three distinct possibilities for the status of bioethics in disciplinary terms. First, bioethics may be considered to be a *branch of an existing discipline*. Of existing disciplines, philosophy is a, if not the, principal contender, as ethics is traditionally a branch of philosophy. Under this interpretation, criticisms of bioethics as a field may be directed against a possible attempt by one discipline to claim a monopoly in answering ethical questions and against the *way* in which it asks and answers ethical questions in this field. This seems to be suggested by Cooter's mention of narrow analytic notions of ethics. I shall return to the role of philosophy below.

Secondly, bioethics may be seen as a *multidisciplinary field*. According to the definition of the International Association of Bioethics (IAB), bioethics is described not as a discipline but as a multidisciplinary *field of study*, involving ethical, legal, social and philosophical aspects (International Association of Bioethics, 2014). The distinction between 'ethical' and 'philosophical' aspects here draws attention to the fact that in bioethical debates some philosophical questions arise that are not ethical, for example, epistemological questions about the limits of knowledge; key conceptual questions about the meaning of terms such as 'life' and 'death'; questions of personal identity.

As already hinted at, there is a potential criticism of defining such a field *as* a distinct field, seeing its purpose as giving a particular status to those who engage in it, viz., bioethicists. Why should social questions not be addressed by social scientists, legal questions by lawyers, philosophical questions by philosophers? To those who take this view, the attempt to define bioethics by the type of questions covered is insufficient. It also raises the problem of credentialling, discussed further below.

Finally, might bioethics be considered *a metadiscipline*? For some of those who work in the field, bioethics is emerging as a discipline or at least as a metadiscipline or transdisciplinary field. According to this view it is possible for those who specialise in bioethics to develop multidisciplinary ways of working beyond their home discipline: to engage properly and effectively in bioethics requires the ability to recognise the different and multiple dimensions that ethical questions have, and to be willing to work collaboratively with other disciplinary perspectives.

The claim that the issues involved in bioethics need a multidisciplinary approach is indeed acknowledged by the IAB definition. To regard it as a field of study rather than a discipline allows for the fact that scholars with different home disciplines can work together to address the issues, without regarding themselves as practitioners of a new discipline. This allows for multiple voices to be heard.

A longer definition than that of the IAB, by Ben Mepham, makes the point about the different fields involved very well:

> bioethics would seem to require the development and integration of several fields of inquiry, which are currently rather disparate. They range from the metaphysical and epistemological questions about the nature of life and humanity; responsibilities for the biosphere, through sociological accounts of the construction of scientific theories; socioeconomic analysis of biotechnological application and consideration of research policy, to the moral, legal and political questions posed by global overpopulation, malnutrition and environmental degradation.
>
> (Mepham, 2014)

Of course, there are still questions about the interactions between them and there is an ongoing debate about the relationship between empirical and theoretical bioethics, about the ways in which different disciplines can work, in parallel or in an integrated way: 'an integrative bioethical blending of historical, practical and ethical considerations of issues, behaviours and actions is necessary to ensure defensible and appropriate responses, social policy and law'(Sodeke, 2012: 17).

The possibility of an integrated metadiscipline, however, raises the question of *bioethicists*, as opposed to sociologists, philosophers or other academics working in the domain.

4.3 Bioethics versus 'bioethicists'

Misunderstandings are apt to arise concerning the relationship between 'bioethics' and 'bioethicists'. In fact, in some circles it is regarded as a joke that no one wants to be regarded as a bioethicist, although many people work on ethical, legal or social aspects of developments in health care and the life sciences. The terms ELSI (ethical, legal and social issues) and ELSA (ethical, legal and social aspects) became fashionable in the 1990s, in relation to genome research in particular, but have been more recently challenged by the term RRI (Responsible Research and Innovation) (Zwart, Landeweerd and van Rooij, 2014).

Bioethics, however, has a longer academic history and a wider remit. There may be a preference for being identified in relation to one's 'home' discipline of philosophy or sociology, bringing this to bear on a specific range of issues, and arguably the terms ELSI and ELSA allow this. But if 'bioethicist' simply means someone who does work on those issues (which may be from one of a number of different perspectives), then why should there be a problem? If 'bioethicist' is taken to mean someone who has a certain type of expertise on the issues, someone who is a professional *qua* bioethicist, however, then it is necessary to be clear about exactly what sort of expertise is involved, without concluding prematurely that there is *no* relevant expertise. The issue of credentialling also becomes central. Indeed this is arguably the most serious challenge facing bioethics today, although discussion of it is not new. What is it that entitles someone to say they are a bioethicist, rather than a philosopher working on bioethical questions?

4.4 Challenges to the role of philosophy in bioethics

Under an interpretation of bioethics that construes it largely as a branch of (applied) philosophy, there are criticisms of bioethics emanating both from within philosophy and from without. Challenges to the practice of applied ethics are not specific to bioethics but range much more widely. From within philosophy, it is important to address the Alasdair MacIntyre question as to whether applied ethics rests on a mistake (MacIntyre, 1984). If applied ethics is understood as 'applying' a set of principles, or a theory, to a practical problem or issue, there are prior questions as to how that question or issue is identified and described, and regarding who construes it as a problem. In the practice of health care, for example, is it for the health care professionals to identify the problems or for philosophers? In so far as it is thought to be the former, the charge of 'collusion' with medicine, as in the passage from Cooter, has to be addressed.

While this is an important question, it will only count as a problem for an account of bioethics which depends on this model of 'application', but whether this is the only possible model needs to be explored. It is also worth noting that similar issues could in principle face other disciplines working in bioethics, depending on the type of work involved.

Critics of bioethics from outside the field of philosophy may have similar concerns, namely that 'armchair philosophers' may be trying to apply theories and principles that have very little relevance to real life practice. It is important to disentangle the particular contribution philosophical ethics has to make to bioethics and the possibility for productive working with other disciplines. On the other hand, the external criticism may be based, not on worries about 'application' in general, but on the view that in bioethics particular approaches have been prioritised, and to this I shall now turn.

4.5 Criticisms of dominant approaches in bioethics

Sometimes, because of the dominance of certain works in the literature, bioethics appears to be caricatured just *as* a particular type of approach. An obvious candidate here is what is known as the 'four principles' approach to the issues. Although these were developed as principles of bio*medical* ethics, rather than as bioethics *tout court*, they are alive and well in bioethics and have been both influential and useful (Beauchamp and Childress, 2013). The nuances of the original text and subsequent editions, however, are sometimes overlooked.

Those critics who have focused on the 'narrowness' of bioethics, whether or not they have the four principles in mind, may not be aware of the diversity of the field. For example, suggestions that bioethics overlooks social issues of power and its distribution in society, and how that affects our understanding of and response to ethical issues, could not justifiably be made about feminist bioethics, at least. Indeed, the repertoire of philosophical theoretical approaches is very diverse, and yet there is some truth in the idea that there was a predominantly individualistic focus in bioethics in the first decades of its development. At the time of writing there is a concerted effort to put public health more firmly on the agenda, although to the extent that justice has been one of the four principles this has never been entirely neglected, as the principle of justice is at stake in issues such as resource allocation, which operates at both the individual and social level. It is fair to say, however, that applied ethics is becoming more specialised. Public health ethics has become a field in its own right, as have nano-ethics, food ethics and nursing ethics, to name but a few, some of which have birthed specialist journals.

To say that bioethics began with a primarily individualistic character does not imply that bioethics itself is *necessarily* individualistic, and certainly does not that imply it is marred by individualism. It is possible to find explanations of why bioethics has been mainly (though not exclusively) concerned with the individual to date, given the history of medical practice, which has been a major factor; and why there is currently a turn to more overtly public health issues. Such issues constitute lively debates *within the field*. It would be a mistake to operate with a picture of bioethics as a discrete and unified field being attacked by the critics. As the following quotation shows, there have long been voices in bioethics pointing to two challenges that need to be addressed:

> how to shift the locus of bioethical dialogue to bring to the foreground implicit assumptions that frame central issues and determine whose voices are to be heard and how to sharpen the vision of a global bioethics to include the perspectives of the marginalized as well as the privileged.
> (Donchin and Diniz, 2001: iv)

Ironically, however, although this multiplicity of voices might be regarded as a healthy sign, and one that is to be found within other disciplines, the different points of view over the meaning of bioethics are regarded as a weakness by Cooter.

4.6 Divisions within the 'discipline'

Interestingly, the point about divisions within the discipline being a weakness is the other side of the coin from the point described above, the caricature of bioethics as one set of principles. Setting on one side for present purposes whether bioethics should be regarded as a discipline, it is nevertheless tempting to ask what discipline does not have divisions, in terms of different schools of thought?

Specific reference is made to divisions over the origin and meaning of bioethics. The history of bioethics is, I think, important, as is its history in specific social contexts. The study of bioethics in context points us to the differences between European and American bioethics, between German and UK bioethics, between East and West – all these and more have been, and remain, fascinating areas, which are informed by the history and nature of the social context. They take us into the realm of the politics of bioethics. A reflexive bioethics does indeed need to be aware of these social factors, but it does not follow from this that the field as a whole is undermined by them, unless one makes the mistake of thinking that the field depends on finding a universally agreed and applicable (bearing in mind the caveat noted above about the limits of 'application') set of principles.

4.7 A global bioethics?

There has indeed been a considerable amount of discussion of the possibility of a global bioethics, and there has been a Universal Declaration about bioethics (UNESCO, 2006). It is not always clear, however, what is meant by global bioethics – whether it involves global in reach or in acceptance or both, and to what extent agreement on a set of principles is sufficient if they are interpreted and/or applied differently (cf. Chadwick and O'Connor, 2014). This debate is arguably outside the remit of the present discussion, as what is at issue is the nature of the field of bioethics. Suffice it to say that the debates about a global bioethics are evidence of the ongoing dialogue within the field and between different schools of thought and cultures, about what bioethics is and should be.

4.8 Framing and social concerns

Attention to social factors, together with the point about 'framing' in the quotation from Donchin and Diniz above, is important and leads to discussion of the next criticism, which is that any theoretical approach 'frames' the issues in a particular way, drawing attention to what the 'framer' considers to be the salient points of a situation. Dominant framings can be blind to the concerns that members of different publics have, whether or not they are key stakeholders in some specific issue, for example by virtue of being a member of a patient organisation.

This is a crucial question for those who use theoretical approaches in bioethics to address, especially where it is claimed that the roots of a given theoretical approach lie in the 'common morality'. What exactly is the 'common morality' and how robust are the claims that a theoretical approach is rooted in it? This point is of course implicit in the criticism of applied ethics discussed above, but it is not directed only at philosophers working in bioethics. It also has bite against members of policy-making committees in the relevant domain, who, for example, think it adequate to address issues using scientific techniques of risk assessment without having regard to what may be more fundamental social concerns. Considerable progress has been made in this area, however, over the last decade and more, in attention to empirical data and public engagement.

4.9 The committee (bio)ethicist

In its relations with public policy, bioethics has come in for a considerable amount of criticism and debate. Within the field, there may be uncertainty among people who are asked to participate in policy-making bodies, as to what their role is. They may be criticised whether they seek to provide answers or whether they do not. They may be confused as to the limits of the debate in which they participate. Are certain options, depending on the context, 'off the table'? The relationship between academic and public policy bioethics is quite complex.

It is crucial in this context to examine the possible senses of ethical expertise. While there is a growing body of literature on the notion and possibility of ethical expertise, an early article by Jenneth Parker (1994) distinguished three different senses of expertise which we might look to in examining the concept. The first is the kind of expertise which refers to having possession of an accepted body of knowledge in the relevant field. The problem in ethics is that there is no one accepted body of knowledge, as there might be, for example, in rheumatology. Of course there may be different schools of thought in medical specialties, notoriously so in psychiatry for example, but in asking for an expert opinion, there is no such thing as an accepted expert opinion on what is the right thing to do – nor is such unison between voices desirable. The ethical expert, in so far as he or she has a relevant body of knowledge, is precisely one who is aware of different approaches to the matter.

The second kind of expertise would be that which is representative of secular opinion on the issues at hand, one who is well versed in the findings of empirical research on the issues in question. This is not generally conceived of as ethical expertise – in fact one of the common criticisms of 'ethical expertise' is that it ignores this, as noted above.

Parker's own suggestion for the relevant kind of expertise is the ability to facilitate debate, rooted in familiarity with a variety of approaches, which enables the 'expert' to ask pertinent questions, query assumptions and draw attention to the ethical dimensions of a situation that might otherwise be overlooked. It must be noted that Parker is concerned with the role of the philosopher as committee ethicist, rather than the bioethicist *per se*, but the distinctions remain helpful in this context, although (as a matter of fact) the position of 'ethicist' on policy-making committees is not exclusive to philosophers.

4.10 Restrictiveness, permissiveness and misconduct

Beyond the discussion of what the role of an ethicist in public policy should be, there has also been criticism of the *performance* of (bio)ethicists in public policy and, indeed, consultancy. They may be criticised for trying to 'stop science' on the one hand and for not stopping anything (by being too liberal) on the other. There may be *ad hominem* criticisms about specific appointments to facilitate certain policy orientations, and so on. In the United States, Republican presidents are unlikely to be advised by the same bioethicists as Democrat ones. In the United Kingdom, the restrictiveness of ethical review by research ethics committees is said to be leading towards ethics fatigue at the very least and possibly hostility towards ethics itself.

Considerations such as these lead to the need to recognise the desirability and urgency of finding a way for bioethics to be facilitative of good research rather than perceived as burdensome and bureaucratic. It is also important, if it is to retain any legitimacy at all, that it not be conceived of as a tool to support particular political agendas.

As with other disciplines and fields of study there may, from time to time, be scandals. In the past few years there have been a number of examples of research misconduct involving fraud in areas such as biological science. In bioethics the alleged issues have concerned, rather, 'getting in bed' with scientists, politicians and/or 'big pharma'. It should not need to be said, however, that even if certain individuals do behave in this way, it does not demonstrate that the field should be regarded as a tarnished 'brand'.

4.11 Conclusions: voices in harmony?

There are many voices in bioethics – voices from different schools of thought, voices from different disciplines, voices from different cultures. Rather than being a weakness, this should be regarded as a strength, because what these different voices have in common is that they are all addressing the same themes. The subject matter, the content, of bioethical debate concerns matters that are important for all human beings, touching on human identity as a living being, in addition to ethical issues that emerge across the life span. It would be a mistake to think that the voices could sing in unison on these topics, and that would not be desirable. It would also be a mistake to think that there is inevitable discord. As said at the beginning, the themes re-emerge and are reinterpreted at different times in different places, as musical themes are taken up by different instruments in a Beethoven string quartet. Of course there is a perennial problem, that some individuals, and even individuals in a position of power, may be 'tone deaf', i.e. they do not 'get' the ethical dimensions of a situation. One of the most important tasks of bioethics, and of ethics more generally, is precisely to draw attention to the ethical dimensions of situations, so that we not only 'get' them but attempt to do something about them.

In order to play a satisfactory part in a professional orchestra or a choir, however, there has to be a demonstrable level of competence. If bioethicists are to be accepted as professional bioethicists, rather than scholars from other disciplines working on a particular set of issues, there needs to be further debate about what that means. While this needs to be the subject of another chapter, it is in itself an ethical issue, and it is important that we 'get' it.

References

Beauchamp, T. and Childress, J. (2013) *Principles of Biomedical Ethics*, 7th edn, New York: Oxford University Press.

Chadwick, R. and O'Connor, A. (2014) 'Ethical theory and global challenges', in D. Moellendorf and H. Widdows (eds), (2015) *The Routledge Handbook on Global Ethics*, Abingdon: Routledge.

Cooter, R. (2004) 'Bioethics', *Lancet*, 364 (9447): 1749.

Donchin, A. and Diniz, D. (2001) 'Guest editors' note', *Bioethics*, 15(3): iii–v.

International Association of Bioethics. (2014) 'Our objectives'. Available HTTP: <http://bioethics-international.org/index.php?show=objectives> (accessed 6 October 2014).

MacIntyre, A. (1984) 'Does applied ethics rest on a mistake?', *Monist*, 67(4): 532–548.

Mepham, B. (2014) *Selected Publications in Bioethics (Volume 1)*, privately published.

Parker, J. (1994) 'Moral philosophy – another "disabling profession"?', in R. Chadwick (ed.), *Ethics and the Professions*, Aldershot: Avebury: 27–41.

Sodeke, S. O. (2012) 'Tuskegee University experience challenges conventional wisdom: Is integrative bioethics practice the new ethics for the public's health?', *Journal of Health Care for the Poor and Underserved*, 32(4): 15–33.

UNESCO (2006) *Universal Declaration on Bioethics and Human Rights*, Paris: UNESCO.

Whittall, A. (2002) 'Harmony', in A. Latham (ed.), *The Oxford Companion to Music*, Oxford: Oxford University Press: 560–563.

Zwart, H., Landeweerd, L. and van Rooij, A. (2014) 'Adapt or perish? Assessing the recent shift in the European research funding arena from 'ELSA' to 'RRI', *Life Sciences, Society and Policy* 10(11) doi:10.1186/s40504-014-0011-x.

Part II
European bioethics in social rooms

5 Personalised medicine: priority setting and opportunity costs in European public health care systems

Jochen Vollmann

5.1 Introduction

Modern medicine now has access to extensive genetic information about humans. In the international *Human Genome Project* the entire human genome was decoded, and technical progress in the field of sequencing technologies enables inexpensive analyses of the complete genome of an individual. Clinical medicine is seeking to utilise these insights from molecular genetics research to treat patients more effectively. In the field of medical diagnostics and treatment, knowledge about the individual genes of a patient is being used to develop custom-tailored, individualised treatments (Chin, Andersen and Futreal, 2011; McDermott, Downing and Stratton, 2011; Phimister, Feero and Guttmacher, 2012; Sledge, 2012). For instance, by determining specific genetic biomarkers in a patient prior to starting treatment, doctors can determine whether or not a cancer drug will be effective against a specific tumour. Ineffective treatments can be excluded from the outset, and patients can therefore also be spared unnecessary adverse side effects. Furthermore, the pharmaceutical industry contends that by avoiding ineffective treatments, considerable health care costs can be saved (Richter-Kuhlmann, 2012a).

This concept of personalised medicine is not only often used in oncology, but also raises hopes of successful treatments for other common diseases, such as cardiovascular diseases, type 2 diabetes mellitus and mental disorders. Frequently, personalised medicine is used as a synonym for progress and the promise of modern medicine *per se* and is presented in an uncritically positive way in research, business and the media (Collins, 2011; Holsboer, 2011; Schwan, 2013). Public research funding has declared personalised medicine to be a priority both at the European and also at the national level (Bundesministerium für Bildung und Forschung, 2010), and large pharmaceutical and biotechnology companies invest billions of euros into this research. Due to new scientific insights and the close cooperation of research, clinics and industry (Collins, 2011; Hüsing, 2010; Mirnezami, Nicholson and Darzi, 2012), modern medicine is facing a new "revolution" (Richter-Kuhlmann, 2012a). The treatment concept also appeals to medical laypersons, as something that is worthy of support. However, are the hopes associated with personalised medicine well founded, and are the high investments justified?

5.2 The concept of a person and "personalised medicine"

The term "personalised medicine" insinuates a kind of medical care which focuses on the health situation and the particular needs of each individual person. This is incorrect and misleading in two ways. First, the molecular genetic complexity of many illnesses makes the possibility of a treatment custom-tailored to each individual person very improbable, while the extremely high efforts and costs of this approach do not appear feasible in the current health care system. What the term connotes is therefore not *personalised* diagnosis and treatment but at best diagnostic and therapeutic approaches which are targeted at specific patient subgroups, for example, groups which have the same tumour biomarkers (*stratified medicine*).

Second, medical care focused on molecular genetic characteristics has nothing to do with medical care oriented to the individual patient. *Individualisation* only takes place at the molecular genetic level, but not at the personal level between doctor and patient. To achieve a personal treatment, the person of the patient should be placed at the centre of treatment, and this is exactly what so-called personalised medicine does not do (Dabrock, Braun and Ried, 2012; Hüsing, 2010). A person is not only distinguished by biological traits, but also by individual psychological and social characteristics and needs. Individuals have their own lifestyles, values and preferences (Yurkiewicz, 2010). Law and ethics emphasise the normative implications of the concept of personhood, as evident in ongoing debates about so-called "personhood" (Lampe, 1998; Mahowald, 1995). As a consequence, in the doctor-patient relationship, the patient is entitled to adequate education and information by the doctor and has the individual right to consent to or to refuse a treatment (Kohnen, Schildmann and Vollmann, 2012). The patient's self-determined decision must be respected, even if it goes against the doctor's advice and against a medical indication, precisely because we ascribe the person these rights (Vollmann, 2008).

This ethical and anthropological understanding of the "person" is expressed by many people in their wishes towards modern medicine. Patients wish to be perceived by their doctors and by medical institutions as individual persons with questions, wishes and normative preferences. In the citizens' report *High-Tech Medicine: What Kind of Health Care Do We Want?* of the German Federal Ministry of Education and Research, citizens demand that medical and nursing staff have better communication skills. Furthermore, alongside the specialist subjects, mental and interpersonal aspects in day-to-day patient care must play an equal role in medical and nursing education and training and in research. The importance of taking time for the patient should be rediscovered in modern medicine (Bundesministerium für Bildung und Forschung, 2011; cf. Koch, 2012; Siegmund-Schultze, 2011). This broader cultural understanding of the term "person" and the wishes of citizens for personal medical care are not considered in so-called personalised medicine. The term sounds appealing but is misleading. The intention of the inappropriate use of the term "person", which is conveyed in numerous texts and images in advertising materials, is to achieve a positive image and wide acceptance in society. It is important to debunk this questionable advertising strategy because it abuses the concept of personhood, perceives patients primarily as carriers of molecular genetically determined traits and suggests a genetic determinism for medicine (Kerr and Cunningham-Burley, 2000; Tauber and Sarkar, 1993) and aims at setting specific priorities in research funding. The latter, in particular, requires a transparent and critical discussion, as well as democratic decision-making.

5.3 Basic research and clinical application

Additional doubts arise with regard to the statement of the U.S. *Food and Drug Administration (FDA)* that after a decade of billions of dollars in investments in the *Human Genome Project* and in subsequent genetic analysis studies, the yield has only been a small number of clinical treatments on the basis of genetic biomarkers (Hüsing, 2010; Marshall, 2011). In addition, for the president of the Max Planck Society, the hope of immediately deriving rapid medical progress from the deciphering of the human genome has hardly been fulfilled (Gruss, 2011). Upon closer scientific observation the reason for this discrepancy is clear. The clinical applications that have been successful until now are mainly in the field of oncology and are limited to a few tumour types for which the molecular genetic biomarkers are known and for which there is a treatment available. This fortunate constellation is the exception in clinical practice; for the majority of patients these new treatments are of no benefit. The scientific explanation for the slow clinical progress lies in the complexity of tumour biology, where the variability and mutation dynamics of the genetic traits of many tumours complicate the development of targeted therapies. Progress in clinical treatment and practice does not necessarily follow from a brilliant treatment approach that is derived from basic research (Browman, Hébert and Coutts, 2011; Burke and Psaty, 2007; Konstantinopoulos, Karamouzis and Papavassiliou, 2009; Ludwig, 2012). Unfortunately, the international experience during the last decade makes rapid clinical progress for the majority of cancer patients very unlikely.

5.4 Medical research and industry under pressure to succeed

This sobering conclusion is contrary to the euphoria about the promise of personalised medicine. After decades without innovation breakthroughs, many biomedical researchers long for significant therapeutic progress (Collins, 2011; Holsboer, 2011; Hudson, 2009). The pharmaceutical industry is in a similar situation – its patents for the strongest selling drugs (so-called "blockbusters") are due to expire in the coming years, and many companies do not have any new, innovative drugs in their development pipeline (Collier, 2011; Greiner, 2012). Rather, the pharmaceutical and biotechnology industries are under pressure from the markets to reduce their high costs for research and development, since these, given the lack of innovation, do not refinance themselves (Aiolfi, 2011; Dhankhar, Evers and Møller, 2012; Hunt, Manson and Morgan, 2011; KPMG, 2011). Compared to the stock price development of other companies, the value of many pharmaceutical companies has declined, while the return on investment from the high expenditures in research and development has been falling for years. As a result, consultants predict tough times ahead for the pharmaceutical industry (Frankfurter Allgemeine Zeitung, 2012).

In this difficult economic situation, many pharmaceutical companies are counting on rapid progress in the new field of personalised medicine. However, the high expectations are contrasted to the sluggish progress in the clinical application of personalised medicine (Ludwig, 2012). In practice, there is a danger that insufficiently tested drugs might be introduced too hastily into clinical care. New "personalised" diagnostics and therapeutics may not have been approved without sufficient proof of their effectiveness. However, validation studies that are required for scientific proof of effectiveness are seldom carried out because these are long-term, complex and costly (Ludwig, 2012). It is commonly argued that in personalised medicine the relevant cost and time-consuming proof of effectiveness does not apply and should be abbreviated to get approval for the drug. But even in small patient groups and targeted treatments, the effectiveness and benefit of new drugs must be scientifically proven to ensure the health and welfare of the patients and to avoid unnecessary health costs (Ludwig, Fetscherand and Schildmann, 2009; Richter-Kuhlmann, 2012a).

For this reason, drugs in the field of personalised treatments must be checked according to normal approval procedures, in order to meet scientific and therapeutic standards. Since current clinical research in the field of personalised medicine is primarily financed by the pharmaceutical industry, conflicts of interest are inevitable (Valachis et al., 2012). To promote the necessary gain in scientific knowledge in this new field, we therefore need more clinical research that is publically funded and is independent from the private sector. This would strengthen serious patient-oriented clinical research that is independent of short-term economic interests (Vollmann, Schildmann and Kohnen, 2011). At present, however, universities and other public research organisations in this field are hardly autonomous and independent, so that the content of research activities and research strategies are often heavily influenced by industry (Dreger, 2011).

5.5 Priority setting and opportunity costs

The high investment costs in research based on molecular genetic criteria raise the question of opportunity costs. This type of research ultimately provides stratified medical care that only benefits subgroups of patients. Investments in this field have been made for more than a decade and, due to many open research questions, will continue to be made in the future (Rauprich, 2010). Given the limited resources in the health care sector, a prioritisation decision is required already at the research level regarding the extent of public resources that shall flow into particular areas of the health care system. A research priority in one area limits the remaining research funds for other medical specialty areas. With regard to the promotion and funding of personalised medicine, this difficult normative and political decision is further exacerbated since there are only a relatively small number of patients who may benefit from these very expensive measures. That is why clinical physicians are concerned that through the prioritised promotion of personalised medicine, other important clinical and health care areas which might be beneficial for many patients will be neglected (Browman et al., 2011; Koch, 2012; Ludwig, 2012; Siegmund-Schultze, 2011). Thus far, only a minority of patients have benefited from this expensive, research- and economics-driven project of personalised medicine (Browman et al., 2011; Deutscher Ethikrat [German Ethics Council], 2012; Hamburg and Collins, 2010). Based on previous experience, high profits can be expected from expensive cancer drugs for small patient groups (so-called "niche busters"), and therefore this approach continues to appear lucrative for the pharmaceutical industry, without taking into account the health needs of the majority of patients in our health care system.

Whereas in oncology at least a small portion of patients have benefited from the innovations of personalised medicine, they have until now brought no benefit for patients in other social and medically important disease groups. For example, for the common disease type 2 diabetes, none of the molecular genetic descriptions of subgroups, biomarkers, etc. are superior to the usual preventive, diagnostic and treatment options and do not improve the health situation of the affected patients (Schulze, 2011). Moreover, screening for type 2 diabetes does not offer any relevant advantages (Simmons et al., 2012). Rather, as our society ages, our nutrition, exercise and lifestyle play an increasingly crucial role in the prevention and treatment of type 2 diabetes (Kurth, 2012; Richter-Kuhlmann, 2012b). For this disease, modern medicine does not primarily require new molecular genetic insights but rather socio-medical care approaches and intensive public health research to enable and support at-risk and affected people to adopt healthy behaviours as individuals. But this research is seriously underfunded in our health care system.

Another example is the increasing importance of mental illness as a public health concern in our society. Mental illness and its treatment and prevention are of great significance for affected patients, health insurance companies, pension fund insurance companies (who bear the cost of rehabilitation) as well as for the labour market. According to the German Federal Ministry of Labour and Social Affairs, the missed days at work due to mental disorders have increased from 6.6 per cent in 2001 to 13.1 per cent in 2010, which is associated with economic costs of approximately €8–10 billion annually. The most important specified causes are higher demands at the workplace, increased personal responsibility, pressure to be flexible, irregular employment relationships and job insecurity (Deutsches Ärzteblatt, 2012). The current care of these patients in our health care system is under criticism due to excessively long sick leave times, also excessive waiting times for psychiatric and psychotherapy treatment and/or in-patient rehabilitation measures and too frequent early retirements due to mental disorders. Investments are therefore required in research to develop new concepts for social-psychiatric prevention and treatment, thus, for example, enabling effective prevention and early intervention at the workplace and improving the cooperation between the company doctor, primary care physician, psychiatrist and hospital, etc. This raises the issue whether we as a society shall respond to the increasing importance of mental illness primarily with high investments in molecular genetic research for "personalised treatment" or invest at least in equal measure in social psychiatric and mental health research, which in current research policy is allocated relatively few funds.

Therefore, from a medical ethics perspective, the existing preference for molecular genetics medicine in personalised medicine in contrast to other research fields in the publically funded health care system needs to be critically examined. In essence, all prioritisation decisions are ethical decisions in which competing values must be weighed (Rauprich, 2010). In doing so, transparency must prevail regarding who decides about what facts matter, which criteria are used and on which arguments decisions are based. Therefore, it is ethically unacceptable that influential individual interests *de facto* determine medical research priorities and resource allocation in the publically funded health care system. But this is exactly what is currently happening under the innocuous label of "personalised medicine". Cost-benefit assessments of the individual treatments – now often discussed – are also insufficient, since, on the basis of empirical data, they only allow statements about the medical benefits and the costs of the treatment area under investigation. Frequently in practice, the selection of the treatment area for research already represents a setting of priorities within the overall spectrum of possible health-promoting measures, without prior reflection on the norms involved. For our health care in the future, what is required are transparent and democratically legitimised superordinate medical and research policy prioritisations.

However, our society leaves crucial research policy decisions to internationally active stakeholders from research and industry. Whereas public funds have invested heavily in basic research (e.g. Human Genome Project), in the field of clinical applications priority setting is left to the discretion of the international pharmaceutical industry. In Germany, universities and other public research organisations have little influence on content prioritisation in this field because, as I noted above, due to the lack of public funding, independent research hardly exists. To be sure, cooperation with the public health authorities is always emphasised in order to coordinate health care and socio-economic priorities. In reality, however, this hardly ever happens. The reason is that international pharmaceutical companies develop diagnostics and drugs for the world market (Dhankhar et al., 2012; Frankfurter Allgemeine Zeitung,

2013; Hunt et al., 2011; KPMG, 2011; Schwan, 2013). However, the health care needs and the financing of the health care systems differ greatly from country to country. For example, the health care market in the U.S. (currently the largest), with its strong private sector orientation and a high proportion of citizens who lack medical insurance, differs greatly from European health care systems. The demographic trend of Western societies contrasts sharply with that of the economically emerging countries such as Brazil and India, with their high proportion of young people in the population and a growing, upwardly mobile middle class that finances its medical care privately (Agarwal, d'Almeida and Francis, 2012). In 2020 the pharmaceutical industry will make the same amount of profit in these so-called *emerging markets* as it does in the current largest market, the U.S. (KPMG, 2011). And these profits will originate from innovative products, including products in the fields of personalised medicine, which are expensive and have to be paid for privately (Griggs, 2009). By contrast, the importance of European health care markets for the development of new drugs is declining.

Given the different socio-economic and health priorities, which vary from country to country, the research and development investments of the pharmaceutical industry will follow international market opportunities, which are not necessarily congruent with health care needs in Germany and other European countries. To provide optimal health care for our population, it is essential to develop our own strategic research and health care policy in the public health sector. To achieve this, those responsible for health and research policy must recognise the existing problems and put them forward for public debate. However, past experience with a public discussion about setting priorities and rationing in the health care system in Germany gives little cause for optimism. A wealthy, shrinking and ageing society does not muster the strength to carry out a reform or to design its own public health system. Thus, society should not complain when global stakeholders set priorities under the lofty-sounding label of personalised medicine – priorities that do not correspond to the society's own health care needs.

5.6 Conclusion

Genetic, biomarker-based personalised medicine does not contribute to a more personal treatment of individual patients, in contrast to patient- or person-centred medical care. Subgroups of patients, for example in oncology, may have medical advantages from the present progress in personalised medicine, but it is unlikely that this will be the case for the overall majority of patients. The promise of less expensive health care through personalised medicine lacks any empirical evidence. Rather, based on past experience, an increase in costs is more likely. A public debate is needed on priority setting in medical research and treatment and about how societies and public health systems can influence the development of the research agenda regarding future health care priorities.

References

Agarwal, S., d'Almeida, J. and Francis, T. (2012) 'Capturing the Brazilian pharma opportunity. Global pharma companies are missing a chance to serve Brazil's increasingly prosperous and growing middle class', *McKinsey Quarterly*, March 2012: 1–4.

Aiolfi, S. (2011) 'Die Pharmaforschung ist zu teuer. Investoren zeigen sich irritiert über einen offensichtlichen Mangel an Effizienz', *Neue Zürcher Zeitung*, 31 December 2011.

Browman, G., Hébert, P.C. and Coutts, J. (2011) 'Personalized medicine: A windfall for science, but what about patients?', *Canadian Medical Association Journal*, 183: E1277.

Bundesministerium für Bildung und Forschung (2010) *Ideen. Innovation. Wachstum – Hightech-Strategie 2020 für Deutschland*, Berlin: Bundesministerium für Bildung und Forschung.

Bundesministerium für Bildung und Forschung (2011) *Bürgerreport: Hightech-Medizin – Welche Gesundheit wollen wir?*, Berlin: Bundesministerium für Bildung und Forschung.

Burke, W. and Psaty, B.M. (2007) 'Personalized medicine in the era of genomics', *Journal of the American Medical Association*, 298: 1682–1684.

Chin, L., Andersen, J.N. and Futreal, P.A. (2011) 'Cancer genomics: From discovery science to personalized medicine', *Nature Medicine*, 17: 297–303.

Collier, R. (2011) 'Bye, bye blockbusters, hello niche busters', *Canadian Medical Association Journal*, 183: E697–E698.

Collins, F.S. (2011) *Meine Gene – mein Leben*, Heidelberg: Spektrum Akademischer Verlag.

Dabrock, P., Braun, M. and Ried, J. (2012) 'Individualisierte Medizin: Ethische und gesellschaftliche Herausforderungen', *Forum*, 27: 209–213.

Deutscher Ethikrat [German Ethics Council] (2012) *Pressemitteilungen: Ethikrat rückt den Patienten in den Fokus der personalisierten Medizin*. Berlin: Deutscher Ethikrat.

Deutsches Ärzteblatt (2012) 'Krankschreibungen: Mehr Fehltage wegen psychischer Erkrankungen', *Deutsches Ärzteblatt*, 109: A-948.

Dhankhar, A., Evers, M. and Møller, M. (2012) *Escaping the sword of Damocles: Toward a new future for pharmaceutical R&D*. Chicago: McKinsey and Company.

Dreger, P. (2011) 'Brief: Priorisierung in der Forschung', *Deutsches Ärzteblatt*, 108: A-2286.

Frankfurter Allgemeine Zeitung. (2012) 'Im Gespräch: Thomas Strüngmann, Unternehmer und Investor in der Pharmabranche', *Frankfurter Allgemeine Zeitung*, 10 April 2012.

Frankfurter Allgemeine Zeitung. (2013) 'Sanofi schmerzt Patentauslauf. Gewinn des Pharmakonzerns könnte 2013 sinken', *Frankfurter Allgemeine Zeitung*, 8 February 2013.

Greiner, W. (2012) 'Ökonomische Herausforderungen der individualisierten Medizin', *Forum*, 27: 203–208.

Griggs, J.J. (2009) 'Personalized medicine: A Perk of Privilege?', *Clinical Pharmacology & Therapeutics*, 86: 21–23.

Gruss, P. (2011) 'Der Faktor Mensch', *MaxPlanckForschung*, 1: 6–7.

Hamburg, M.A. and Collins, F.S. (2010) 'The path to personalized medicine', *New England Journal of Medicine*, 363(4): 301–304.

Holsboer, F. (2011) *Biologie für die Seele: Mein Weg zur personalisierten Medizin*. München: dtv.

Hudson, T.J. (2009) 'Personalized medicine: A transformative approach is needed', *Canadian Medical Association Journal*, 180: 911–913.

Hunt, V., Manson, N. and Morgan, P. (2011) 'A wake-up call for big pharma: Pharmaceuticals and medical products practice', *McKinsey Quarterly*, December 2011: 1–6.

Hüsing, B. (2010) 'Individualisierte Medizin – Potenziale und Handlungsbedarf', *Zeitschrift für Evidenz, Fortbildung und Qualität im Gesundheitswesen*, 104: 727–731.

Kerr, A. and Cunningham-Burley, S. (2000) 'On ambivalence and risk: Reflexive modernity and the new human genetics', *Sociology*, 34: 283–304.

Koch, M. (2012) 'Arzt-Patienten-Beziehung: In falsches Fahrwasser geraten', *Deutsches Ärzteblatt*, 109: A-20.

Kohnen, T., Schildmann, J. and Vollmann, J. (2012) 'Patients' self-determination in "personalized medicine": The case of whole genome sequencing and tissue banking in oncology'. In: *Individualized medicine between hype and hope*. Hg. P. Dabrock; M. Braun; J. Ried. Zürich: Lit Verlag, 97–110.

Konstantinopoulos, P.A., Karamouzis, M.V. and Papavassiliou, A.G. (2009) 'Educational and social-ethical issues in the pursuit of molecular medicine', *Molecular Medicine*, 15: 60–63.

KPMG. (2011) *Pharmaceuticals: Future pharma. Five strategies to accelerate the transformation of the pharmaceutical industry by 2020*. London: KPMG.

Kurth, B-M. (2012) 'Erste Ergebnisse aus der "Studie zur Gesundheit Erwachsener in Deutschland"' (DEGS), *Bundesgesundheitsblatt*, 55: 980–990.

Lampe, E-J. (1998) 'Persönlichkeit, Persönlichkeitsphäre, Persönlichkeitsrecht'. In: *Persönlichkeit, Familie, Eigentum: Grundrechte aus der Sicht der Sozial- und Verhaltenswissenschaften*. Hg. E-J Lampe. Opladen: Westdeutscher Verlag, 73–102.

Ludwig, W-D. (2012) 'Möglichkeiten und Grenzen der stratifizierenden Medizin am Beispiel von prädiktiven Biomarkern und "zielgerichteten" medikamentösen Therapien in der Onkologie', *Zeitschrift für Evidenz, Fortbildung und Qualität im Gesundheitswesen*, 122: 11–22.

Ludwig, W-D., Fetscher, S. and Schildmann, J. (2009) 'Teure Innovationen in der Onkologie – für alle? Überlegungen zu Voraussetzungen für eine rationale Pharmakotherapie und ethische Herausforderungen', *Der Onkologe*, 15: 1004–1014.

Mahowald, M.B. (1995) 'Person'. In: *Encyclopedia of Bioethics*, 4th edn. Reich, W.T. (ed.) New York: Simon & Schuster and Prentice Hall International, 1934–1940.

Marshall, E. (2011) 'Waiting for the revolution', *Science*, 331: 526–529.

McDermott, U., Downing, J.R. and Stratton, M.R. (2011) 'Genomics and the continuum of cancer care', *New England Journal of Medicine*, 364: 340–350.

Mirnezami, R., Nicholson, J. and Darzi, A. (2012) 'Preparing for precision medicine', *New England Journal of Medicine*, 366: 489–491.

Phimister, E.G., Feero, G.W. and Guttmacher, A.E. (2012) 'Realizing genomic medicine', *New England Journal of Medicine*, 366: 757–759.

Rauprich, O. (2010) 'Rationierung unter den Bedingungen der Endlichkeit im Gesundheitswesen'. In: *Endliches Leben Interdisziplinäre Zugänge zum Phänomen der Krankheit*. Hg. G. Thomas; M. Höfner; S. Schaede. Tübingen: Mohr Siebeck, 229–256.

Richter-Kuhlmann, E. (2012a) 'Pränataldiagnostik: Paradigmenwechsel', *Deutsches Ärzteblatt*, 109: A-1306.

——— (2012b) 'Gesundheitssurvey des Robert-Koch-Instituts: Zivilisationskrankheiten nehmen zu', *Deutsches Ärzteblatt*, 109: C-1171–1172.

Schulze, M. (2011) *Programme of the international symposium: predictive genetic testing, risk communication and risk perception: Value of genetic. Information for diabetes risk prediction*, Berlin: Robert Koch Institut.

Schwan, S. (2013) 'Die Dividendenhoffnungen bleiben intakt', *Frankfurter Allgemeine Zeitung*, 14 January 2013.

Siegmund-Schultze, N. (2011) 'Versorgung von Krebspatienten: Menschliche Zuwendung aufwerten', *Deutsches Ärzteblatt*, 108: A-932.

Simmons, R.K., Echouff o-Tcheugui, J.B., Sharp, S.J. et al. (2012) 'Screening for type 2 diabetes and population mortality over 10 years (ADDITION-Cambridge): A cluster-randomised controlled trial', *Lancet*, 380: 1741–1748.

Sledge, G.W. (2012) 'The challenge and promise of the genomic era', *Journal of Clinical Oncology*, 30: 203–209.

Tauber, A.I. and Sarkar, S. (1993) 'The ideology of the Human Genome Project', *Journal of the Royal Society and Medicine*, 86: 537–540.

Valachis, A., Polyzos, N.P., Nearchou, A. et al. (2012) 'Financial relationships in economic analyses of targeted therapies in oncology', *Journal of Clinical Oncology*, 30: 1316–1320.

Vollmann, J. (2008) *Patientenselbstbestimmung und Selbstbestimmungsfähigkeit: Beiträge zur klinischen Ethik*, Stuttgart: Kohlhammer.

Vollmann, J., Schildmann, J. and Kohnen, T. (2011) 'Onkologie: Sehr gut recherchiert', *Deutsches Ärzteblatt*, 108: A-2341.

Yurkiewicz, S. (2010) 'The prospects for personalized medicine', *Hastings Center Report*, 40: 14–18.

6 Phage-ethics: a 'depth' bioethical reading of Sinclair Lewis's science novel *Arrowsmith*

Hub Zwart

6.1 Introduction

Arrowsmith (published in 1925) is an intriguing novel for various reasons, and may be read from various perspectives.[1] My personal fascination with this 500-page romance stems from the fact that it is often regarded as the first real *science novel*, devoted to experimental laboratory research as a practice, a profession, an ideology, a worldview, a 'prominent strand in modern culture' (Schorer, 1961: 414), a way of life.[2] Named after its key protagonist Martin Arrowsmith, it records an important event in the history of biomedicine: the discovery of the 'bacterium-eating' virus, the bacteriophage. But it also addresses a moral ambivalence that runs through biomedicine as a research field, namely the tension between the exacting demands of 'pure' research, on the one hand, and its various (more or less benevolent) applications in medical practice, on the other. The novel stages a series of dramatic moral conflicts between the duties of Martin Arrowsmith as a physician (working for the benefit of his patients) and as a researcher (working for the benefit of future generations, of 'humankind'). Thus, *Arrowsmith* serves as a paradigm of a whole genre, and Lewis's lively descriptions of science communication, priority conflicts, funding strategies, research ethics and laboratory rivalries are still relevant today. First and foremost, however, the novel allows us to discern how, beneath biomedicine's manifest aspiration to promote human well-being, there is a 'deeper' impulse, a disconcerting obsession at work that may prove highly disruptive, not only for test animals, research subjects and patients, but also for the scientists themselves. Biomedicine's fuelling desire, its *cupido sciendi* (its 'will to know') is not predominantly to save, but rather to *control* life, and the aim of a 'depth bioethical' reading is to bring this subliminal dimension to the surface.

Sinclair Lewis (who was awarded the Nobel Prize for literature in 1930) wrote what is perhaps his best novel in collaboration with science writer Paul de Kruif,[3] a graduate from the University of Michigan who had worked as a bacteriologist ('microbe hunter') at the Rockefeller Institute for Medical Research in New York[4] and was well underway to become a prominent author himself.[5] He would publish his (still famous) best-selling book *The*

Microbe Hunters in 1926. Whereas Lewis (son of a general practitioner) was responsible for the descriptions of marital, domestic, professional and civic life in the United States a century ago, de Kruif added the scientific ingredients (the biomedical jargon and the intricate details of laboratory research). But he also portrayed one of the most intriguing characters of the book, namely Max Gottlieb: a 'blend' (de Kruif, 1962: 93, 102), or 'amalgam' (Markel, 2001: 372), or *Mischperson* as Freud calls it (1900/1942: 299) of Frederick G. Novy (de Kruif's professor of bacteriology at the University of Michigan) and Jacques Loeb, the famous biologist of German-Jewish descent (1859–1924) who joined the Rockefeller Institute in 1910 (Pauly, 1981; Fangerau, 2006).[6] Lewis and de Kruif toured the Caribbean together on a 'literary safari' (de Kruif, 1962), combining furious writing with heavy drinking, collecting ample materials for their masterpiece along the way.[7] And while de Kruif offered Lewis a crash course in bacteriology, Lewis provided de Kruif with an apprenticeship in non-academic writing.

Arrowsmith is a must for bioethicists because it portrays the relentless (and potentially disruptive) will to power that drives life science research. Whereas on the 'manifest' level biomedicine aspires to do good, there is a 'mysterious and unreasoning compulsion' (Lewis, 1925/2002: 146) at work that cannot be reduced to purely altruistic motives. This is underlined by a disconcerting quote from Paul de Kruif (who passed on his own research ethos on Martin Arrowsmith) about the 'nihilism' of scientific inquiry:

> Why had I stopped the study of medicine and switched to bacteriology? ... [What did] my years of cool butchery of thousands of rabbits and guinea pigs show but a lack of reverence for life? I was destructive. I [was] a nihilist, period. For me, the world was too full of people and animals. And having no spark of reverence for all life, I had no ethics.
> (1962: 39)

To bring this 'deeper' impulse to the fore, I will read the novel from a psychoanalytic angle, using methods and concepts borrowed from Freud and Lacan. A 'depth bioethical' reading may help us to discern, and come to terms with, this disconcerting normative 'flaw' at the core of what is purported to be the 'science of life'. But before explaining the design of my chapter more fully, let me first provide an outline of the plot.

6.2 Plot outline

Like Lewis himself (born in Sauk Centre, Minnesota, in 1885) Martin Arrowsmith grows up in the American Mid-West at the turn of the century, but as a young adult, his biography more closely resembles that of Paul de Kruif (1890–1971). Like him, he is a medical student at the University of 'Winnemac' (≡ Michigan) at 'Maholis' (≡ Ann Arbor), a 'factory designed to produce physicians much like the Ford Motor Company produces cars'

(Lewis, 1925/2002: 8). Here, Martin becomes infected with the spirit of pure science, personified by Max Gottlieb (≡ Jacques Loeb), a *Fremdkörper* in professional medicine: a professor of bacteriology rather than a physician, who puts his life in the service of an obsession, a fatal addiction: 'pure', basic research. His goal is to synthesise antitoxins *in vitro* to free humanity from the scourge of infectious disease, but also to free laboratory researchers from the laborious use of test animals (as impure and unreliable models). Martin wants to follow in his footsteps and become a bacteriologist himself: a devotee, a believer in the 'religion' of science.

But as he meets a female nurse (Leora) and becomes a married man, he has to choose between a career as a general practitioner (that will provide him with social respectability and an income) and the uncertainties of a life devoted to science-for-its-own-sake. Somewhat reluctantly, he opts for the former, thus betraying his true calling, suppressing his persistent feelings of discontent with heavy drinking. Martin gives in to the reality principle, as it were, allowing himself to become enwrapped in civic, marital and professional life. Yet, he keeps up his habit of spending long and lonely nights tinkering in his home-made laboratory. At a certain point he investigates a local outbreak of cattle disease, publishes his results in the *Journal of Infectious Diseases* and sends a reprint to Gottlieb, who now works as a principal researcher at the McGurk Institute (≡ the Rockefeller Institute) in New York. Gottlieb invites Martin to join him at McGurk and Martin eagerly accepts the invitation.

During his research there, he coincidentally discovers a strange invisible 'something', a mysterious 'principle X' which destroys bacteria, and he decides to study it meticulously, in accordance with the rigorous methods of his mentor. Unfortunately, while being engrossed in his analyses, but experiencing serious inhibitions when it comes to putting his findings to paper, Felix d'Herelle of the Pasteur Institute announces his discovery of what he refers to as the 'bacterium-eating' virus, the bacteriophage. After recovering from this serious drawback (the loss of priority), Martin is urged by Gottlieb to continue his phage research, but to focus on practical applications instead, using these predators of bacteria as 'allies' in the war against disease. When the fictitious Caribbean island of St. Hubert is struck with bubonic plague, and McGurk is called upon for help, Martin is sent there (accompanied by his wife Leora and a drinking companion, the public health specialist Sondelius) to conduct a field trial designed to determine whether 'phage' can effectively be employed in fighting lethal pathogens. The result is a moral clash between the island's administrators (who had expected a life-saving doctor) and Martin's own objective as a scientist, intent on using the population as 'material' for his trial. Thus, he finds himself confronted with an ethical dilemma: as a physician, it is his duty to vaccinate as many inhabitants as possible, but as a researcher, he is in need of an (untreated) control group to demonstrate the effectiveness of his vaccine. This means dividing the illiterate population of a village into two equal halves: the saved and the doomed.

Initially, he remains loyal to the experimental rigour instilled in him by Gottlieb, but after the tragic death of both Sondelius and his wife the physician in him gains the upper hand and he contaminates the experiment that was supposed to bring him everlasting fame. He still manages to publish his results, but tampers with his sloppy data so as to make his story sufficiently convincing. He marries again, this time to an affluent socialite widow who kindly provides him with a lavishly equipped laboratory of his own. Yet, utter dislike of the social life of the New York elite, in combination with marital unease, presses him to leave both wife and child behind and to escape to the wilderness of Vermont, where, together with a former colleague, he lives out his mania for 'pure' research, virtually undisturbed, in an isolated forest cabin.

In the following sections, key dimensions of the novel will be subjected to a psychoanalytical reading, treating Martin Arrowsmith as a case study (*Fallgeschichte*). Successively, I will focus on: (a) the organisational and occupational hazards of a biomedical career; (b) the 'cupido sciendi' of pure science as a 'divine madness'; (c) Martin's grand moment of discovery (the bacteriophage as the intrusion of the 'real'); (d) the core medical-ethical dilemma (the bacteriologist as a physician and as a researcher) and (e) cabin science: Martin's escape to a reclusive, scientific Walden, the novel's final act. Finally, I will address the question of how analysing *Arrowsmith* may add to bioethical discourse.

6.3 Medical practice and its discontents

For young Martin Arrowsmith, becoming a doctor involves an extended process of socialisation into the medical profession. Although courses in bacteriology and immunology are indispensable ingredients of his training, they nonetheless represent something which, in essence, remains at odds with professional medicine, namely basic research: science for the sake of science (seeing human beings as research subjects rather than as patients). The pure scientist (Max Gottlieb) is an oddity on the campus, eager to recruit a small number of students (the elect 'few') – or even one single student, Martin. This means luring Martin away from a normal professional career, converting him to the spirit of pure science.[8]

Thus, the novel depicts a failed process of socialisation. Martin continues to waver between the world of medical professionals (from country doctors up to metropolitan hospital surgeons), on the one hand, and the international subculture of 'pure' scientists on the other: nomads really, contemptuous of 'worldly success' (Lewis, 1925/2002: 11), speaking a strange, artificial language, migrating from one laboratory to the next, convening at international conferences and publishing dense quantitative analyses in esoteric journals. Sooner or later, Martin will have to choose between the 'profane' world of medical practice and the 'sacred' world of laboratory work, with McGurk, the 'immaculate' laboratory, towering as the ultimate 'sanctuary' of science (Lewis, 1925/2002: 310): a 'Heavenly laboratory in which good scientists may spend eternity in happy and thoroughly impractical research' (Lewis, 1925/2002: 147).

Just a few years before *Arrowsmith* was published, Sigmund Freud (1921/1940) elaborated his views on socialisation in 'Massenpsychologie und Ichanalyse' ('Group psychology and the analysis of the ego'). How can an organised group of people (an 'organised crowd') sustain itself in view of the fact that, for individuals, participation in groups comes with a price: they must relinquish private interests and short-term rewards to pursue distant goals that can only be collectively achieved? How can self-centredness, individualism and discontent in modern mass societies be overcome? For Freud, the key to understanding the functioning of well-organised groups (as opposed to unorganised groups, the *crowds* or *mobs*, intimidating, but prone to panic) is identification. Groups need leaders: parental figures embodying the collective ideal and endowed with sufficient charisma and prestige for anonymous group members to identify themselves with these leaders. And this is precisely the weakness of professional medicine as depicted in Lewis's novel – and the cause of Martin's failure. The various father figures (representatives of organised medicine) are relentlessly ridiculed, one after the other. Only Loeb escapes the pervasive atmosphere of satire.

In the early twentieth century, group behaviour had become an urgent topic. Societies were becoming mass societies; modern media were creating mass audiences; politics had become the domain of mass movements; and even science itself was expanding in scope and scale: new universities were established and new types of scientific institutions were founded (such as the Rockefeller, in 1901). The question of how to manage and organise large groups was not a purely academic one.

In *Arrowsmith* we see a chronic tension/collision between two types of groups (two types of calling), highly dependent on one another, and yet apparently mutually exclusive, namely ('impure') medical practice and basic ('pure') research. For Martin, there are many incentives for choosing a medical career: the income and respectability of the profession, the possibility of marriage and of upward social mobility, in combination with the public acknowledgement of the relevance of this type of work. Yet, what is lacking, to a deplorable extent, is inspiring personalities. One by one the father figures in Lewis's novel (representing medicine and public health) are ridiculed as hypocrites, endorsing unsubstantiated claims and leading uninspiring lives. On top of that, Martin himself is not a good physician at all, lacking 'bedside manners' and communicative skills, while his drinking habits are symptomatic of his ambivalence: his repressed yearning for pure inquiry.

Gottlieb, by contrast, seems to stand out as a beacon of integrity, a scientific prophet, a window into the future. Their first meetings give rise to 'imprinting', as it were. No matter how hard Martin tries to 'repress' his admiration for his hero, his exposure to Gottlieb prevents him from developing a whole-hearted commitment to medical practice. Indeed, although he had 'given up Gottlieb-worship and his yearning for the laboratory . . . something of Gottlieb's spirit remained' (Lewis, 1925/2002: 115).

Having mesmerised Martin during his lectures, and subsequently during the laboratory hours they spent together, Gottlieb continues to draw Martin towards him.[9] Gottlieb considers 'medical science' a contradiction in terms. He is the genuine scientist, devoting his life to intellectual aspirations, willing to work excessively hard and to accept the risk of failure. Martin is in awe of Gottlieb, the ideal 'father figure' he is looking for (Parry, 2008: vii), an ego-ideal or intellectual conscience, encouraging him to work harder. Indeed, Gottlieb 'indoctrinates him into the religion of a scientist' (ibid: viii).

A 'rapport' is created in very first lecture he attends, and Martin identifies himself with his life-long mentor. The novel describes how, at the beginning of the lecture, Professor Max Gottlieb is about to assassinate a guinea pig with anthrax germs, displaying his masterful technical dexterity, claiming that 'technique is the beginning of all science' (Lewis, 1925/2002: 36). As Lewis phrases it, the class was 'a mob' (ibid: 35), 'shuddering' (ibid: 36) in response to the idea that even a small sample of anthrax bacilli could easily produce a lethal infection. But Martin is simply enthralled by Gottlieb. Indeed:

> Martin Arrowsmith already saw himself doing the same experiment and, as he remembered Gottlieb's unerring fingers, his hands curved in imitation . . . . He had begun, perhaps in youthful imitation of Gottlieb, to work by himself in the laboratory at night.
>
> (ibid: 38–39)

He mimics and copies Gottlieb's words and gestures. And via Gottlieb, who studied with Helmholtz and idolises Koch, Martin extends his identification to his master's masters.

This fascination for scientific truth hampers his professional career, causing a chronic sense of ambivalence: 'Martin remained doubtful, he admired the insistence on the physician's immediate service to mankind, but he could not forget the cool ascetic hours in the laboratory' (ibid: 119). As a symptom of this ambivalence, he insists on having a makeshift laboratory of his own where he continues his habit of conducting experiments, usually at night, although this is barely tolerated by his social environment.

His research position at McGurk (where he joins his ego-ideal again), his dramatic expedition to the Caribbean and, finally, his retreat into the woods are all instances of a 'return of the repressed'. Having been exposed to the quest for pure science, he cannot really become socialised into normal civil society any more. Indeed, in *Arrowsmith*, bacteriology is presented as an infectious 'affliction', spreading from the laboratories of Pasteur and Koch into the United States, with researchers such as Gottlieb as 'carriers' or 'vectors'.[10] As Freud argues in 'Massenpsychologie und Ich-analyse', there is a strong desire in infected individuals to confer their infection to others, for why should they alone be excluded from the benefits of social life and condemned to an ascetic existence of toil and hardship (Freud, 1921/1940: 134)? But what exactly makes laboratory research so 'infectious' (for individuals 'susceptible' to it), so alluring?

6.4 *Cupido sciendi*: pure science as a divine, infectious madness

Arrowsmith contains numerous descriptions of biomedical research settings with racks of test-tubes, Bunsen burners, constant temperature baths, centrifuges, autoclaves, note-books and so on, but this in itself does not explain the fatal attraction these *loci* of truth exert on individuals such as Martin. Rather, what attracts him in science is the aura of a quasi-religious calling. This is underlined by an improvised sermon by Gottlieb, with Martin (who has just entered McGurk) 'at his feet' (Doctorow, 2008: 453), explaining that science, extremely demanding and error-prone, is essentially a religion:

> I make many mistakes. But one thing I keep always pure: the religion of a scientist. To be a scientist [is] like mysticism . . . it makes its victims all different from the good normal man . . . The scientist is intensely religious – he is so religious that he will not accept quarter-truths, because they are an insult to his faith . . . he is a man that all nice good-natured people should naturally hate! . . . [The authentic scientist is] the only real revolutionary . . . He lives in a cold, clear light . . . Not all the men who work at science are scientists. So few! . . . To be a scientist [there are] two things you must do: work twice as hard as you can, and keep people from using you. I will try to protect you from success . . . May Koch bless you!.
> (Lewis, 1925/2002: 292–293)

Science means perseverance, loneliness. Research had not yet evolved into the large-scale, pre-programmed phenomenon it has become today. Discoveries are made by solitary individuals at their benches, preferably after hours, during the night.[11] McGurk encourages individuals to pursue their goals in splendid isolation. Research is 'pure', researcher-driven, and intolerant towards the 'quarter-truths' abounding in the real world outside the lab.

As a general practitioner struggling in the fuzzy, dreary outside world, Martin tries to forget about Gottlieb, who continues to haunt him like a phantom. As a doctor, Martin is deprived of something – and of someone. The repressed attachment continues to cast a shadow[12] and his ego is split into two halves: on the one hand the married, heavy-drinking professional, on the other hand the would-be researcher, tormented by his intellectual conscience (his ego-ideal), failing to live up to his true vocation. His entering McGurk as a research associate entails a moment of euphoria and triumph, of reconciliation and atonement: a spiritual 'inflammation'. He and Gottlieb (the 'demon' of pure science) are finally on speaking terms again.

In *Arrowsmith* the ethos of science is described as a divine madness, a θεία μανία, as Plato phrased it (*Phaedrus*, 244–256). Inside their laboratory, similar to Plato's philosophers, scientists behold a realm of truth which is invisible for untrained senses, a transcendent region only discernible to the initiated mind, although there are many who, after much toil and hardship, leave the field without gaining even a glimpse of this higher reality (ibid; 248B). Because of their desire for truth, true scientists cannot sleep at night. They must distance themselves from the common 'herd' of mankind, ignoring their neighbours, who rebuke them for apparently having gone mad. In *Arrowsmith*, this madness does not give access to a 'higher' realm (of ideas), as in Plato, but rather to a 'deeper' realm of microbes, only accessible via microscopes. The topology has changed: rather than striving upwards, the modern scientist aims to dive deeper, but a similar amount of persistence is required. Only those who, like Martin, persevere in their tedious, repetitive activities will experience the 'joy' (Lewis, 1925/2002: 43), the 'rapt quietude' (ibid: 125), the 'beautiful precision and dullness' (ibid: 40) of laboratory work. They will 'sink blissfully into the laboratory' (ibid: 270), 'beyond sounding in their experimentation' (ibid: 305), so that their lab becomes a 'perfect world' (ibid: 295).

On the verge of the discovery of his 'principle X', Martin becomes completely absorbed in his work. He forgets about night and day, becomes unconscious of the world, completely exhausts himself, until he goes literally mad: 'He was completely fagged, perhaps a little insane' (ibid: 326). Indeed, he works himself into a state of 'neurasthenia':

> Martin watched himself, in the madness of overwork, drift toward neurasthenia . . . From irritability he passed into a sick nervousness in which he missed things for which he reached, dropped test-tubes, gasped at sudden footsteps behind him . . . Then he was obsessed by the desire to spell backward all the words which snatched at him from signs . . . At last Fear closed in on him. [It began] with terror of the darkness. Footsteps in the hall were a creeping cutthroat . . . When in the street below he did actually see a man standing still, he was cold with panic. Every sky glow was a fire . . . He knew absolutely that his fears were absurd, and that knowledge did not at all keep them from dominating him. Till the safe dawn brought back a dependable world.
>
> (ibid: 332–333)

As a consequence of his fatigue, he suffers from a wide range of symptoms: insomnia, agoraphobia, claustrophobia, pyrophobia, siderodromophobia (i.e. the fear of railway journeys) and, most of all, anthropophobia, and yet he realises that, sooner or later, his crazy experiment will turn 'from overwhelming glory into sane . . . routine' again (ibid: 335). What is it that, during this episode of self-imposed mental suffering, reveals itself to him? What is this 'gold' which he seems about to find (ibid: 336)?

6.5 The bacteriophage as the intrusion of the 'real'

Arrowsmith makes it sufficiently clear that experimental laboratory work is oftentimes quite tiresome and repetitive. Researchers redo their experiments over and over again, under various conditions, in order to confirm and verify their results. As World War I is gliding into its final, most sinister act, Martin quietly attends the beautiful, grapelike microbes named staphylococci, which he cultivates in vitro.[13] All of a sudden, something completely unexpected happens, thwarting his expectations in a rather dramatic fashion. What went wrong?

The purpose of laboratories is to keep the unexpected and disturbing at bay, allowing researchers to achieve maximal control over nature. The experimental setting is designed to immunise against disturbances and intrusions ('noise'). The real world (out there, beyond the confines of the lab) is kept at a safe distance. Research facilities are purified, streamlined versions of reality, devoid of debris, processing tiny, artificial samples of nature that can be meticulously studied, such as strains of bacteria in test-tubes, carefully cultivated, protected, isolated, controllable and predictable to a considerable extent, with the help of measurements and mathematical equations.

But now, in the midst of this tedious, repetitive, quantitative work, something highly unusual occurs, something which cannot be ignored. 'I have hit something' (Lewis, 1925/2002: 323), Martin aptly exclaims, something 'at the mysterious source of life' (ibid: 321), something which is not mentioned in the manuals or journals of normal science. A violent, disruptive, completely unknown dimension of nature suddenly opens up to him. A peaceful strain of staphylococcus bacteria, which should be flourishing and multiplying in their flask, is suddenly missing. Instead of a colony of bugs, he discerns a 'clearing' (ibid: 325). The microbes have all disappeared: a most uncanny situation. Under his microscope, he sees 'nothing but shadows of what had been bacteria: thin outlines, the form still there but the substance gone; minute skeletons on an infinitesimal battlefield' (ibid: 323). While World War I is raging, Martin hovers over a perennial battlefield (existing since time immemorial) on the microbial level, spotting the ghostly remainders of his perished troops (with test-tubes turned into trenches). Something has dissolved them, wiped them out. It looks as if they committed 'suicide' on the spot (ibid). Something is relentlessly preying on these peaceful herds; something violent has entered the lab, reminiscent of Heraclites' maxim that warfare (πόλεμος) is the essence of being. What is this intruding 'something'?

Jacques Lacan would have called it 'the real': something which cannot be discerned directly, but intrudes and flouts our expectations, something alien, amorphous, unknown and uncanny; something we were *not* looking for. All of a sudden, something is missing which should be there (something is *Fort* which should be *Da*): a researcher is suddenly deprived of his microbes. They are reduced to phantoms: ghostly, emptied organisms, bodies without organelles. Nothing survives the intruder's attack. The real is that which is discovered by coincidence, which resists the normal functioning of scientific practice (Lacan, 2007: 29) but cannot be ignored any longer; something profoundly alien and 'other'.[14] It can only be tamed if embedded in the symbolic order, by identifying, naming, counting and analysing it: the basic objective of laboratory research.[15]

Martin's discovery of the bacteriophage is also a turning point in the movie version (Ford, 1931). In mid-winter,[16] with Manhattan covered in snow, Martin places three flasks in a refrigerator, thick with bugs. Returning to his laboratory later that evening, unable to detach himself from his work, he discovers that in one of them, the bugs have completely vanished. Instead of being turbid, the fluid is clear. Under his microscope, which he handles with professional ease, he discovers the remnants of what had been a thriving colony of bugs. Nothing like this had ever happened before. Was it good or bad? Bad, because it ruins his experiment, but he quickly considers the option that it might be something 'good', something 'better'. Bugs don't commit suicide: what slaughtered them? It must be *something*. In fact, it turns out to be the greatest *thing* that ever happened to him. 'I have found *something*', he triumphantly exclaims, 'but don't ask me what it *is*,' After days of prolonged labour, Gottlieb glances though his notes and says: 'Martin, you have a big *thing* here, a great *thing* . . . You must find out what it *is* . . . You will begin working in earnest'.

Techno-scientific artefacts create a man-made, controllable reality, but the disconcerting real is never completely annihilated. It persists in the folds and margins of the laboratory world,[17] offering resistance to complete 'assimilation' (Lacan, 1973: 65), revealing itself as a gap, a crevice, a rupture, something totally unexpected (Lacan, 1991/2001: 58), unacknowledged, unnamed, unmeasured, unvisualised. The real is basically an intrusion, a disruption: that which resists our expectations. It is the 'inexorable' (Lacan, 2013: 565). As Heraclites phrased it, many centuries ago: real nature is wont to hide herself, but sudden revelations may prove quite disconcerting (Lacan, 2004: 90ff). The real is that which, from the point of view of normal science, seems utterly impossible (Lacan, 2011: 141).

A first important step towards the 'symbolisation'/domestication of the real is the act of naming. Martin uses a provisional, empty signifier for his strange entity: 'Principle X'.[18] In the struggle over priority which unfolds, d'Herelle emerges victoriously, not only because he is the first to publish his results, but also because he gives the new entity a convincing name: the virus that preys on bugs, the *bacteriophage*. By coining this signifier, which aptly conveys (in shorthand) what the mysterious entity actually *does*, he definitely makes a name for himself. We see science at work: with scientists achieving immortality by successfully adding a new signifier to the network of names, concepts and symbols which Lacan refers to as the 'symbolical order'. By providing it with a name, the bacteriophage (or 'phage', as Americans soon prefer to call it (Cairns et al, 1966)) becomes something that can be analysed and normalised, something scientists can relate and refer to: equations can now be drafted; the anomaly becomes embedded in discourse.[19]

Why didn't Martin publish his findings earlier? Because the scientific method, personified by Gottlieb (his 'conscience'), prevented him from doing so. No preliminary results, however intriguing, even if they bring you everlasting fame: that is Gottlieb's ethos. More research is always needed.

As a super-ego (*Über-Ich*), Gottlieb proves too demanding. He does not let Martin *enjoy* the fruits of his sacrifices, his late-night hours. Martin never seems to have laboured enough. With Gottlieb peering over his shoulder, he feels paralysed when it comes to putting his findings on paper. As Freud (1921/1940) phrased it, the leader of the organised group (the collective conscience or ego-ideal) is reluctant to grant his co-workers their personal triumphs, as this would set them apart from others and reward their striving for independence. Gottlieb already said it in his sermon: 'I will try to protect you from success.' Whereas Director Tubbs urges Martin to hasten and publish his results, Gottlieb keeps discouraging him from doing so. And when the latter walks into Martin's lab to tell him the bad news about d'Herelle's publication (according to Gottlieb's rigid standards a premature, sloppy publication, no doubt), he is ambivalent about it. Although he deplores the fact that Martin (and, by implication, the Institute) has lost the race over priority, the sublime ethic of pure science nonetheless stood its ground, rather than compromising itself by hastily running into print, merely to attain worldly fame. Martin, the researcher in the trenches as it were, is sacrificed to these lofty ideals. And rather than regretting his reluctance, Martin himself experiences relief for not having published a 'premature' paper (Lewis, 1925/2002: 345). He doesn't revolt against Gottlieb's sinister regime: not yet, but continues to produce more knowledge, work harder, even risk his life, by travelling to plague-ridden St. Hubert, where his devotion to the lofty ideals of science will be put to the test even more relentlessly.

6.6 The medical-ethical dilemma (the bacteriologist as researcher and physician)

The history of the bacteriophage is closely connected with World War I. Bacterial viruses were discovered in 1915 by the English microbiologist F.W. Twort, who discontinued his research because of the war effort. Two years later, in 1917, the phage was discovered for a second time[20] by French-Canadian Félix d'Herelle at the Pasteur Institute. In d'Herelle's original publication, he calls the bacteriophage a potential panacea, a 'microbe of immunity'. Therapeutic trials proved unsuccessful, however, and 'phage therapy' (the use of phage as a bacterium-killer, as a soldier in the 'war' against infectious diseases) eventually gave way to more effective means: penicillin and other antibiotics (Dublanchet and Bourne, 2007).[21]

The bacteriophage itself became essentially a lab organism: a tool for basic research in molecular biology, and achieved world-renown through the work of Max Delbrück at Caltech (Pasadena) who employed it as a 'minimal organism' (the 'hydrogen atom of biology'). His phage summer course at Cold Spring Harbor[22] put young James Watson on the road to success (Watson, 1966). In Lewis's novel, phage research is still in its earliest, 'applicatory' stage. With de Kruif providing the necessary scientific details, *Arrowsmith* follows actual history quite closely, as if d'Herelle and Arrowsmith are really contemporaries, stumbling over bacterial viruses at different locations (Paris and New York) more or less simultaneously.

Seeing the struggle for priority lost,[23] Gottlieb urges Martin to reorient his agenda towards applied research. The outbreak of bubonic plague in the Lesser Antilles provides him with a perfect opportunity to test his phage *in vivo*. His motives are scientific rather than medical and he sets off on an expedition which is not meant to save lives, but rather to produce a landmark publication. the time has come to test his principle X in an outdoor setting, exposing it to the reality principle as it were. Bacterial viruses are still untried in the real world outside the lab. Will the vaccine work in the messy and complex environment called reality? The inhabitants of St. Hubert are seen as research subjects rather than suffering patients. The population of a remote village (providing optimal conditions for a field trial) is divided into two samples: the experimental condition (receiving the phage vaccine) and the control group (denied the life-saving serum and treated with traditional methods) – a strategy which Pasteur and his followers had successfully adopted in their experiments with cattle (Zwart, 2008: 177ff).[24] Indeed, the experiment (purportedly for the benefit of mankind, but primarily conducted on behalf of the prestige of McGurk) is performed by Americans at the expense of non-white, native human 'bodies' (Lynch, 2000). Moreover, as the phage vaccine begins to show results, it becomes increasingly difficult to uphold the experimental design in practice.

Initially, Martin is bent on conducting high-quality research sufficiently robust to render (friendly but powerless) doctors obsolete for good, but in the end he acknowledges that he is 'too human to be a satisfactory experimenter'. The panic-stricken controls (the anonymous, indigenous masses) secretly move over to the experimental sample, and finally, due to the death of Martin's two most significant others (Western individuals with a name and a face, namely Sondelius and Leora),[25] Martin becomes aware of the disruptive logic of 'pure' biomedical research that endangers rather than safeguards life. He now gives his phage vaccine to everybody, ignoring Gottlieb's instructions (his inflexible ego-ideal in command). The objective is reversed from conducting experiments to beneficence. With a scientific conscience weakened by inconsolable remorse, tropical heat and heavy liquor, he fails the test. Giving in to emotional pressures, he proves unable to uphold his unconditional allegiance to pure research.

There are dramatic examples in real history of similar conflicts between the roles of physician and researcher (between caring for severely ill patients and trying to find a magic bullet), for instance in the case of AIDS. Another famous example is the discovery of cyclosporine to prevent rejection of organ transplants (Starzl, 1967, 1992/2003). After the heroic first stage of organ transplantation (during the 1950s and 1960s), a severe crisis emerged in the 1970s. Implants were rejected, immune systems were ruined. Cyclosporine seemed to offer a miracle cure. Prospects for patients improved dramatically. But in order for the new product to become available, it had to be tested in randomised trials, allowing the results from the experimental condition (the 'saved') to be compared with those of the controls (the 'doomed').

Martin continues to waver between both roles. Initially, he remains loyal to the gospel of randomised trials preached by Gottlieb, but eventually he botches his experiment and spoils his results, assuming the role of 'saviour' of the desperate. The plague disappears from the island, but it is no longer possible to conclusively prove that it was the phage vaccine that did it (as plagues always have the tendency to disappear after a while, even in the absence of any biomedical intervention whatsoever).[26] Thus, his final big opportunity to acquire everlasting fame is thwarted. Martin's fatal flaw is his incapacity to consistently uphold his loyalty to one of these two incommensurable deontologies: the demands of scientific rigour versus the principles of professional medical ethics – although the deontology of science seems the dominant one because an *Über-Ich* is 'introjected' (as Freud calls it) into his psyche, personified by Gottlieb. He feels haunted by the latter's critical gaze, experiences any concessions to his duties as a physician as moral weakness and sees his West Indies expedition as a failure because he put the well-being of people above research (Parry, 2008: ix).

Beneath his 'manifest' allegiance to Gottlieb, however, a 'latent' Oedipal conflict is clearly at work as well. Throughout the novel, Martin struggles to distance himself from Gottlieb-the-father, attempting to evade the inevitable Oedipal collision that awaits him should they remain too close. This is what makes him leave the (promising) field of bacteriology to become a country doctor: an independent, married adult with an income, craving to free himself from the tyranny of 'Gottliebism' (Lewis, 1925/2002: 116). Yet, Gottlieb crosses his path again and Martin, tormented by discontent, now eagerly subordinates himself to his found-again father-figure, wasting two long years on dreary, repetitive, meaningless lab work, without any output of significance. When suddenly the perennial microbial battlefield opens up before his eyes, for the first time in biomedical history, Gottlieb proves an excessively stern father, notably towards his 'favourite' (ibid: 64), standing in the way between Martin and his international breakthrough, consciously retarding and discouraging his publication, so that the competition over priority is lost. Gottlieb effectively hinders Martin to seize the one big opportunity to 'make a name for himself', as Tubbs phrases it: gaining international recognition and achieving intellectual independence as a department head (a position offered to him by Tubbs, but withdrawn as soon as the news of d'Herelle's publication reaches New York).

This is also reflected by Gottlieb's comments on this occasion: 'Something has happened, not altogether bad.' Martin fails to step out of his long shadow even now, and is sent on a gloomy errand, all for the glory of Gottlieb himself, whose life-work he is supposed to fulfil: the St. Hubert expedition, although at a certain point he is overwhelmed by an outburst of male, Oedipal protest: 'To Hell with experiments! To Hell with Gottlieb!', as the movie version phrases it.

66 Hub Zwart

Upon his return to New York City, he bursts into Gottlieb's office to make a fully-fledged 'confession': 'I did not add to knowledge. I did the humane thing. I lost sight of science'. But he can't get through to Gottlieb any more: he has become senile, so that Martin cannot be 'cleansed' (Lewis, 1925/2002: 422). Instead of accepting his father's place (the position of department head is now offered to him once again), he flees from McGurk for good, taking his microscope with him – an item which functions as a phallic symbol, an enabling contrivance, complementing the deficiencies of a faltering personality – to follow a fugitive colleague into the forest. His final gesture is a refusal to accept endorsement by the professional, institutional, symbolic order. After the death of the father, Martin flees from the role he is expected to play, and from the claustrophobic embrace of his wealthy spouse, who mothers him and bereaves him of what is left of his independence.

6.7 A scientific Walden: the ideal world of cabin science?

Martin is torn between the profane world of everyday existence and the sacred realm of science. The normal world is depicted in a cynical and sarcastic manner. Only heavy drinking allows the hero to survive this empire of imperfection, of love, marriage and human company, where real-life people oftentimes prove disappointing and abusive.

In the realm of science, Martin finds purity and precision, instead of sloppiness and contamination. The two realms compare to one another as newspapers and popular magazines compare to the *Journal of Infectious Diseases*. But in the scientific realm, the death-drive reigns: Martin studies bugs in order to systematically eradicate them (to destroy these 'amiable' pathogenic germs, with their 'lovely flagella' (Lewis, 1925/2002: 41)), while staggering numbers of test animals (rabbits and guinea pigs) are 'sacrificed' on behalf of (often quite pointless) research, without any ethical review procedure whatsoever. At a certain point, Martin even starts using chimpanzees for a two-year project that ends in failure, although 'murdering monkeys proves expensive and grim' (ibid: 440). And finally, on St. Hubert, human beings are sent to death like guinea pigs for the sake of upholding the rigorous logic of randomised trials, represented by a highly charged term: the word 'control'[27] – the novel's basic 'signifier', the most powerful noun Martin as a student adopted from Gottlieb, playing a decisive role in the structuring of the plot.

For Martin, the conflict seems unsolvable. One is *either* a scientist, *or* a doctor (Clarfield, 2007). The normal, professional world ('reality') is a wasteland of boredom – a waste of time. The 'religion' of science promises personal redemption, but this can only be achieved by conducting experiments, almost as a 'religious exercise' (Löwy, 1988).

As a final solution, in a desperate quest for salvation, Martin prefers *flight* over *fight*, into the forest, the outdoors world, where a self-made cabin laboratory is installed. Thus, Martin moves from rural medicine (North Dakota) to public health (a small town in Iowa) to bacteriology (a fashionable Chicago clinic) to basic research (New York, the 'ultimate' city) and finally to 'pastoralism' (Doctorow, 2008: 456). Here, in a drastically simplified world (in stark contrast to the extravagantly furnished laboratory organisation at McGurk),[28] he can finally *act out* his ideal of uncontaminated inquiry, albeit in a rather imaginary manner, since life in this tiny scientific hermitage (this 'shrine': Lewis, 1925/2002: 467) is almost completely out of touch with what is happening in the world at large. Here, in isolation, he can really begin working in earnest, continuously, day and night.[29] As a stranded researcher conducting experiments which seem bereft of all purpose, he continues to respond to what Lacan sees as the basic commandment of modern science: Go on, continue to produce more knowledge (1991: 120)![30] It is the attitude of the neurotic who, unable to deal with the conflicting demands and tensions of the real world (i.e. the world of contracts, relationships, professional expectations, rivalling claims, priority conflicts and so on), decides to drastically simplify his life. Only in this manner can he live up to his fantasy of pure, uncontaminated activity, instilled in him during his student days by Gottlieb.

6.8 Conclusion

Arrowsmith addresses a basic divide running through biomedicine, a clash between two (incommensurable) 'deontologies': the principles of medical ethics on the one hand and the demands of experimental research on the other. Although biomedicine is allegedly motivated by the objective to promote well-being (enhancing the effectiveness of clinical practice), *Arrowsmith* emphasises that there is another, rather disruptive impulse at work as well: a violent will to control life, endangering rather than protecting the well-being not only of research animals, but also of patients and, eventually, of biomedical researchers (such as Martin Arrowsmith) themselves. They must choose between two options, both of which are presented as morally unsatisfactory: on the one hand medical practice, portrayed as fundamentally insincere (permeated by *mauvaise foi*, to use the Sartrean term), on the other hand the methodology of randomised trials, depicted as inconsiderate and ruthless. After a series of fiascos, Martin's 'solution' is simplification and escape (*flight* instead of *fight*).

One may ask whether this 'nihilistic' portrayal of the moral dichotomy is inevitable. In real life, the relationship between medical practice and basic research can perhaps be seen in a different light: as a host-virus interaction, for instance, so that the one cannot really function without the other. In splendid isolation, pure science may become thin and empty, may find itself deprived of its 'mechanisms of defence' against the relentless drive towards control that fuels the quest for knowledge. And perhaps one may even argue that the novel's grim message was inspired by Oedipal motives (with Lewis denouncing his father's medical occupation, and de Kruif settling his accounts with the Rockefeller Institute, which sacked him because of his budding journalistic aspirations).

But this would be too easy. The chronic tension is there for real. In Lacanian terms: the phage is Martin Arrowsmith's *object a*: the cause of his desire, that which gives meaning to his life, that which makes him move and act. Suffering, desperate patients are not his primary source of inspiration. He is motivated by an invisible, faceless laboratory phenomenon, inexorable and uncanny, hovering between living and non-living, and more addictive than heavy liquor. The phage is the one thing he wants to control, but which is actually controlling him. In his craving to transform it into a predictable tool, a working vaccine would merely have been a by-product in this struggle for power between the researcher and his virus. He hopes the phage will end his discontent, his anonymity, by making him famous, turning his life into a success story after all. Medical benefit functions as a mere façade, a pretext for his urge to dominate nature down to her most elementary (viral) dimensions, working himself into a state of neurasthenia – in accordance with Dostoyevsky's insistence that intellectual activity is, in the final instance, a 'disease' (1864/1972: 18).

In short, we are not confronted with a moral 'dilemma' (a problem that can be 'solved' by developing and abiding to rules and regulations, such as ethical principles of research with human subjects). Although these may allow us to subdue the tension, making it more manageable, they cannot abolish it. The desire to control life is addictive in itself and cannot be reduced to altruistic motives. As a science novel, *Arrowsmith* opens up and dramatises this basic divide. By doing so, it may further the sensitivity of physicians, scientists and bioethicists to the gap between what basic research produces and what clinical medicine basically needs.

Notes

1 As a portrayal of medical practice in the American Mid-West in the early twentieth century, for instance, or of the devastating consequences of alcoholism, or of the obsessive concern of contemporary Western civilisation with (public) health.
2 '*Arrowsmith*, the first major American novel to concern itself with the culture of science . . . brought to the reading public of the 1920s the news of science' (Doctorow, 2008: 455–456).
3 'To Dr Paul de Kruif I am indebted not only for most of the bacteriological and medical material in this tale but equally for his help in the planning of the fable itself – for his realisation of the characters as living people, for his philosophy as a scientist' (Lewis, 1925/2002: 2).
4 The Rockefeller Institute, with its 'sumptuously plush research facilities', is depicted by de Kruif as a 'scientific emporium' and as 'that ivoryest of all ivory towers of medical science' (1962: 14).
5 Although his 'dissociation experiments' (comparing virulent and attenuated streptococci) resulted in publications in the *Journal of Experimental Medicine*, he was fired by the Institute's director Simon Flexner (Dr A. DeWitt Tubbs in the novel) for publishing *Our Medicine Men*: a critical journalistic review of contemporary medical practice in the United States ('A montage of what I'd seen, heard, read, felt, and experienced': 1962: 35), written at night while experimenting during daytime. Flexner notably objected to

de Kruif's view that relentless *competition* rather than disinterested *collaboration* lies at the heart of scientific research.
6 'Max Gottlieb was [a] melange of my revered chief, Professor Novy, and of Jacques Loeb, my master in a mechanistic conception of life' (de Kruif 1962: 109). While Martin Arrowsmith was modelled on de Kruif himself to some extent, Leora was a 'replica' of his wife Rhea (ibid).
7 Their collaboration was drenched in 'epic' alcohol bouts and subsequent hangovers. In his memoirs, de Kruif explains that during these 'drunken combats' his assignment was 'to keep our genius [Lewis] on this side of delirium tremens . . . on this side of going off a deep end – though there were times, mornings, when his shaky hands poured some of his Scotch onto the table and some into the glass' (1962: 94).
8 Like Jacques Loeb (1859–1924), Gottlieb was a contemporary of Freud, trained by the German physiological school, although Freud focused on neurology and language (aphasia) and Gottlieb on psychophysics, before turning to immunology. Like Martin, Freud dropped out of academia to become a practising therapist, re-entering the world of research by initiating a research field of his own making: the study of the unconscious.
9 Lewis originally intended to call his novel *In the Shadow of Max Gottlieb* (Fangerau, 2006).
10 Immunology and psychoanalysis seem comparable. There is a famous anecdote, told by Lacan, who allegedly had it from Jung, that (as their ocean liner entered New York harbour) Freud gloomily told the latter that they were 'bringing the plague' to America. Psychoanalysis has often been depicted as an 'infection', disrupting academic life and therapeutic practice (or even society at large), for instance by de Kruif, who claimed that Pavlov 'immunised me against the peril of what I came to call the "analism" promulgated by Sigmund Freud, just then beginning to taint American psychiatry and even psychology' (1962: 122).
11 Cf. 'In Betreff der intellektuellen Leistung bleibt bestehen, daß die großen Entscheidungen der Denkarbeit, die folgenschweren Entdeckungen und Problemlösungen nur dem Einzelnen, der in der Einsamkeit arbeitet, möglich sind' (Freud, 1921/1940: 89).
12 'Der Schatten des Objekts [i.e. Gottlieb] ist auf das Ich gefallen' (1921/1940: 120).
13 'He was so absorbed in staphylolysin that he did not realise the world was about to be made safe for democracy. He was a little dazed when America entered the war' (Lewis, 1925/2002: 315).
14 The Real is not 'reality'. The latter term refers to the world of normal experience; that which functions, the world as we know it, worked-over, restructured, reorganised and transformed into something which is sufficiently accessible and predictable: objective reality, a product of human culture, of science and technology most of all. A world, a techno-social 'habitat': to a considerable extent man-made. We have been working hard to transform the terrifying Real into an environment we may safely inhabit, in which we function. Fire, for instance, has been domesticated with the help of pyro-technology, but the looming threat is still there (cf. the *Towering Inferno* archetype).
15 During his days as a country doctor, an infectious disease raged among farm animals, and the situation quickly got out of hand. Martin managed to tame the threat with the help of his makeshift laboratory.
16 In the novel, the discovery is made during a 'fine, wide August morning' (Lewis, 1925/2002: 326).
17 'Le réel est à la limite de notre expérience' (Lacan, 1994: 31).
18 Martin starts taking notes: 'I have observed a principle which I shall temporarily call the X Principle' (Lewis, 1925/2002: 328). Indeed, 'after years of stumbling he . . . had visions of his name in journals and text books; of scientific meetings cheering him. He had been an unknown among the experts of the Institute, but now he pitied all of them. But when he was back at his bench the grandiose aspirations faded and he was . . . the impersonal worker. Before him, supreme joy of the investigator, new mountain-passes of work opened' (ibid: 329).

19 The discovery of the bacteriophage as an intrusion of the 'Real' is different from the famous Eureka-experience (of Archimedes and others) when pieces of a puzzle suddenly fit together and the missing link is found. The intrusion of the Real is something unpleasant, something we try to ignore or to explain away: that which does *not* fit our theories, enforcing itself upon us, until we 'give in', forced to acknowledge that we have 'hit' something. This is also underscored by d'Herelle (1917) who explains how he isolated the 'invisible microbe' from the faeces of a patient recovering from dysentery; the unexpected finding emerges in that which is rejected, abhorred: the (infectious) waste.
20 'Perhaps independently, perhaps not' (Stent, 1966: 3).
21 'By the middle of the 1930s . . . the widely propagandized control of bacterial diseases by means of bacteriophages had failed to materialize' (Stent, 1966: 5). This may change, however, as new ways of using viruses and microbes to address societal concerns are currently developed: a revival of d'Herelle's approach (Keen, 2012). Dublanchet and Bourne (2007) likewise argue that, in view of the increase in antibiotic resistance, phage therapy becomes topical again.
22 Pasadena (Los Angeles) and Cold Spring Harbor: the 'Mecca and Medina' of phage-research (Cairns et al, 1966: ix).
23 While the conflict over priority between Twort and d'Herelle is still a matter of dispute among historians, the Arrowsmith-d'Herelle conflict resurged in the struggle over priority that unfolded in the 1980s between Robert Gallo (of the National Cancer Institute in Bethesda, Maryland, who also did research on viral pathogens in the Caribbean) and Luc Montagnier (of the Pasteur Institute) over the discovery of HIV.
24 'There may have been in the shadowy heart of Max Gottlieb a diabolic insensitivity to . . . suffering mankind. He who had lived to study the methods of immunising mankind against disease had little interest in actually using those methods' (Lewis, 1925/2002: 365).
25 Leora dies from smoking a cigarette carelessly left behind by Martin in his lab, infected by spillage from a test-tube.
26 'Playing the savior, he had been a traitor to Gottlieb and all that Gottlieb represented . . . he did not have complete proof of the value of the phage . . . The more they shouted his glory, the more he thought about what tight-minded scientists in distant laboratories would say of a man who had had his chance and cast it away' (Lewis, 1925/2002: 414–415).
27 'He had learned from Gottlieb the trick of using the word "control" in reference to the person or animal or chemical left untreated during an experiment, as a standard for comparison . . . When a physician boasted of his success with this drug or that electric cabinet, Gottlieb always snorted, "Where was your control?"' (Lewis, 1925/2002: 43).
28 In the novel, but even more so in the film, McGurk is depicted as a streamlined laboratory in a futuristic institute in a futuristic building in a futuristic city: on the uppermost floors of a skyscraper, a majestic office building located in the metropolitan quarter from which New York ruled the world; a topology emphasising the steep vertical aloofness of 'top' science.
29 'When they had worked all night, they came out to find serene dawn lifting across the sleeping lake' (Lewis, 1925/2002: 468). And when his wife (in a final desperate effort to make him change his mind) seeks him out in his hide-out and asks him whether he hasn't become a bit insane, he answers: 'O absolutely! And how I enjoy it!' (ibid: 469).
30 Cf. the final sentence of the novel: 'I feel as if I were really beginning to work now . . . We'll plug along for two or three years . . . and probably we'll fail' (Lewis, 1925/2002: 471).

References

Cairns, J., Stent, G., Watson, J.D. (eds.) (1966) *Phage and the Origins of Molecular Biology*, Cold Spring Harbor: Cold Spring Harbor Laboratory of Quantitative Biology.
Clarfield, A.M. (2007) 'Novel medicine: *Arrowsmith*', *Journal of the Royal Society of Medicine*, 100: 286.

d'Herelle, F. (1917) 'Sur un microbe invisible antagoniste des bacilles dysentériques', *Les Comptes rendus de l'Académie des Sciences*, 165: 373–375.
Doctorow, E.L. (2008) 'Afterword'. In: Lewis, S. (1925/2008) *Arrowsmith*. New York: New American Library, 451–456.
Dostoyevsky, F. (1864/1972) *Notes from Underground*, London: Penguin.
Dublanchet A., Bourne S. (2007) 'The epic of phage therapy', *Canadian Journal of Infectious Diseases and Medical Microbiology*, 18(1): 15–18.
Fangerau H.M. (2006) 'The novel *Arrowsmith*, Paul de Kruif (1890–1971) and Jacques Loeb (1859–1924): A literary portrait of "medical science"', *Medical Humanities*, 32: 82–87.
Ford, J. (1931) *Arrowsmith* [the movie], Goldwyn Meyer.
Freud, S. (1900/1942) Die Traumdeutung. *Gesammelte Werke II/III*. London: Imago.
——— (1921/1940) Massenpsychologie und Ich-analyse. *Gesammelte Werke XIII*. London: Imago, 71–162.
Keen, E. (2012) 'Felix d'Herelle and our microbial future', *Future Microbiology*, 7 (12): 1337–1339.
Kruif, P. de (1926) *The Microbe Hunters*. New York: Harcourt.
——— (1962) *The Sweeping Wind: A Memoir*. London: Hart-Davis.
Lacan, J. (1973) *Le Séminaire XI: Les quatre concepts fondamentaux de la psychanalyse*. Paris: Éditions du Seuil.
——— (1991/2001) *Le séminaire VIII: Le transfert*. Paris: Éditions du Seuil.
——— (1991) *Le séminaire XVII : L'envers de la psychanalyse*. Paris: Éditions du Seuil.
——— (1994) *Le séminaire IV: La relation d'objet*. Paris: Éditions du Seuil.
——— (2004) *Le séminaire X: L'angoisse*. Paris: Éditions du Seuil.
——— (2007) *Le séminaire XVIII: D'un discours qui ne serait pas du semblant*. Paris: Éditions du Seuil.
——— (2011) *Le Séminaire XIX: . . . Ou pire*. Paris: Éditions du Seuil.
——— (2013) *Le Séminaire VI: Le désir et son interprétation*. Paris: Éditions de la Martinière et Le Champ Freudien Éditeur.
Lewis S. (1925/2002) *Arrowsmith*. In: *Arrowsmith/Elmer Gantry/Dodsworth*. New York: Literary classics of the United States. Original publication: Lewis, S. (1925) *Arrowsmith*. New York: Harcourt Brace.
Löwy I. (1988) Immunology and literature in the early twentieth century: Arrowsmith and the doctor's dilemma. *Medical History*, 32: 314–332.
Lynch, L. (2000) Arrowsmith goes native: Medicine and empire in fiction and film. *Mosaic: A Journal for the Interdisciplinary Study of Literature*, 33: 193–209.
Markel, H. (2001) Reflection on Sinclair Lewis's 'Arrowsmith': The great American novel of public health and medicine. *Public Health Reports*, 116: 371–375.
Parry, S. (2008) 'Introduction'. In: Lewis, S. (1925/2008) *Arrowsmith*. New York: New American Library, v–xii.
Pauly, Ph. J. (1981) *Jacques Loeb and the Control of Life: An Experimental Biologist in Germany and America, 1859–1924*. Ph.D. Johns Hopkins University Pittsburgh/London: University of Pittsburgh Press.
Plato (1914/1995) Phaedrus. In: Plato, I *Euthyphro, Apology, Crito, Phaedo, Phaedrus* [Loeb series]. Cambridge, MA: Harvard University Press, 405–579.
Schorer, M. (1961) *Sinclair Lewis: An American Life*. New York/Toronto/London: McGraw-Hill.
Starzl, T.E. (1967) Ethical problems in organ transplantation. In: Elkinton, J.R. (ed.) *The Changing Mores of Biomedical Research: A Colloquium on Ethical Dilemmas from Medical Advances*. *Annals of Internal Medicine*, 67: 32–36.
——— (1992/2003) *The Puzzle People. Memoirs of a Transplant Surgeon*. Pittsburgh: University of Pittsburgh Press.

Stent, G. (1966) 'Introduction: Waiting for the paradox'. In: Cairns J., Stent G., Watson, .D. (eds.) *Phage and the Origins of Molecular Biology*. Cold Spring Harbor: Cold Spring Harbor Laboratory of Quantitative Biology, 3–5.

Twort, F.W. (1915). An investigation on the nature of ultra-microscopic viruses. *The Lancet* 186 (4814): 1241–1243.

Watson, J.D. (1966) 'Growing up in the Phage Group'. In: Cairns J., Stent G., Watson, J.D. (eds.) *Phage and the Origins of Molecular Biology*. Cold Spring Harbor: Cold Spring Harbor Laboratory of Quantitative Biology.

Zwart, H. (2008) *Understanding Nature. Case Studies in Comparative Epistemology*, Dordrecht: Springer.

7 Voices carry? The voice of bioethics in the courtroom and the voice of law in bioethics

Richard Huxtable and Suzanne Ost

7.1 Introduction

Both bioethics and law have valid (and invalid) ways of telling stories. They can sometimes tell these stories with one another, thereby enriching the worldview of each. Judge-made law has made some positive contributions to the shaping of bioethics as a discipline, providing a real-world testing ground for moral arguments, issuing the judicial 'products' with which bioethics engages, and emphasising the importance of observing due process. And bioethics can have a positive impact on law when law engages with, for example, the principle of respect for autonomy. But, importantly, bioethics and law each has its own domain (and associated language and 'voice') and, on occasion, this can lead to obscuration and disharmony. The courtroom is an adversarial arena, not always ideally suited to the resolution of ethical conflict, and its concern with actions that satisfy attainable standards can fall short of the aspirations set in philosophical ethics. Indeed, sometimes the ethical dimensions of the case at hand are misinterpreted or wholly neglected in the courtroom. So much of what judges do involves interpretation (of the facts of the case, the story of legal precedent and of the particular ethical dilemma) and translation (of ethical issues into law's discourse). Likewise, bioethics involves its own narrative discourse; real life situations are interpreted into substantive ethical controversies. Consequently, whilst both bioethics and law can reveal more of the story than one alone, the presence of narrative construction in both means that there is no one 'truth' but, rather, numerous interpretations of the critical scenario.

This chapter explores the interaction between bioethics and law in the specific theatre of the courtroom. No matter what some judges say, the courtroom has long been a location in which law and bioethics interact, not least in seminal health care law cases such as *Re A (Children) (Conjoined Twins: Surgical Separation)* [2001] Fam 147 and *R v Arthur* (1981) 12 BMLR 1. By way of a case study, the chapter first argues that the voice of bioethics in the courtroom can be obscured because of the drama of the case. Secondly, however, it acknowledges that the voice of bioethics will sometimes transfer through to the courtroom and law, both covertly and overtly. Moreover, thirdly, we will suggest that a reciprocal transfer can also be detected, when we hear echoes of law's products, processes and practices in bioethics. Finally, through an exploration of narrative construction and interpretation in law and bioethics, we argue that there is no one truth but, rather, that the voices of law and bioethics offer multiple narratives of cases involving bioethical conflict – and that, accordingly, each field can benefit by ensuring that it is ready to receive the insights the other has to offer.

7.2 Drama and the doctor in the dock

In 1981, highly respected paediatrician Dr Leonard Arthur faced trial for the murder of John Pearson, a baby with Down's syndrome. The charge was subsequently reduced to attempted murder and, at the end of the trial, he was acquitted. According to newspaper reports (Osman, Ferriman and Timmins, 1981: 1), there were cries of 'Thank God' from the public gallery as the verdict was announced. The Down's Children's Association expressed fears that the case would cause more parents to reject children with Down's and be 'sufficient reason to let them die' (Ferriman, 1981: 3). The subject matter of the case, a doctor dedicated to caring for children charged with a baby's murder, is certainly dramatic. It is thus unsurprising that Dr Arthur's case attracted much media attention. It gave rise to a series of challenging moral problems, numerous bioethical papers and a whole book, Raanan Gillon's *Philosophical Medical Ethics*, in 1986. But, as we will see, the responses of the medical profession and the judge's directions to the jury suggest that, in such high profile criminal law cases, fundamental ethical issues are evaded and hidden under the cloak of professional definitions of proper medical treatment. Thus, the voice of the medical profession joins with the voice of law to mask the voice of bioethics.

The charge against Dr Arthur arose from his management of the baby, who died 69 hours after he was born. The post mortem revealed that he had died of bronchopneumonia and a toxic level of a powerful painkiller was found in his blood (Osman, 1981: 2). During a police interview, Dr Arthur stated: 'I am fully responsible, no one else. I do not want to be a martyr and I do not want the nurses brought into it' (ibid). That initial reaction helped shape the image of a conscientious doctor caught in the wheels of the criminal law. There was no suggestion that Dr Arthur had any venal motive. Although he may have been wrong (at least legally) in the care he provided, he did not have the appearance of a 'bad' man.

In a contemporary newspaper report, it is stated that the baby's mother 'rejected the child because it was mentally retarded' (ibid). Following discussion with both parents, Dr Arthur wrote on the nursing notes 'Parents do not wish to survive. Nursing care only'. He prescribed 5 milligrams of dihydrocodeine to be administered every four hours. The prosecution alleged that this drug would have suppressed the baby's appetite and repressed his ability to breathe independently. In prescribing an unnecessary drug and withholding food, the Crown argued, Dr Arthur sought to bring about the baby's death at the parents' request. The defence contended that Dr Arthur's prescription of dihydrocodeine and the alleged withholding of food and treatment amounted to acceptable medical practice. They were too remote from the death to amount to the *actus reus* of attempted murder and Dr Arthur had no intention of bringing about John Pearson's death. Rather, these measures were a 'holding' tactic, so that the baby's condition could be reviewed and in case the mother changed her mind.

Whilst it was the Crown's case that John Pearson had been a healthy baby, save for Down's syndrome, the defence produced slides which showed that the baby had serious brain and lung damage. Cross-examination of witnesses revealed that the baby had lost no weight during his brief life. Therefore, he had not been starved to death. There was thus a lack of reliable evidence that Dr Arthur's management was a significant contributory factor in causing the baby's death, so the murder charge was withdrawn and the prosecution then pursued a charge of attempted murder ((1981) 12 BMLR 1, 9–10). The prosecution's flawed telling of the story must have impacted on the jury, especially since the case against Dr Arthur for attempted murder fared no better. There was no apparent evidence that Dr Arthur knew that the baby had numerous abnormalities when he prescribed dihydrocodeine and instructed that only nursing care be given. On the evidence available, at most all that could be suggested was that he might have considered the possibility that because the baby had Down's syndrome, he could have had further impairments. Notwithstanding the destruction of the prosecution's case, the ethical issues remained exactly the same. Although expressed too simply, the central question of principle remained: did John Pearson have the same rights to life-sustaining care as a baby born without Down's?

In directing the jury, Farquharson J stated:

> I imagine you will think long and hard before deciding that doctors, of the eminence that we have heard, representing to you what medical ethics are, and apparently have been over a period of time in that great profession, have evolved standards which amount to committing crime.
> (ibid, 17)

It may seem that the judge comes close to suggesting that doctors define ethics and the boundaries of crime are set by these ethics, as long as the defendant doctor has no apparent venal motive. But just before this sentence, he reminded the jury that the medical profession's ethics cannot, alone, ensure the non-criminality of an act or omission. Earlier in the directions, he said that doctors are not given 'extra protection' from the criminal law (ibid, 4). Yet, given the weight of the expert evidence, did the jury hear this message?

Four eminent experts gave evidence for the defence to the effect that Dr Arthur's management of John Pearson fell within the bounds of acceptable medical conduct. According to his peers' testimonies, Dr Arthur had done no wrong. That said, the evidence reveals uncertainty as to whether all medical professionals would have considered Dr Arthur's management appropriate. One of the expert witnesses said:

> If a doctor puts such a child on a regime which will inevitably end with its death that could be described as taking steps. I would not do it myself, but in this extremely grey area doctors may arrive at inconsistent decisions.
>
> (ibid, 15)

Another considered what Dr Arthur did fell 'within acceptable paediatric policy' (ibid, 16). Although the professional evidence was not overwhelmingly supportive, neither was it condemnatory.

Alongside the possible seeds of doubt this evidence may have sowed in the jury's minds, prominence was attached throughout to Dr Arthur's good character. In the concluding paragraph of his directions, the judge noted that 'seldom in a court could one have heard so many testaments to a man's good character' (ibid, 18). He went on to say that this did not make the doctor incapable of committing a crime, but he ended with the following statement:

> in a case of this kind, when we are talking about medical attitudes and treatment, his own career must stand him in good stead, as to whether he is a man who would do what the prosecution submit he has done.
>
> (ibid, 16)

Essentially, the jury were asked: was Leonard Arthur a bad man? It was the man and not the (other) ethical issues that shaped the trial. Further, it might seem that, in a sense, the child was on trial too. The judge described the baby as a 'mongol' and 'it', and accepted the bleakest of prognoses for the life of a child with Down's (ibid, 3; Huxtable, 2007: 110–112). Mason and Laurie dismiss *Arthur* as being poor precedent and telling us nothing ultimately about the law relating to the treatment of severely disabled infants (Mason and Laurie, 2011: 479–480). They are right (cf. Huxtable, 2007: 125–126). Later cases heard in the Family Division, such as *Re J (a minor) (medical treatment)* [1993] Fam 15, give much more coherence to the law relating to the care of very sick neonates than Dr Arthur's trial (Mason and Laurie, 2011: 481–488). The trial – and no doubt others (e.g. *R v Bourne* [1939] 1 KB 687; *R v Adams* [1957] Crim LR 365) – reveals that when the criminal law intervenes, drama can obscure the voice of bioethics in the courtroom.

7.3 The voice of bioethics in the law?

Even beyond the criminal law, there is reason to doubt that the voice of bioethics is heard sufficiently when bioethical conflict transfers from the clinic to the courtroom. The courts will sometimes hear from *amici curiae*, intervening parties and others who seek to advance distinctive principled positions: for example, the Pro-Life Alliance, Care Not Killing, Dignity and Choice in Dying and the British Humanist Association have all been involved in recent proceedings (e.g. *Re A (Children) (Conjoined Twins: Surgical Separation)* [2001] Fam 147; R *(on the application of Purdy) v DPP* [2009] EWCA 92 (CA); R *(on the application of Nicklinson and another) v Ministry of Justice; R (on the application of AM) v The Director of Public Prosecutions* [2014] UKSC 38). Yet, bioethics' academic orators – 'bioethicists' – are seldom heard (James, 2008: 68). Even when exceptions are made, so too are errors. In 2000, in *Re A (Children) (Conjoined Twins: Surgical Separation)* [2001] Fam 147, the Court of Appeal contemplated the surgical separation of conjoined twins: to do so would immediately mean the death of the weaker twin; but not to do so would apparently mean the death of both girls within a matter of months. Favourable references were made to John Keown's (1997) work on the sanctity of life, which the court seemed inclined to apply. Yet, in the event, the judges' reasoning owed more to an ethic that is most concerned with judging the quality (rather than the inviolability) of life and is thus quite at odds with the one Keown espouses (Huxtable, 2002).

Of course, this is not to say that medical law is entirely divorced from medical ethics. Even leaving aside jurisprudential questions about whether law (in principle) involves a moral commitment, the ethical dimensions of law (in fact) are inescapable. Sometimes the judges are relatively open about (and to) this: Lord Coleridge CJ famously stated that 'It would not be correct to say that every moral obligation involves a legal duty; but every legal duty is founded on a moral obligation' (*R v Instan* (1893) 1 QB 450, 453). Equally, the courts are not averse to receiving direct inputs on 'formal' and 'semi-formal' (Miola, 2004: 253) medical ethics from professional organisations such as the General Medical Council (e.g. *W v Egdell* [1990] Ch 359, 390–392, 412–414, 416, 420–423). Less commonly, judges may engage with critical medical ethics, as did Butler Sloss P (as she was then) in her endorsement of respect for the gravely disabled patient's subjective experience of her condition in *B v NHS Trust* [2002] EWHC 429 (Fam), para 94 (cf. Atkins, 2000). Note also Hoffmann LJ's more critical ethical approach in the Court of Appeal in *Bland*, in which the judges agreed that clinically assisted nutrition and hydration could be withdrawn from a patient in a persistent vegetative state (*Airedale NHS Trust v Bland* [1993] 1 AC 789, 824–834). But other times, as we see in *Re A*, the judges are less open: Ward LJ insisted that 'this is a court of law, not of morals' ([2000] 4 All ER 961, 969), albeit before proceeding to analyse (but misapply) the sanctity of life position in considerable detail. It seems that, no matter what the judges say, medical law is replete with the 'stigmata cases' to which Lee and Morgan have referred, i.e. cases that 'require courts to develop a social, even a moral vision with which to respond to the dilemmas created by the social and cultural revolution of contemporary medicine' (Lee and Morgan, 2001: 298).

The 'moral vision' will occasionally be clear to all, such as when direct appeals are made to the aforementioned sanctity of life or to the principle of respect for autonomy. Yet, even when the moral vision is clouded – and the ruling in question more technical and correspondingly 'de-moralised' – it can usually be detected (Montgomery, 2006). For example, in Dr Arthur's trial we see hints of the *Bolam* standard, borrowed from the civil law of clinical negligence, which holds that a defendant is not negligent if he or she has acted in accordance with a responsible body of medical opinion (*Bolam v Friern Hospital Management Committee* [1957] 1 WLR 582). The standard has long had a stranglehold on medical law. This might appear to be a descriptive paradigm, according to which an individual clinician's behaviour is compared or contrasted with that of his peers. But this inevitably involves an ethical judgment: it is, therefore, also an evaluative standard, premised on the idea that one ought to do what one's 'responsible' peers would do. The judges have recently sought to remind defendants that they (not the defendants) will be the ultimate arbiters of responsible practice (*Bolitho v City and Hackney Health Authority* [1997] 4 All ER 771). But whoever does the judging, the standard unavoidably involves just this i.e. a judgment, with inescapable ethical undertones.

On this view, (bio)ethics does indeed enter law, both overtly and covertly. Indeed, like Miola, one might view ethics and law as united in a 'symbiotic' relationship (Miola, 2007). But does the reverse hold? In other words, how, if at all, does law enter bioethics?

7.4 The voice of law in bioethics?

There are three legal locations in particular from which law's voice has projected into bioethics: the products, processes and practices of law (Huxtable, 2015). First, the products of law, as they pertain to the biosciences, will undoubtedly make a considerable contribution to bioethics and its development. Law can, therefore, provide some of the raw materials with which bioethicists will work. There will be rulings, statutes and codes that have a direct and specific bearing on an issue of bioethical import, such as when a jurisdiction seeks to govern the uses of human tissue, practices in reproductive medicine, or physician-assisted dying. There are, of course, many more examples that could be cited. Very often, as we suggested above, the legal materials in question will adopt a particular principled position. As Callahan has suggested, law is 'ready to take on ethics if that is what gets served up to it for the making of decisions' (Callahan, 1996: 34). Bioethicists will, understandably, seek to reflect critically on such developments. Sometimes the judges will even advance ethical practice, such as when a clinician's recommendation of the creation of clinical ethics committees was endorsed by the New Jersey Supreme Court adjudicating on the fate of Karen Ann Quinlan (*In re Quinlan* (1976) NJ 355 A 2d 647). As Spielman (2007: 41) observes, this 'endorsement provided a crucial boost to the fledgling ethics committee movement'. There will also be a plethora of other rules and regulations not directly aimed at the biosciences whose influence is nevertheless felt. Although medical (or, more broadly, health care) law is nowadays a recognised body of law in its own right, it continues to gain sustenance from its roots in criminal law, tort law, public law, human rights law and European Community law, amongst others. Sometimes, retracing (and even replanting) these roots will help the parties to navigate their way out of bioethical difficulty (e.g. R *(on the application of Watts) v Secretary of State for Health* [2003] EWHC 2228/[2004] EWCA Civ 166, *Malette v Shulman* (1990) 67 DLR (4th) 321 (Ont CA), *Airedale NHS Trust v Bland* [1993] 2 WLR 316 and *Re A (Children) (Conjoined Twins: Surgical Separation)* [2001] Fam 147).

Secondly, law makes a distinctive contribution to bioethics in its insistence on due process. Commenting on the United States, Jonsen (1998: 343) cites Annas' claim that:

> American bioethics has been driven by the law . . . The stress on autonomy and self determination comes from our Bill of Rights, our Declaration of Independence and the whole common law tradition. And law's primary contribution to bioethics is procedural. Lawyers are expert at procedure. The common law itself is based on deciding individual cases and using these cases as the basis of creating law. Bioethics has adopted this technique. In the United States, with its pluralism of beliefs and people, the law is what holds us together. There is no other ethos . . .

His comments chime with experiences elsewhere. Casuistry – case-based reasoning – is a method also adopted by bioethical practitioners outside the United States (Ashcroft et al, 2005). Indeed, the influence of law here should not be surprising, as bioethics is a wide, multi- and inter-disciplinary discipline, whose practitioners have long included lawyers (Schneider, 1994). We see this not only in the pages of specialist journals, but also in bioethics' more overtly practice-orientated and public-facing endeavours, such as the work of national organisations like the Nuffield Council on Bioethics (e.g. Nuffield Council on Bioethics, 2006). Despite such input, there are some who believe that the lessons of the law should be better heeded in bioethical practice. In the UK, for example, Sheila McLean (2008) has appealed to the due process associated with legal proceedings in her critique of clinical ethics services. In this jurisdiction, research ethics committees are formally constituted and regulated (a development which owes much to the European Union's European Clinical Trials Directive 2001/20/EC) but clinical ethics committees, from which advice may be issued on cases of ethical complexity, remain relatively *ad hoc*, despite their growing number (85 by 2014) (UK Clinical Ethics Network, 2014). McLean (2008) perceives a 'due process wasteland', which she believes would be best redeveloped by architects schooled in pertinent principles of law.

Thirdly, law's intrinsic connection to practice enables it to make a distinctive contribution to bioethics. In the words of Lon Fuller (1969: 96), law is 'the enterprise of subjecting human conduct to the governance of rules'. In its preoccupation with human conduct, law can therefore provide a real world testing ground for concepts and approaches in bioethics. 'Moral philosophers are not obliged day by day to solve the real problems of real people', notes Birks (2000: 2–3), 'nor are they called to daily account to justify to those same real people the substance of their tenets and the even hand-edness of their procedures'. Bioethics is, by its nature, also a practice-facing endeavour, such that it is not wholly beholden to the sometimes abstract theorising of moral philosophy. However, for many, bioethics remains essentially tethered to this branch of philosophy, since it involves 'the systematic study of the moral dimensions – including moral vision, decisions, conduct, and policies – of the life sciences and health care, employing a variety of ethical methodologies in an interdisciplinary setting' (Reich, 1995: xxi). Legal officials like the judges, meanwhile, must often do more than study, deliberate or theorise – they must *decide*. And, McLean (2007: 196) continues,

> irrespective of the ethical views of decision-makers – legal or medical – there are rules under which they must operate, like it or not. Whether or not they are based on moral obligations . . . they nonetheless are superior (in practical terms) to the outcome predicted by adherents to one ethical school of thought or another.

What law thus offers to bioethics is the crucible of experience: a space in which action-directed theories and approaches can be tested.

Law's voice has therefore projected into bioethics, correspondingly influencing its theoretical and practical expressions. But that does not mean that each can fully hear the other's voice; to borrow Carl Schneider's (1994) terminology, we should be wary of those limits that 'crimp the usefulness of law's language as a vehicle for bioethical discourse'. Three particular limits – concerning angst, action and aspiration – suggest that we should be cautious.

First, when we mention angst, we mean to refer to the adversarial process that is central to law, at least as it is associated with court proceedings. Certainly bioethics will often engage with conflict, whether between principles, positions or parties. But bioethics need not resolve such conflicts in an all-or-nothing fashion; law courts, however, tend to position parties as adversaries and ultimately to divide them into winner and loser (Meller and Barclay, 2011: 619). We see this quite vividly in the trial of Dr Arthur, in which he appears to emerge victorious, over both the prosecutors and, some might say, John Pearson. Even the judges have appreciated that this model is not wholly suited to addressing the dilemmas that can arise for patients and the professionals caring for them (e.g. *Portsmouth NHS Trust v Wyatt* [2005] EWCA Civ 1181, *per* Wall LJ, para. 86).

Secondly, in its preoccupation with action and with rules, law seems likely to miss other pieces of the moral jigsaw. The 'native language' of bioethics is much richer than law's, as one might expect, given its wider reach; as Schneider (1994: 16) says, bioethics contemplates 'the most basic and intractable issues about human life and the most intricate and intimate issues about human relationships', with the result that 'a rich vocabulary of ethical considerations, styles, and approaches is necessary'. Although there will be areas of agreement, it is likely there is no *lingua franca* for bioethics, and this need not be a bad thing *per se* (Derse, 2000). Nor should we expect this. Pluralistic contemporary societies lack a common conception of the good; there is, for example, no shared moral consensus on the meaning of 'beneficence'. Indeed, Engelhardt (1996) argues that the only *lingua franca* for modern bioethics is the language of consent.

Of course, some of the rich vocabulary of bioethics, including the language of consent, will be amenable to translation into the language of law: action-directed approaches, like consequentialism and deontology, appear so amenable, particularly the latter, given its concern with duties and rights. Yet, other words might be lost; for example, law will struggle to express the values associated with virtue, character and emotion. Some suggest that action and character can be related (e.g. Feldman, 2000; van Zyl, 2002; Solum, 2003), but Slote (1995: 91) observes that,

> [b]ecause virtue ethics is supposed to concentrate more on the inner life of the individual than either consequentialism or deontology, one can easily wonder whether the former is really capable of doing justice to law or to any sort of objective or real constraint upon human action.

The constraints to which Slote refers give rise to the third area of concern, regarding the aspirations of bioethics, of which law will often fall short. In the words of Mark Twain, 'Laws control the lesser man . . . Right conduct controls the greater one'. Law, on this account, is more often concerned with minimal standards, rather than high level aspirations. The English case law pertaining to 'informed' consent was long a case in point, because the judges effectively signalled that doctors could disclose what other doctors in their position would disclose – not necessarily what the patient wanted to know (Fovargue and Miola, 2010). Here, as elsewhere, *Bolam* appeared to reign supreme. Although the jurisprudence in this area is now developing along more robustly pro-autonomy lines (e.g. *Chester v Afshar* [2004] UKHL 41), we might still doubt that the judges have given due critical attention to the model(s) of autonomy they seek to defend (Coggon, 2007). Indeed, it is not difficult to detect inconsistent approaches throughout medical law, with some such inconsistencies attributable to a failure to attend to the ethical dimensions of the given problem (e.g. Huxtable, 2007; 2012).

Perhaps law's failures are forgivable and explicable, given the aforementioned absence of a bioethical *lingua franca*. If only autonomy and non-interference command a consensus in bioethics, then it should not be surprising – and may even be commendable – that law seeks, at a minimum, to give effect to such liberal ideals. Of course, as we indicated previously, the ethical lexicon cannot be *reduced* to these concerns and neither is there bioethical consensus on *how* such ideas are to be understood. There are, therefore, ongoing challenges for bioethics, in ensuring its lexicon is appropriately rich and in generating the most robust ethical models. The challenge for law, meanwhile, involves setting the (ethical) bar at the appropriate height. Given the nature of law, coupled with the ethical dissensus to which we have referred, we suspect that law is likely to set the bar a few rungs lower than it might be set by some critical bioethicists.

Bioethics is, after all, 'a critical discipline', says Brownsword (2008: 15): 'bioethics tries to sort out the moral wheat from the non-moral chaff'. As Dawson and Wilkinson (2009: 36) elaborate, philosophical practical ethics comprises: 'appraisal of ethical arguments using the techniques of analytic philosophy'; 'conceptual analysis, which seeks to clarify and explain the role of particular ethical concepts and terms'; and 'the formulation and critical assessment of ethical principles or normative theories about how we should behave'. Logical analysis – and thus clarity and consistency – seems to play an important role in this endeavour (e.g. Pollock, 1988). Similar analytical approaches might, of course, be adopted by legal scholars, such as those inquiring into the requirements associated with the 'internal morality of law' or the 'Rule of Law' (see Brazier and Ost, 2013: Chapter 8).

Although there will be areas of overlap (including overlapping concerns with consistency and the like), the standards and requirements of law and bioethics will nevertheless continue to differ. We have suggested that, whilst each undoubtedly influences and enriches the other, bioethics and law have different voices and speak different languages. Implicit in some of what we have said here might appear to be the idea that the two must inevitably remain in competition, clamouring to be loudest. However, this need not be the case, as we will explore in the next section.

7.5 Different voices, different stories?

The voices of bioethics and law can sound different and sometimes dissonant because of the presence of interpretation in both fields. Often the cases involving bioethical conflict are ones in which we engage in narrative thinking in order to reach comprehension. According to Bruner (1996: 39),

> [t]here appear to be two broad ways in which human beings organize and manage their knowledge of the world . . . one seems more specialized for treating of physical 'things,' the other for treating of people and their plights. These are conventionally known as *logical scientific thinking* and *narrative thinking*. . . .

We suggested, above, that law and bioethics will sometimes tend towards logical approaches and appraisals. But these might not be entirely appropriate concerns; instead we might find it more fitting to rely on narrative discourse to make sense of cases involving people and their plights, such as the end of life, abortion and the selling of organs. In bioethics, this is the domain of narrative ethics, the exploration of meaning and interpretation of human events, of narrative knowledge, construction and storytelling in bioethics, which can involve embracing disciplines such as literary criticism, sociology and psychology (Charon, 1994: 260).

According to this view, the voices of bioethics and law are involved in the process of narrative discourse, offering meanings, solutions and challenges that are subject to interpretation throughout the story. The role of interpretation is important here, for interpretation is an essential element in the narratives that the voices of bioethics and law play a part in shaping.

As we noted earlier, some of the decisions taken by the courts may appear to be illogical and fail to harmonise the voices of bioethics and the law. But there is a reason for this. Charon (1994: 272) highlights the existence of differing interpretations in bioethics, noting that ethical issues regularly come to light because of a conflict between the interpretations of an issue and the available actions. When the law intervenes, a conflict in interpretations of the ethical issue often exists and the law attempts to resolve the case, although it can only do so in the specific legal context. So the application of law in *Re A* resolved the legal dilemma presented by the bioethical conflict that the precipitating event gave rise to – whether benefiting one twin or not harming the other should take priority.

When law is applied to bioethical dilemmas, the ethical issue must be interpreted and translated into legal discourse, principles and concepts in order to (legally) resolve the case. Thus, we observe Brooke LJ moulding the case before him into one in which the doctrine of necessity could apply, to justify operating on the conjoined twins and thereby killing Mary (*Re A (Children) (Conjoined Twins: Surgical Separation)* [2001] Fam 147, 219–240). And judges interpret the case law in light of the ethical dilemma before them: the defence of necessity had never before been available in response to a case involving the deliberate ending of life (*R v Dudley and Stephens* (1884) 14 QBD 273; *R v Howe* [1987] AC 417). Brooke LJ interpreted the criminal law jurisprudence surrounding necessity to involve policy considerations not present in *Re A*, which therefore made it an exceptional case. It was not a case where one person was being a judge in his own cause of the value of his life, nor one in which allowing necessity to justify the taking of an innocent life would cause the law to be absolutely divorced from morality (*Re A (Children) (Conjoined Twins: Surgical Separation)* [2001] Fam 147, 239). So interpreted, necessity could be an available defence, thereby differentiating the case before him from previous cases. Thus, Brooke LJ chose an interpretation that responded to the specific and unique elements in the case, a reflection of Dworkin's 'law as integrity' thesis (Dworkin, 1998: 238–239).

Through his interpretation and application of law-lore, Brooke LJ became a co-author of the story of criminal law; the case before him became a chapter of this story. His translation of ethical conflict into a legal story involving necessity offered a resolution. Thus, even in such hard cases, although the task of finding a resolution is especially taxing, it has still proven possible for judges to find, interpret and apply a legal principle such as necessity that apparently offers the least detrimental outcome.

Turning to bioethics, ethicists and health care lawyers interpret real life situations into substantive ethical controversies, interpreting a factual situation and framing the ethical theories and principles to tackle the situation. Thus, for example, a case involving the donation of a man's organs on the condition that they would go to a white recipient is presented as an ethical controversy of autonomy versus justice (Department of Health, 2000; Cronin and Price, 2008). Following a hospital's refusal to provide in vitro fertilisation treatment to a woman (R v Ethical Committee of St Mary's Hospital (Manchester), ex p Harriott [1988] 1 FLR 512), her former status as a prostitute is emphasised in the bioethical and health care law literature. The case can thereby be narrated as an ethical controversy involving reproductive autonomy versus discrimination (Freeman, 1988: 3; Brahams, 1990: 857). Whilst this may narrow the bioethical debate, such narrowing might be necessary to enable a legal decision to be reached. This suggests that some sort of compromise is necessary to enable law and bioethics to work in harmony. Interpretation is thus crucial in ensuring the evolution of narratives that construct the reality, which the voices of bioethics and law help shape, and in facilitating congruence between the two disciplines. It is therefore highly unlikely that there will be one generic interpretation of an event and, consequently, there is no one 'truth': there are, instead, multiple stories.

7.6 Conclusion

Practitioners of bioethics and of law can speak in different voices and will sometimes tell very different stories. Occasionally, as one can detect in some depictions of widely publicised and dramatic court proceedings, legal officials will be willing to hear what bioethic(ist)s have to say, citing some principle or other as a means of resolving the case at hand. Equally, one can also detect bioethics' reception of law's concerns, when the former field addresses what law has to say on a substantive matter of moral import, or problems of process. But any dialogue (such as it is) is unlikely to be entirely mutually enriching. Law courts are adversarial arenas, in which ethical nuance and laudable aspirations might lose out in the quest to determine a victor; legal answers tend also to be directed towards action, rather than concerns about character, virtue and the like that might be voiced in the bioethical forum. As such, when faced with questions associated with moral conflict, law and bioethics are capable of replying as one, but their answers can also be discordant and can speak past one another. Practitioners in each field need not despair, however. Rather, we suspect that there will be much to be gained from recognising that each has their own story to tell, guided by their own narrative norms. Neither can necessarily claim superiority or access to the 'truth' of the matter. However, each will be likely to gain greater insight by opening a dialogue with the other, telling and re-telling the story, so that the voices of one forum can carry over into the other.

References

Annas, G.J. (1991) 'Ethics committees: From ethical comfort to ethical cover', *Hastings Center Report*, 21: 18–21.
Anon. (1981) 'Dr Leonard Arthur: His trial and its implications', *British Medical Journal*, 283: 1340–1341.
Ashcroft, R., Lucassen, A., Parker, M., Verkerk, M. and Widdershoven, G. (2005) *Case Analysis in Clinical Ethics*, Cambridge: Cambridge University Press.
Atkins, K. (2000) 'Autonomy and the subjective character of experience', *Journal of Applied Philosophy*, 17(1): 71–79.
Birks, P. (2000) 'Rights, wrongs, and remedies', *Oxford Journal of Legal Studies*, 20(1): 1–37.
Brahams, D. (1990) 'Ethics and the law: The law and assisted conception', *British Medical Bulletin*, 46(3): 850–859.
Brazier, M. and Ost, S. (2013) *Medicine and Bioethics in the 'Theatre' of the Criminal Process*, Cambridge: Cambridge University Press.
Brownsword, R. (1993) 'Towards a rational law of contract', in T. Wilhelmsson (ed.), *Perspectives of Critical Contract Law*, Aldershot: Dartmouth, 241–272.
—— (2008) 'Bioethics: Bridging from morality to law?', in M. Freeman (ed.), *Law and Bioethics: Current Legal Issues 2008, Volume 11*, Oxford: Oxford University Press, 12–30.
Bruner, J. (1996) *Actual Minds, Possible Worlds*, Cambridge, MA: Harvard University Press.
Callahan, D. (1996) 'Escaping from legalism: Is it possible?', *Hastings Center Report*, 26(6): 34–35.
Charon, R. (1994) 'Narrative contributions to medical ethics: Recognition, formulation, interpretation, and validation in the practice of the ethicist', in E. Dubose, R. Hamel and L. O'Connell (eds.), *A Matter of Principles: Ferment in US Bioethics*, Valley Forge, PA: Trinity Press International, 260–283.
Coggon, J. (2007) 'Varied and principled understandings of autonomy in English law: Justifiable inconsistency or blinkered moralism?', *Health Care Analysis*, 15: 235–255.
Cronin, A. and Price, D. (2008) 'Directed organ donation: Is the donor the owner?', *Clinical Ethics*, 3(3): 127–131.
Dawson, A., and Wilkinson, S. (2009) 'Philosophical clinical ethics', *Clinical Ethics*, 4: 36–37.
Department of Health (2000) *An Investigation into Conditional Organ Donation, the Report of the Panel*, London: Department of Health.
Derse, A.R. (2000) 'Is there a *lingua franca* for bioethics at the end of life?', *The Journal of Law, Medicine & Ethics*, 28(3): 279–284.
Dworkin, R. (1998) *Law's Empire*, London: Hart.
Engelhardt, H.T. (1996) *Foundations of Bioethics*, 2nd edn, Oxford: Oxford University Press.
Feldman, H.L. (2000) 'Prudence, benevolence, and negligence: Virtue ethics and tort law', *Chicago-Kent Law Review*, 74: 1431–1466.
Ferriman, A. (1981) 'Down's group fear case will cause deaths', *The Times*, 7 November.
Fovargue, S. and Miola, J. (2010) 'One step forward, two steps back? The GMC, the common law and "informed" consent', *Journal of Medical Ethics*, 36: 494–497.
Freeman, M. (1988) 'Introduction', in M. Freeman (ed.), *Medicine, Ethics and the Law*, London: Stevens & Sons, 1–8.
Fuller, L.L. (1969) *The Morality of Law*, revised edn, New Haven, CT: Yale University Press.
Gillon, R. (1986) *Philosophical Medical Ethics*, Chichester: Wiley.
Huxtable, R. (2002) 'Separation of conjoined twins: Where next for English law?', *Criminal Law Review*, 459–470.
—— (2007) *Euthanasia, Ethics and the Law: From Conflict to Compromise*, Abingdon: Routledge-Cavendish.

―――― (2012) *Law, Ethics and Compromise at the Limits of Life: To Treat or not to Treat?*, Abingdon: Routledge.

―――― (2015) 'Friends, foes, flatmates: On the relationship between law and bioethics', in A. Cribb, J. Ives and M. Dunn (eds.), *Empirical Bioethics: Practical and Theoretical Perspectives*, Cambridge: Cambridge University Press.

James, T. (2008) 'The appeal to law to provide public answers to bioethical questions: It all depends what sort of answers you want', *Health Care Analysis*, 16: 65–76.

Jonsen, A.R. (1998) *The Birth of Bioethics*, Oxford: Oxford University Press.

Keown, J. (1997) 'Restoring moral and intellectual shape to the law after *Bland*', *The Law Quarterly Review*, 113: 481–503.

Lee, R. and Morgan, D. (2001) 'Regulating risk society: Stigmata cases, scientific citizenship and biomedical diplomacy', *Sydney Law Review*, 23(3): 297–318.

Mason, K. and Laurie, G. (2011) *Mason and McCall Smith's Law and Medical Ethics*, 8th edn, Oxford: Oxford University Press.

McLean, S.A.M. (2007) 'Law, ethics and health care', in R. Ashcroft, A. Dawson, H. Draper and J. McMillan (eds.), *Principles of Health Care Ethics*, 2nd edn, Chichester: John Wiley and Sons, 193–198.

―――― (2008) 'Clinical ethics committees: A due process wasteland?', *Clinical Ethics*, 3: 99–104.

Meller, S. and Barclay, S. (2011) 'Mediation: An approach to intractable disputes between parents and paediatricians', *Archives of Disease in Childhood*, 96: 619–621.

Miola, J. (2004) 'Medical law and medical ethics – complementary or corrosive?', *Medical Law International*, 6: 251–274.

―――― (2007) *Medical Ethics and Medical Law: A Symbiotic Relationship*, Oxford: Hart.

Montgomery, J. (2006) 'Law and the demoralisation of medicine', *Legal Studies*, 26(2): 185–210.

Nuffield Council on Bioethics (2006) *Critical Care Decisions in Fetal and Neonatal Medicine: Ethical Issues*, London: Nuffield Council on Bioethics.

Osman, A., Ferriman, A. and Timmins, N. (1981) 'Women cry "Thank God" as Dr Arthur is cleared', *The Times*, 6 November.

Osman, A. (1981) '69-hour life of a mongoloid child', *The Times*, 14 October.

Pollock, L. (1988) 'Evaluating moral theories', *American Philosophical Quarterly*, 25(3): 229–240.

Reich, W.T. (1995) *Encyclopedia of Bioethics, Volume I*, New York: Macmillan.

Schneider, C.E. (1994) 'Bioethics in the language of the law', *Hastings Center Report*, 24(4): 16–22.

Slote, M. (1995) 'Law in virtue ethics', *Law and Philosophy*, 14(1): 91–113.

Solum, L.B. (2003) 'Virtue jurisprudence: A virtue-centered theory of judging', *Metaphilosophy*, 34(1/2): 178–213.

Spielman, B. (2007) *Bioethics in Law*, Totowa, NJ; Humana Press.

Twining, W. and Miers, D.R. (1991) *How to Do Things with Rules*, 3rd edn, London: Butterworths.

UK Clinical Ethics Network (2014) 'Clinical ethics committees'. Available HTTP: <http://www.ukcen.net/index.php/committees/introduction> (accessed 28 November 2014).

van Zyl, L. (2002) 'Euthanasia, virtue ethics and the law', *New Zealand Bioethics Journal*, 3(1): 18–27.

8 A (social) room with a view (to the future): advance decisions and the problem of personhood

Tom Hayes

8.1 Introduction

This chapter discusses advance decisions to refuse medical treatment (hereafter 'advance decisions') and a specific challenge to their legitimacy that has been made based on certain conceptions of personhood. I argue that the alternative conceptions of personhood on which these challenges are based are incompatible with the democratically mandated end of the legal recognition of advance decisions.

Focusing on English law, I begin by explaining what advance decisions are, how they were developed, how they fit into the legal corpus and how they function (although it should be remembered that advance decisions also function in other jurisdictions (Lewis, 2006: 225–227)). Following this, I outline some of the main theories of personhood that have been used as a basis for contesting the legitimacy of advance decisions, through the suggestion that the creator of the advance decision is not to be considered the same person as (or lacks a sufficient connection to) the individual to whom the advance decision may apply in future. This problem, termed by DeGrazia as the 'someone else problem' (1999: 376) will be of profound concern to ethicists and lawyers alike.

However, I will argue that the acceptance of some conceptions of personhood would, in practical terms, defeat the right to make autonomous decisions over one's future self in the way that the British Parliament intended. Its acceptance would therefore be to ignore the successful political struggle for the recognition of advance decisions, which was part of the political movement for patient rights and empowerment. Furthermore, it is questionable why the argument for the adoption of certain philosophical models of personhood should be advanced and accepted selectively, with respect to advance decisions, if it is not also to be adopted in other areas of law where it could clearly apply. I will therefore suggest that it would be inconsistent to adopt a model of personhood for one particular area of law without adopting the same model in other areas of law, such as the criminal law, contract law and the law of wills. Adopting an alternative model of personhood would not be impossible, but would entail dramatic changes in other areas of law and it is far from clear that there would be popular support for such changes.

8.2 Advance decisions

At the outset it should be noted that in England and Wales advance decisions have also been known by other terms such as 'advance directives' and 'living wills' in the past and may be known by different terms where they are recognised outside England and Wales (see Lewis, 2006: 225–227). I will employ the term 'advance decision' both for the avoidance of ambiguity and as it is the phrase now used in English law in the Mental Capacity Act 2005 (hereafter 'MCA') (Royal College of Physicians, 2009: 2).

In English law, the term 'advance decision' simply refers to a legally binding anticipatory decision to refuse medical treatment. Advance decisions can be made by an adult person with capacity and only become binding in the event that the capacity to make a particular decision contemporaneously is lost, therefore they only have practical significance where they purport to refuse treatment that would otherwise be provided in the best interests of the patient. These points will be examined and elaborated upon later.

However, in order to understand advance decisions in a meaningful way, we must have regard to some of the significant developments which led to their recognition. As part of this exercise it is germane to consider the development of the right to refuse treatment contemporaneously, because advance decisions are considered to be an extension of this right. Therefore I will also give some indication of the context in which this right to make advance decisions has arisen.

Legally, advance decisions are based on the right to refuse medical treatment (s. 26(1) MCA) and this is a right that rests on a venerable body of civil and criminal case law. One of the earliest reported decisions in English law to highlight consent as a precondition of lawful medical treatment was from 1767, in the case of *Slater v Baker and Stapleton* (1767) 95 ER 860 (see Mayberry and Mayberry, 2003: 33–34). More recently, one of the most significant points in the development of the doctrine of consent was reached after the Nuremburg Code was drawn up in 1947 and since then, in the post-war period, patient rights have been given greater protection in Britain and beyond (e.g. Article 3 Charter of Fundamental Rights of the European Union) (UN Economic and Social Council, 2000: General Comment 14 (discussing Article 12 of the International Covenant on Economic, Social and Cultural Rights); see also Horn, Huxtable and Jox, 2013).

Voluntarism (i.e. the principle that demands respect for the voluntary will of the decision maker, such that it should be ensured that decisions are made freely and in absence of coercive influence) is designed to be guaranteed through the consent process and has been cemented at the core of medical practice with both the civil and criminal law safeguards. Failure to explain the nature or purpose of a given procedure before embarking upon it will constitute a battery, which is both a criminal offence in English law as well as a civil wrong, i.e. it is both prohibited as a wrong against the state and a wrong between citizens (*Airedale NHS Trust v Bland* [1993] AC 789, 882, *per*

Lord Browne-Wilkinson). Failure to explain the mere risks associated with a procedure may alternatively result in a civil negligence claim (*Chatterton v Gerson* [1981] 1 All ER 257), if it can be proven that the medical practitioner breached their duty of care and caused the claimant a loss. The standard of care expected of doctors was once based on the question of whether the treatment provided was in accordance with the expectations of a reasonable body of medical professionals (*Bolam v Friern Hospital Management Committee* [1957] 2 All ER 118), but it has since been made more explicitly subject to the approval of the court (*Bolitho v City and Hackney Health Authority* [1998] AC 232). After proving that the medical practitioner owed a duty of care that has been breached, the claimant must also demonstrate that they suffered a loss. However, latterly, the requirement to prove that loss was suffered has been given a generous interpretation, where it has appeared to run counter to the doctrine of informed consent (*Chester v Afshar* [2004] UKHL 41). As a result of modern requirements such as these, patients can expect to receive far more information about their treatment today than ever before. In addition to the standard level of information given to patients about their treatment, they can also expect to be provided with truthful answers to their questions (*Pearce v United Bristol Healthcare NHS Trust* [1998] EWCA Civ 865) and information about the risks and consequences associated with alternative treatments (*Birch v University College London Hospital NHS Foundation Trust* [2008] EWHC 2237). These developments led to the recognition of the right to *informed* consent in English law (see e.g. *Chester v Afshar* [2004] UKHL 41 [14], *per* Lord Steyn; see also Hayes, 2012: 202–203).

Even though these rights to information have been significantly strengthened, there remains an important qualification to the right to refuse treatment. Namely, the right only exists where the patient has the mental capacity to make the particular decision in question. If the patient lacks this capacity, treatment can be given to them in accordance with their best interests, notwithstanding any objections that the patient may have. In English law, best interests are to be determined in accordance with s.4 of the MCA. This provision requires various factors to be taken into account, including the patient's past and present wishes, but a combination of other factors, such as whether the person will at some time have capacity in relation to the decision (s.4(3)(a) MCA), can outweigh the will of the patient. Consequently, the law still allows considerable scope for treatment to be provided on paternalistic grounds. However, the scope for paternalism can be limited through the creation of an advance decision.

8.3 Advance decisions in English law

In defining advance decisions, a distinction must first be drawn between 'advance decisions', which are defined within the MCA, which are legally binding, and other anticipatory instruments such as 'advance directives' and 'advance statements', which are not legally binding insofar as they purport to do anything other than to refuse medical treatment, for example, where they request certain treatment (R *(On the Application of Oliver Leslie Burke) v GMC* [2005] 3 WLR 1132). As such, Buchanan's example of a request made to have one's life sustained while in a Persistent Vegetative State ('PVS') for the purposes of becoming an organ donor (1988: 278) would not constitute an advance decision in English law.

As noted above, the principal exception to the right to refuse treatment is that the right is only available for those with mental capacity. The determination of mental capacity is governed by the MCA. This law largely codified the pre-existing common law (Brazier and Cave, 2007: 125), with some modifications. It enshrined a presumption that everyone has capacity (s.1(2)) unless the contrary is proven through an assessment of capacity. The test for capacity is a functionalist assessment (Brazier and Cave, 2007: 126) and asks whether the person is able to comprehend and retain information, as well as whether they are capable of weighing that information in the balance in order to make a decision and to communicate their decision (s.3(1)). If any of these requirements cannot be met because 'of an impairment of, or disturbance in the functioning of, the mind or brain' (s.2(1)), the person being assessed will be deemed to lack capacity. The law is clear that any such conclusion is to be made on the basis of an assessment on the stated criteria and not on the person's 'age or appearance' (s.2(3)(a)). Nor can 'the tail of welfare wag the dog of capacity' and a person be deemed to lack capacity merely because they appear to make a poor or an unwise decision (*Heart of England NHS Foundation Trust v JB* [2014] EWHC 342, [7], *per* Peter Jackson J).

Ordinarily, when a person lacks capacity to make a specific treatment decision, treatment may be given to them in accordance with (what is deemed to be) his or her best interests. Deciding what is in a person's best interests involves following the process of inquiry specified in s.4 MCA. That process requires that, *inter alia*, the past and present wishes of the patient be considered (s.4(6)(a)), but does not require those wishes to be determinative of the final treatment decision. Hence, in the absence of an advance decision to refuse treatment, it is entirely possible that treatment will be given to a patient who lacks capacity, which he or she does not wish to receive. For instance, Jehovah's Witnesses might be expected to refuse blood transfusions under any circumstances, even if doing so meant that they would die and even though a blood transfusion might well be in his or her best interests (e.g. *Newcastle Upon Tyne Hospitals Foundation Trust v LM* [2014] EWHC 454 (COP)). With advances in medical treatment making it possible to sustain life for long periods even where there is a very low level of mental functioning, it is possible that some people would not wish to be kept alive in such a state even though it may be considered in their best interests (e.g. *W v M* [2011] EWHC 2443).

Advance decisions provide those who anticipate being given unwanted treatment in his or her best interests once they have lost capacity with a way to refuse treatment prospectively. It should be noted that it is also possible to create a Lasting Power of Attorney ('LPA') (s.9 MCA), which gives authority to a nominated person (or persons) to make decisions on behalf of a person should they lack capacity in future. However, decisions made under an LPA must be made in accordance with the best interests of the patient (s.9(4)(a)) and therefore the power conferred under an LPA is less than the power that a patient has to decide on their own medical treatment contemporaneously or anticipatorily. Thus, although there are similarities between LPAs and advance decisions, they present their own set of challenges, the discussion of which is beyond the scope of this chapter.

The idea of legally binding advance decisions has been attributed to an argument made by US lawyer Luiz Kutner in the 1960s (Huxtable, 2012: 65). In English law, support for the recognition of binding anticipatory refusals of treatment was expressed in the seminal case of *Airedale NHS Trust v Bland* [1993] AC 789 (which is discussed below in greater detail) and has now been codified by the MCA (ss.24–26). The recognition of the right to make advance decisions was controversial, as some argued that it could lead to "'euthanasia by the back door'" (Joint Committee on the Draft Mental Incapacity Bill 2003: [196]). However, these arguments were not upheld and the Bill passed into law (under its revised title) and so confirmed the right to create advance decisions.

English law stipulates a number of requirements that must be met before an advance decision will be considered binding. First, the creator of the advance decision must be aged 18 years at the minimum. Secondly, advance decisions must be made while the creator has capacity to make the decision (s.24(1) MCA). As any advance decision can be withdrawn at any time without the need for writing by its creator (s.24(4) MCA), advance decisions can be invalidated if they are expressly withdrawn by the competent author (s.25(2)(a)). However, they may also be invalidated if the author does anything that is 'clearly inconsistent' with the decision (s.25(2)(c), for example, marrying into a faith that espouses views that are inconsistent with those expressed in the decision: MCA explanatory notes [87]). If an LPA is created after the advance decision, it will invalidate any part of the advance decision which is covered by the decision-making powers given to the donee under the terms of the LPA (s.25(2)(b)).

The MCA also makes clear that an advance decision will not be applicable in certain circumstances. Most obviously, the advance decision will not apply if the circumstances anticipated have not arisen (s.25(4)(b)) or if the treatment proposed is not that which has been specifically refused (s.25(4)(a)). In addition, if circumstances have arisen that would have affected the decision (had the author been aware of them at the material time) and there are reasonable grounds for believing this, the advance decision will not be applicable (s.25(4)(c)). Advance decisions pertaining to either life-saving or life-supporting treatment will not be applicable unless they are made in accordance with the formalities set out in ss.25(5)–(6), which require the decision to be made in writing, for it to be signed and witnessed and for the written acknowledgement that the decision should apply even if it would result in a risk to life.

If these conditions are met, the advance decision may then take binding effect once the patient loses capacity to make the decision (s.25(3)). Consequently the advance decision has the same legal force as a contemporaneous decision to refuse treatment by an adult with capacity (s.26(1) MCA). This means that a medical professional who provides treatment, which involves touching a patient in defiance of a valid and binding advance decision, commits a criminal battery.

8.4 The case for recognising advance decisions

It is important to acknowledge that one of the main motivators for the recognition of advance decisions has been the improvements in the technical ability of medical treatment to sustain life. While many such medical advances have improved the quality of patients' lives and have allowed people to enjoy longer lives, these advances have also given rise to ethical dilemmas. These are particularly apparent in cases in which the technical ability to keep a patient alive exists, but the condition of the patient cannot be improved, such that they will be continuously dependent on medical intervention merely to stay alive. Anthony Bland's case provides the paradigm illustration of this.

Following the injuries he sustained in the Hillsborough disaster (in which people in a football stadium were crushed to death and injured as a tragic result of overcrowding), Anthony was being kept alive by artificial means, but there appeared to be no prospect of recovery. Hence the question arose as to whether, in those circumstances, he should be kept alive (and indeed whether the cessation of the medical treatment that was supporting his life would give rise to any liability). As a measure of the complexity of the matters raised in the case, it was appealed to the House of Lords (at the time, the highest domestic court). There it was decided that treatment could be lawfully withdrawn as its continuation was deemed to no longer be in Anthony's best interests. This kind of dilemma is not unique to English law, as similar cases have come before courts elsewhere in Europe (e.g. *Englaro*; see Moratti, 2010) and in other parts of the world (e.g. *Quinlan* and *Schiavo*; see Fine, 2005; Jox et al, 2012).

Airedale NHS Trust v Bland [1993] AC 789 is a seminal case for medical lawyers and Butler-Sloss LJ placed a heavy emphasis on 'the right of self-determination' in her judgment in the Court of Appeal: 'The starting point for consideration, in my view, is the right of a human being to make his own decisions and to decide whether to accept or reject treatment, the right of self-determination' (ibid, 816).

This right has echoes of the frequently cited principle of respect for autonomy found in bioethics (indeed it is perhaps the dominant principle in bioethics: Callahan, 2003: 288), but differences between the two concepts can be identified, depending on which conception of autonomy is used as a comparator. For instance, some accounts of autonomy might not admit irrational decisions as being autonomous and, on a Kantian account, autonomy is a property of decisions rather than a right held by individuals (O'Neill, 2002: 83). Another potential difference between some philosophical and bioethical conceptions of autonomy and the idea of self-determination propounded in *Airedale NHS Trust v Bland* [1993] AC 789 (and developed in later cases) can be found in the proposition that a person has the right to self-determine the kinds of medical treatment to refuse should they ever lose capacity. Butler-Sloss LJ, again in the Court of Appeal, asserted that this was uncontentiously possible in law: 'Counsel all agree that the right to reject treatment extends to deciding not to accept treatment in the future by way of advance directive or "living will"' (ibid, 816).

This view would indeed be accepted by some philosophers, such as Ronald Dworkin (1993: 227), who view 'precedent autonomy' as capable of taking on binding force following the loss of capacity for further autonomous decisions to be made. However, some philosophers and bioethicists remain unconvinced that autonomy can provide a complete justification for recognising advance decisions as binding, especially if there should be a lengthy interlude between the making of the decision and its application (e.g. Dresser, 1995; Maclean, 2006; Wrigley, 2007). Objections to such advance decisions can be made on several grounds (see Buchanan, 1988: 278–279; Fagerlin and Schneider, 2004). For instance, it might be argued that autonomy is not adequately safeguarded, because of the greater likelihood that the creator of the advance decision would be ill-informed about his or her decision compared to the contemporaneous decision-maker (Dresser, 1995: 35). Of course, however, the problems of lacking information and misunderstanding are not unique to advance decisions and could occur in respect of contemporaneous medical treatment. The English law of informed consent, for example, merely requires a non-negligent disclosure of the nature and purpose of the treatment (*Chatterton v Gerson* [1981] 1 All ER 257) and the risks associated with the treatment and the condition (*Birch v University College London Hospital NHS Foundation Trust* [2008] EWHC 2237). There is no requirement for the healthcare professional to ensure that the patient actually *understands* the information disclosed to them before the law will recognise the consent (*Al Hamwi v Johnston* [2005] EWHC 206). Consequently, this line of objection is not unique to advance decisions, but merely a matter of greater concern in relation to them than perhaps in relation to other decisions.

Similarly, it has been argued that people should not be able to bind their future selves as they cannot anticipate the potential for medical advances (Joint Committee on the Draft Mental Incapacity Bill, 2003: [198]). They may, for example, be unable to envision possible improvements in medical science and medical techniques, which may alter the prognosis or the quality of life that can be expected with a particular condition. English law gives a degree of recognition to these concerns, but only where circumstances stated in the decision are absent (*W v M* [2011] EWHC 2443) or new circumstances have actually arisen that give reasonable grounds for believing these would have altered the decision (s.25(4)(c), MCA). To maintain an objection to advance decisions *per se* on the grounds that medical advances or changes in circumstances might affect a decision is unwarranted, given that such material changes will not always eventuate. Moreover, we must remember the ambulatory nature of advance decisions: any significant medical advances that are made in the period intervening the creation of the decision and the loss of capacity can be taken into account by the creator of the decision, who can then decide whether to alter or revoke their advance decision in light of those developments.

However, a greater problem for advance decisions is that, as discussed, they are often seen as a mere extension of the right to refuse treatment, they are similarly thought to be based on the concept of autonomy and: 'If advance directives are predicated on the basis of personal autonomy then . . . their authority only applies to an individual if he or she is the same moral entity that created the directive' (Maclean, 2006: 298).

Thus, a personhood problem arises, which poses a challenge to the moral legitimacy of advance decisions, since it suggests that the creator of the decision and the person to whom it applies are distinct moral beings. Accepting a different model of personhood to the one tacitly adopted could sweep away the central justificatory pillar of the right to make advance decisions in that they are designed to protect personal autonomy.

8.5 Personhood

Personhood is a concept that allows for a distinction to be drawn between a mere biological organism and an organism which is recognised as having certain rights. Drawing this distinction is far from novel. In ancient Greece, a person could be recognised as having separate aspects of their being in a *bios* and a *zoē*, i.e. their political and their biological being (Agamben, 1998: 9). Different theories of personhood have emerged in moral philosophy (for an overview, see Goodman, 1988) that suggest different criteria for the recognition of personhood (e.g. consciousness, the capacity for self-awareness or simply being biologically human) and, of greatest concern for current purposes, for when personhood changes over time. Within the confines of this chapter it is not possible to consider all such theories in detail and so the discussion will centre on those theories of personal identity and personhood that have been drawn upon to critique the right to make advance decisions.

The theories that describe the points at which changes in personhood occur may be crudely divided into two categories. One branch is termed *animalist*, the other *psychological*. Animalist theories suggest that personhood is determined by biological persistence (Wrigley, 2007: 386–387). On this basis, personhood persists as long as the organism maintains biological identity, i.e. provided that the organism remains biologically the same. Here there is obvious scope for disagreement over the definition of biological identity in terms of how much biological change can be tolerated before we can say that identity is lost (Parfit, 1987: 234–236). However, if a generous view is taken (perhaps looking at genetic markers as a measure of identity), we may be reasonably sure that the person creating the advance decision is the same as the person to whom it applies. But accepting this as a universal principle of law would have far-reaching implications. For instance, a person who has just died might have biological or genetic identity with the person they were when they were alive. If that can be so, then should not the deceased body have the same rights as the living body? The law would not recognise this; for example, one cannot murder a corpse in the same way that one can murder a living human person (R v Malcherek [1981] 2 All ER 422).

Other theories suggest that personhood is *psychologically* contingent. Locke was one of the chief proponents of this view. He claimed that it is our consciousness that forms our personhood (2008: [9]). Locke provides counterarguments to the biological theories of personhood, which certainly carry intuitive force. He suggests that alterations to our biological make-up, or 'substance', do not cause a change in our personhood. For example, if someone's hand is cut off, they would not thereby become a new person (ibid: [13]). However, as personhood is tied to consciousness, Locke makes the further claim that 'whatever has the consciousness of the present and past actions, is the same person to whom they both belong' (ibid: [16]). This means that, to remain the same person, one must be able to remember one's previous states of consciousness. Thus, the person who develops dementia and cannot remember their prior state of consciousness must be treated as a new person.

Parfit's theory shares some common ground with that of Locke, in as far as he contends that our personhood is derived from our psychological make-up. However, Parfit eschews the contention that moral continuity derives from psychological *identity*. Instead, using a series of thought experiments involving cerebral transplantation, cloning and teleportation (e.g. Parfit, 1987: 267–270, 253–266), he suggests that moral continuity is based on the degree of psychological connectedness between persons at different points in time. This degree of connectedness is what matters in the continuation, or survival, of personhood. In other words, provided that there is a sufficient degree of connectedness at two points in time, two entities can be considered to be the same person. Parfit terms this sufficient degree of connectedness 'R' (for a critical discussion on Parfit's use of this term see Belzer, 1996).

As such, Parfit's psychological theory of personhood posits that identity is not what matters when considering whether the present self is responsible for the acts of the past self (Parfit, 1987: 245–280). Consequently Parfit's theory avoids some of the objections that might be raised against Locke's theory. For instance, for Parfit, but not for Locke, a mere inability to remember one's state of mind whilst drunk or enraged does not preclude responsibility being apportioned to the later incarnation of the self, as long as there is a sufficient psychological connection between the two. Similarly, for the purposes of advance decisions, it would be permissible for a person to bind their future self as long as the future self retained this kind of psychological connection.

However, Parfit's normative demarcator, 'relation R', is not accompanied by a precise means for identifying and measuring connectedness. His method for measuring this is to count the number of 'quasi-memories' (Parfit, 1987: 220) of past experiences the current self has of its ancestor, but this would seem unsatisfactory if equal weight were to be given to all memories: surely the recollection of the train journey to work would be less important than the recollection of one's wedding day. Moreover, in circumstances where dementia patients retain long-term memories but have poor short-term memory recall it is unclear that the capacity for long and short-term memory should be attributed the same importance. If they are not to be attributed the same weight, it is equally unclear as to how value should be assigned to different categories of memory. Such questions and uncertainties are significant impediments to the practical adoption and employment of Parfit's theory of personhood.

Even if there were a reliable and practical way of measuring R, it would be difficult to reconcile Parfit's rejection of the 'all-or-nothing' approach to personal identity (Buchanan, 1988: 294–296). This reflects Parfits's argument that the important moral question here is not whether the current self is *the same as* the past self, but rather the degree to which the current self *is connected to* the past self. However, adopting psychological connectedness as the preferred criterion for determining the continued survival of personhood would require 'far richer data than we ordinarily have or could acquire, even with great cost and effort' (Buchanan, 1988: 296) for the purposes of its assessment. As psychological connectedness is a question of degree, it would also be incompatible with law's functional desire to obtain a clear demarcation between the different categories and statuses it propounds (e.g. guilty/not-guilty, has capacity/lacks capacity).

Compounding these practical problems is the fact that determining whether psychological connectedness persists would necessitate a psychological test at two stages: the moment at which the advance decision is made and the moment at which it becomes applicable. At present, the test to be applied at these points in time is one of capacity, which is a functional test with a binary outcome. Even with such a test, practical problems in requiring capacity tests at both points in time have been noted (Donnelly, 2009), especially in relation to conditions such as dementia, where capacity tends to fluctuate (Holm, 2001: 155–156). However, to a certain degree, these difficulties are alleviated by the fact that the MCA contains a presumption of capacity (s.1(2)), which means that, although there may be some advance decisions made by people who would have been declared incapable of making them, had they been assessed, the presumption can resolve the problem. A similar presumption of 'sufficient connectedness' might be used as a part of a test of psychological connectedness, but defining what constitutes 'sufficient' psychological connectedness in abstract legal terms would be onerous and could be considered to be such a personal question that each case would have to be decided on its facts. This would leave all advance decisions open to challenge and would consequently be a great burden on the courts. Thus, from a practical perspective, there would be significant barriers to implementing Parfit's model of personhood.

Additionally, it would be 'strange' and counterintuitive if our connection to our future selves were dependent on Parfit's claim about personhood, because we can observe that people are treated as being the same person throughout their lives within different social networks (Holm, 2001: 157). So, it must be questioned whether these kinds of arguments could realistically be employed in other areas of law. Could the debtor plausibly argue that she is no longer to be bound by her debts because they were incurred by a previous self? Or that she is only liable for the debt in proportion to her degree of connectedness to the person who incurred the debt? Could the murderer plausibly claim that since having adopted a new religious belief she should not continue to be punished for her crime because she is a new person (or that she lacks sufficient connection to her former self to continue be held responsible for the crime)? It is true that, in English law, some of the partial defences to murder such as loss of control and diminished responsibility (ss.54–55 and 52 Coroners and Justice Act 2009, respectively) may relate to a certain recognition that the defendant acted 'out of character', but even if there was such an out of character act there is no possibility of arguing that it follows that the defendant should not be responsible for her actions because she is a different person (or lacks sufficient connection to a previous self). Could the husband plausibly argue that since meeting his new love he has become a new person (or lacks sufficient connection to a previous self) and therefore is no longer bound by his wedding vows (see Wrigley, 2007: 387)? If we are to accept Parfit's view of personhood in relation to advance decisions then, as a matter of consistency, we would be obliged to accept it in respect of contracting parties, criminals and spouses, to name but a few. It is not suggested that it would be impossible to do this, but merely that such a course of action would entail radical changes for the law, for which there is no democratic mandate, and which would risk 'societal havoc' (Rhoden, 1990: 854).

Perhaps the closest legal analogy to the advance decision is to be found in the will, i.e. the legal document that provides instructions to be carried out after the death of its creator. Here again, we might ask whether it might be possible to reconcile the law's tacit conception of personhood with Parfit's theory. Although it can be noted that certain life events (notably marriage, s.18 Wills Act 1837, and civil partnerships, s.18B Wills Act 1837) render a will void under English law, there is no scope for arguing that a deceased octogenarian's will is invalidated in whole or in part, merely by the fact that her will was executed when she was in her twenties. The law is predicated on the understanding that the person who executes a will remains the same person until their death however great the length of time between those events and whatever psychological change may take place during that period. To hold otherwise would require an assessment of the degree to which the person had changed and from that the extent to which it would be fair to bind their estate by the terms of the will. This would be immensely complicated and destructive of the certainty that wills can afford their creators.

Thus, in each of the areas of law discussed, even if the law was not framed in terms of personal identity or personhood, there is a tacit conception of personhood that is relied upon in order that the law can operate in practice. In so far as any theory of personhood is advanced as being preferable to the law's tacit operating conception of personhood, it is for the proponents of any new theory of personhood to make the case for the adoption of their theory. As part of this task, they must also explain how any alternative theory could be enacted. This is an appropriate debate to have as part of the legislative process.

Similar problems may occur with a model based on the biological test, using the reductionist approach (Parfit, 1987: 234–236). In respect of advance decisions, one would have to complete a biological examination prior to making the decision and again at the time the advance decision purported to apply, in order to determine whether any change had occurred and whether that change had been sufficiently great to invalidate the advance decision. The point at which any change becomes significant would be of crucial importance and it is unclear as to how this could be determined in a non-arbitrary way. Such a test would additionally institute a potentially costly and time-consuming barrier to the creation of advance decisions.

Maclean (2006) has examined some of the theories on personhood that have been presented here and endorses the idea that often there may not be a sufficiently strong relationship between the creator and the subject of an advance decision for the decision to be treated as binding. However, he acknowledges that there is certainly a relationship between the two (2006: 314–316). He characterises this relationship between the two selves as a caring one, akin to that of parent and child, and reminds us that relationships entail certain obligations (2006: 315). In particular, parents may make decisions on behalf of their children, but can only make decisions which are in the best interests of the child. On this basis Maclean concludes, in keeping with others (e.g. Wrigley, 2007), that the case for binding advance decisions is ethically deficient and that any statement purporting to refuse treatment beyond the point at which capacity is lost should only be followed in so far as it accords with the best interests of the patient, when the decision becomes relevant.

Remembering that the only reason for making an advance decision is in order to *avoid* being provided with treatment in accordance with the 'best interests' standard, acceptance of Maclean's argument would entirely defeat the purpose of the advance decision as currently recognised in English law. Of course any statement made might be taken into account in the 'best interests' assessment, but the *raison d'être* of advance decisions is that they should be binding and allow the patient to have the final say over their treatment, rather than be merely a persuasive component of the medico-legal calculus of best interests. There is a strong political case for this position, especially now that the common law, which first made possible the creation of binding advance decisions, has been codified in a democratically enacted statute. Neither the law nor society has committed itself to a model of personhood that would contradict this political aim.

As has been discussed, there is also a strong case that the theories of personhood considered here would not be consistent with the tacit legal understanding of personhood. The law's conception of personhood may be informed by biological and metaphysical arguments, but it is not determined by them (e.g. consider the way that companies can have legal standing and liabilities as persons: see e.g. Machen, 1911). Moreover, in respect of advance decisions, the law has plainly made some attempt to accommodate the kind of concerns that the personhood arguments raise.

In particular, the English law contains a provision to invalidate an advance decision if the author has 'done anything else clearly inconsistent with the advance decision remaining his fixed decision' (s. 25(2)(c)). This provision is based on the case of *HE v NHS Trust A and AE* [2003] EWHC 1017 under the old common law (i.e. the law as it was developed through legal precedent, prior to the enactment of the MCA), in which the advance statement to refuse blood transfusions made by a person who was once a Jehovah's Witness, but who later married in the Islamic faith, was struck down as being invalid. The current law requires something to be done, which implies an external act rather than merely for the individual to say something that would be inconsistent with their advance decision. In addition, concerns about the temporal interlude between the making of an advance decision and its application may be allayed by the fact that it is very easy for a person to change or revoke an advance decision that they have made. This can be done at any point following its creation while they retain capacity (s.24(3) MCA). As this is the case, it can be argued that, even if an advance decision was created decades ago, its creator would always have had the opportunity to amend or withdraw it prior to their loss of capacity. Therefore, the relevant time-points, in terms of personhood, are the moment immediately before decision-making capacity is lost (rather than the moment the decision was made) and the moment when the decision becomes applicable. This will be a shorter period of time than the period between the creation of the advance decision and its application and ought, therefore, to lessen the potential for morally significant changes in personhood Therefore even if we were to accept Parfit's model of personhood as an organising theory for the law, it would not necessarily be incompatible with the recognition of advance decisions made many years before they are called upon.

8.6 Conclusion

The criticisms of the right to make advance decisions grounded in philosophical conceptions of personhood present a fundamental challenge to the system of advance decisions that currently operates in English law. If the legitimacy of advance decisions rests on a conception of personal autonomy, then their authority is predicated on personal identity (or connectedness). If we are also prepared to view personhood as changeable over time, and, consequently, that the author of the advance decision might not be the same person (or sufficiently connected to) the person to whom the decision applies, then the legitimacy of legally binding advance decisions would appear to rest on shaky ground.

However, as I have argued, although these conceptions of personhood may inform the legal construction of personhood, they are by no means determinative of it. This is hardly surprising given the ongoing disputes within philosophy surrounding the way in which personhood and identity should be defined and the fact that law necessarily operates in society, rather than on an abstract plane of thought. Lawmakers must, therefore, have regard to the practical implications of the rules they create. Adopting some of the models of personhood discussed in this chapter would have serious practical consequences for other areas of law. These consequences would be incompatible with some of the core operations of the legal system, including the criminal justice system and the freedom to contract.

If the law on advance decisions is inconsistent with certain conceptions of personhood, it is surely as incumbent on the voices in the philosophical and bioethical rooms to ask themselves why the concepts of personhood that they espouse are not met with democratic approval, as it is for those in legal rooms to account for any philosophical deficiencies in the law and the models of personhood that it tacitly espouses.

In the case of the Mental Capacity Act 2005, it is quite apparent that Parliament intended that people should be able to make legally binding advance decisions and formed this intention in the knowledge that people change their minds and that significant life events may change people's views on their anticipated end-of-life choices, as evidenced by specific provisions in the Act dealing with these potentialities. Thus, adopting a form of personhood that would make advance decisions subject to a 'best interests' rider would defeat the will of Parliament, as well as the will of advance decision makers.

References

Agamben, G. (1998) *Homo Sacer: Sovereign Power and Bare Life* (trans. D. Heller-Roazen), Stanford, CA: Stanford University Press.
Belzer, M. (1996) 'Notes on Relation R', *Analysis*, 56(1): 56–62.
Brazier, M., and E. Cave (2007) *Medicine, Patients and the Law*, 4th edn, London: Penguin Books.

Buchanan, A. (1988) 'Advance Directives and the Personal Identity Problem', *Philosophy & Public Affairs*, 17: 277–302.
Callahan, D. (2003) 'Principlism and Communitarianism', *Journal of Medical Ethics*, 29(5): 287–91.
DeGrazia, D. (1999) 'Advance Directives, Dementia, and "the Someone Else Problem"', *Bioethics* 13(5): 373–391.
Donnelly, M. (2009) 'Capacity Assessment under the Mental Capacity Act 2005: Delivering on the Functional Approach?', *Legal Studies*, 29: 464–491.
Dresser, R. (1995) 'Dworkin on Dementia: Elegant Theory, Questionable Policy', *Hastings Center Report*, 25(6): 32–38.
Dworkin, G. (1988) *The Theory and Practice of Autonomy*, Cambridge Studies in Philosophy, Cambridge: Cambridge University Press.
Dworkin, R. (1993) *Life's Dominion: An Argument about Abortion and Euthanasia*, London: HarperCollins.
Fagerlin, A., and Schneider, C.E. (2004) 'Enough: The Failure of the Living Will', *Hastings Center Report*, 34(2): 30–42.
Fine, R.L. (2005) 'From Quinlan to Schiavo: Medical, Ethical, and Legal Issues in Severe Brain Injury', *Proceedings (Baylor University. Medical Center)*, 18(4): 303–310.
Goodman, M.F. (1988) *What Is a Person?*, Clifton, NJ: Wiley Humana Press.
Hayes, T.P.C. (2012) 'Informed Choice over Informed Consent: Cracking the Old *Chester*nut?' in N. Priaulx and A. Wrigley (eds.), *Ethics, Law and Society: Volume V*, Farnham, Surrey: Ashgate, pp. 201–208.
Holm, S. (2001) 'Autonomy, Authenticity, or Best Interest: Everyday Decision-Making and Persons with Dementia', *Medicine, Health Care and Philosophy*, 4(2): 153–159.
Horn, R.J., R. Huxtable and R.J. Jox, (2013) 'European Perspectives on Ethics and Law in End-of-Life Care', in J.L. Bernat and H.R. Beresford (eds.), *Ethical and Legal Issues in Neurology, Handbook of Clinical Neurology*, Amsterdam: Elsevier, pp. 155–165.
Huxtable, R. (2012) *Law, Ethics and Compromise at the Limits of Life: To Treat or not to Treat?*, London: Routledge.
Joint Committee on the Draft Mental Incapacity Bill (2003) session 2002–2003, *Volume 1*, HL Paper 189-I, HC 1083-I.
Jox, R.J., K. Kuehlmeyer, G. Marckmann and E. Racine (eds.) (2012) *Vegetative State: A Paradigmatic Problem of Modern Societies*, Munster: LIT.
Lewis, P. (2006) 'Medical Treatment of Dementia Patient at the End of Life: Can the Law Accommodate the Personal Identity and Welfare Problems?', *European Journal of Health Law*, 13: 219–234.
Locke, J. (2008 [1690]) 'Of Identity and Diversity', in J. Perry (ed.), *Personal Identity*, 33–53, Berkeley and Los Angeles: University of California Press.
Machen, A.W. Jr. (1911) 'Corporate Personality', *Harvard Law Review*, 24(4): 253–267.
Maclean, A.R. (2006) 'Advance Directives, Future Selves and Decision-Making', *Medical Law Review*, 14(3): 291–320.
Mayberry, M. and J. Mayberry (2003) *Consent in Clinical Practice*, Abingdon: Radcliffe Medical.
Moratti, S. (2010) 'The Englaro Case: Withdrawal of Treatment from a Patient in a Permanent Vegetative State in Italy', *Cambridge Quarterly of Healthcare Ethics*, 19(3): 372.
O'Neill, O. (2002) *Autonomy and Trust in Bioethics*, Cambridge: Cambridge University Press.
Parfit, D. (1987) *Reasons and Persons*, Corrected paperback edn, Oxford: Clarendon Press.
Rhoden, N.K. (1990) 'The Limits of Legal Objectivity', *North Carolina Law Review*, 68: 849–865.
Royal College of Physicians (2009) 'Advance Care Planning', *Concise Guidance to Good Practice: A Series of Evidence-Based Guidelines for Clinical Management*, Number 12, February 2009.

UN Economic and Social Council (2000) 'The Right to the Highest Attainable Standard of Health (Article 12 of the International Covenant on Economic, Social and Cultural Rights)' Substantive Issues Arising in the Implementation of the International Covenant on Economic, Social and Cultural Rights. *United Nations Committee on Economic, Social and Cultural Rights, Twenty-Second Session, Geneva, 25 April–12 May 2000, Agenda Item 3*, E/C.12/2000/4.

Wrigley, A. (2007) 'Personal Identity, Autonomy and Advance Statements', *Journal of Applied Philosophy,* 24(4): 381–396.

Part III

European bioethics in clinical rooms

9 Physicians' perspectives on patient preferences and advance directives in England and France: other countries, other requirements?

Ruth Horn

9.1 Introduction

Since the Nuremberg Code (1947), international attempts have been made to strengthen patient rights and autonomy by focusing on the requirement of free and informed consent for medical treatment or participation in research. In the same way as a patient can chose to consent to a medical intervention, he or she can chose to refuse treatment. The 1997 European Convention on Human Rights and Biomedicine, which came into force in 1999, specified that a patient can withdraw consent at any time (article 5). Furthermore, article 9 of the Convention stipulates that, where a patient has lost competence, the physician should take into account previously expressed wishes and preferences with regard to medical treatment. Although the Convention considers previous wishes not to be legally binding, the Council of Europe in 2009, and again in 2012, urges all member states to adopt legislation on previously expressed and written wishes and preferences of patients, also called advance directives (ADs). Several European countries have adopted legislation on ADs which refuse treatment. However, depending on the value a country attributes to patient autonomy, ADs may be legally binding, or they have only advisory value.

This chapter aims to examine the status and practice of ADs in England and France, two countries that value patient autonomy differently. In England, a country that emphasises respect for individual wishes, 'advance decisions to refuse treatment' have long been considered binding at common law (*Re T (adult: refusal of treatment)* [1992]; *Re C (adult: refusal of treatment)* [1994]; *Re AK (medical treatment: consent)* [2000]). Since the Mental Capacity Act 2005 fully came into force in 2007, ADs to refuse treatment have become a part of the statutory law. ADs are now legally binding if they were issued voluntarily by a competent and sufficiently informed patient, and apply to the circumstances that have arisen (Mental Capacity Act 2005, ss. 24–26). In a case where the AD concerns the withdrawal of life-sustaining treatment, the Act additionally requires that the directive must be written, signed and witnessed, and clearly states that the decision is to apply even if life is at risk. Under the Act, the patient can also appoint a 'lasting power of attorney'. This clause allows patients to empower someone to make health care decisions on their behalf when they have lost the capacity to decide for themselves (Mental Capacity Act 2005, ss. 9–14).

The French situation reflects a culture that promotes the protection of the vulnerable person, even if this is to the detriment of the person's autonomy. The option for patients to write an AD was introduced in 2005 by the law on patients' rights and on the end of life (Loi n° 2005-370). There is no evidence that anticipatory treatment refusals were previously recognised in French jurisprudence. As now stipulated in article L. 1111–11 of the Public Health Code, the doctor can take ADs into account but is not obliged to do so. The patient's will, as expressed in such a directive, is indicative rather than determinative (Feuillet Le-Mintier, 2011). The law states that the doctor alone makes the decision to withdraw life-sustaining treatment. Yet, he or she is advised to consult a colleague, the patient's representative, the family, close persons and, if one exists, the AD. Despite its non-binding character, an AD must have been issued less than three years previously. In the absence of an AD, there is no specific requirement to find out what the patient's wishes would have been. A comparison of European states has found that France also confers the weakest power on proxies or surrogates in decision-making (Lautrette et al., 2008).

In spite of the different legal value accorded to ADs in England and France, the number of written directives is insignificant in both countries (Pennec et al., 2012; Schiff, 2000; Seale, 2006a; 2006b). Even countries such as the United States, where the Patient-Self-Determination Act has accorded legal force to ADs since 1990, report problems in the uptake of these documents (Hanson and Rodgman, 1996). Some authors relate these problems to miscommunications between physicians and patients, including the difficulty associated with articulating future wishes, and fears that the AD could be misinterpreted or disregarded (Fagerlin and Schneider, 2004).

The concerns regarding possible misinterpretations and doctor-patient miscommunications raise two overarching questions regarding the role of physicians in discussing ADs. First, how do physicians discuss future treatment options with patients and how do they support them in expressing their wishes? And, secondly, how do physicians take into account patient preferences in decision-making, and what are the arguments and underlying social values for doing (or not doing) so in different legal contexts?

I will argue that, if we want to better understand why English and French physicians may promote (or not promote) the writing of such directives, it appears appropriate to take into account, not only their views on ADs, but also their general attitude towards patient preferences as well as underlying cultural traditions, which may result in legal and practical constraints regarding the use of ADs (Cartwright et al., 2007; Meñaca et al., 2012; Evans et al., 2013). This chapter explores the problems physicians from different contexts report with regard to end-of-life decision-making and shows how the place accorded to patient preferences influences the potential role of ADs in clinical decision-making in England and France. A better understanding of national differences may help to further develop and implement ADs in the European context.

9.2 Methods

This chapter presents the results of 28 semi-structured, face-to-face interviews on physicians' views on ADs, and more generally on their views about end-of-life decision-making for incompetent patients. In 2011, 14 English and 14 French physicians were recruited from university hospitals (n = 2 in England, n = 3 in France) in two different cities in each country. The focus was on doctors working in services which take care of seriously or terminally ill patients (specifically, geriatrics, intensive care, nephrology, neurology, oncology, palliative care, rheumatology and surgery). Ethical approval for the study was sought and obtained in England from an NHS Research Ethics Committee (REC reference number: 10/H0106/56); in France, the Commission Nationale de l'Informatique et des Libertés confirmed that no specific approval procedure was needed for this study. However, in France recruitment of physicians was negotiated with the head of the hospital services and appropriate standards for interviews were agreed with these heads, including guarantees of the anonymity of the participants. In England, according to the requirements of the local research ethics committee, physicians were approached after initial contact by the medical director of each hospital, who invited them to contact the researcher if they wished to participate in the study. Each participant received an information sheet about the study and written consent was obtained prior to the interviews.

Interviews were conducted by an experienced sociologist in a quiet room in hospitals. Each interview lasted approximately 45 minutes. Each interview was audio recorded and transcribed. The aim of the interviews was to better understand the importance for the physician of a previously stated treatment preference, including the potential role of ADs. For this purpose, the interviews examined the following broad themes: first, the problems that emerge when deciding to withdraw or withhold life-sustaining treatment from both conscious and unconscious patients; secondly, decision-making procedures and the participation of proxies/relatives; thirdly, previous experience with ADs and the participants' views on their usefulness; and, finally, perspectives on improving the decision-making processes in question. The analysis of data gathered within each theme involved numerous readings of the transcribed interviews, followed by identification and refining of comparable recurrent themes and patterns in English and French physicians' attitudes and experiences.

In what follows, participants are identified according to their nationality (En/Fn), gender (m/f) and their medical specialty (geriatrics: ger; intensive care: intens; nephrology: neph; neurology: neur; oncology: onc; palliative care: pall; rheumatology: rheum and surgery: surg). Without aiming to make generalised claims about 'all' English or 'all' French physicians, the data echo tendencies which are also apparent in each country's legislation, public debates and professional guidelines (Horn, 2012).

9.3 Findings

The 14 English physicians included three oncologists, three neurologists, three palliative care specialists, three nephrologists, and two geriatricians. In France, of the 14 physicians, three were oncologists, three neurologists, three palliative care specialists, two nephrologists, two geriatricians and one was from intensive care. Seven of the 14 English physicians and five out of the 14 French physicians were women. The small sample size does not allow us to show differences between physicians of different specialties or according to gender or age; most physicians, with one exception of a younger physician in her early 30s, were between 40 and 55 years old.

9.4 Respect for patient preferences when deciding to withdraw or withhold life-sustaining treatment

As explained earlier, respect for a competent patient's wish to refuse treatment is legally required in England and France. Yet, legislation in each country introduces different limitations to this right in order to balance respect for autonomy against the duty to protect a vulnerable person. These limitations introduce some ambiguities with regard to respecting a patient's wish to refuse life-sustaining treatment, which appears evident in physicians' attitudes.

9.4.1 English physicians' difficulties in implementing the ideal concept of autonomy

English physicians, when asked about difficulties they encounter when deciding to discontinue treatment for both competent and incompetent patients, reported problems regarding patient consent, the timing of making such a decision and the prognosis. All 14 English doctors interviewed in this study explained the importance of discussing decisions to withdraw or withhold treatment with the patient.

These participants valued absolute respect for patients' decisions in situations where they 'can be sure that the patient understands the situation' [E13/m/onc]. One English physician explained that, if he has given accurate information and the patient refuses the treatment as a result, he feels

> very comfortable with that [because] it's a sign of a strong, as well as empowered patient, if they feel they can turn around and say, 'That's not for me'. I just want to find out whether there is something I could change.
> [E1/m/onc]

Supporting this view, another physician explained that

> a 'bad decision' – as I would see it – from the patient does not mean that they should be overridden or that they don't have capacity. [. . .] The issue is . . . does the patient really understand and was the decision made at a time when they had capacity?
>
> [E4/m/ger]

These participants tended to reflect similarly on this issue, arguing that professional duties are not limited to clinical criteria. Rather, they perceived their duty as one of serving the patient according to that individual's needs and preferences.

Even in the case where a patient is incompetent and there is no valid AD, most English doctors (10/14) reported that they try to take into account all opinions, such as those expressed in previous statements or statements by the family, friends, carers or the general practitioner. This attitude echoes the recommendations regarding the assessment of best interests as defined in the Mental Capacity Act, which state that physical well-being should be balanced with emotional and psychological factors, by taking into account the incapacitated person's values, past preferences or present feelings (Mental Capacity Act 2005, s. 4).

Most physicians (8/14) explained that it is important to get the family 'on board', to discuss the decisions with them and to get to know their views. Yet, all of these physicians explained that they would never entirely rely on the family's opinion because families do 'not always act in a patient's best interests' [E8/f/neph] or propose decisions according to the patient's wishes. They explained that most families do not really consider previous values but insist on treatment 'partly out of fear that they'll be seen as the agent of the death of somebody they love' [E2/m/nep]. As such, a physician [E5/f/rheum] revealed that, although she discusses decisions with the family, she makes clear that she alone bears the responsibility for deciding (see also Kitzinger and Kitzinger, 2012).

Although English physicians highly value patients' wishes, in practice, most doctors who were interviewed (8/14) explained that patient wishes are not always known, partly because it is difficult to know the 'right' time to have discussions with the patient. The doctors explained that often they get to know their patients when they are already 'quite a long way down the road' and can 'have no meaningful conversation anymore' [E4/m/ger]. Other physicians (3/14) acknowledged that, even if their patients are competent, they might delay discussion about future treatment because to do otherwise means 'acknowledging that life is now limited' [E1/m/onc].

One doctor explained that she uses 'the lack of information [about possible outcomes] as excuse' not to confront the patient – and herself – with the reality of a poor prognosis. This doctor explained that it is difficult to discuss treatment withdrawal, partly because it's not always bad, and partly because we've not found the words; and partly because it's pushing stones uphill. I think quite a lot of this is just an excuse for not facing our own mortality, rather than a really good reason for not raising the subject.

[E3/f/pall]

This physician and her colleagues use uncertainty about the course of a disease to avoid facing deeper concerns, such as the patient's – and their own – mortality.

The interviews suggest that English physicians seem to be torn between their wish to respect patient preferences, which is emphasised in law and professional guidelines (General Medical Council, 2008, 2010; Liverpool Care Pathway, 2012; Neuberger, 2013), and their unease about communicating a bad prognosis. In medical practice, as well as in jurisprudence (Coggon and Miola, 2011), the implementation of autonomy is not always self-evident. Autonomy often remains a theoretical ideal, which is not always realised in practice.

9.4.2 French physicians' concern for social values

In contrast, none of the French doctors expressed concerns about making decisions without being able to discuss them with the patient. One physician suggested that he does not need a patient's opinion as to whether or not to stop treatment, since he alone makes the decision:

I don't need my patients' opinion to withdraw treatment [. . .] If I think that the patient shouldn't be resuscitated, that she has no chance, I don't need her opinion for this.

[F11/m/onc]

This physician refers to the above-mentioned law of 2005 specifying a physician's right to withdraw or withhold life-sustaining treatment. Although the law emphasises that medical decisions should be informed by patient preferences, it also makes clear that in the end the judgment about the appropriateness of a treatment is the privilege of the physician (see article L.1111–4 Public Health Code; Thouvenin, 2011).

However, another physician [F7/f/onc], who is less supportive of treatment limitations, told me that she 'never' stops treatment, because, for her, withdrawing treatment means making 'a moral judgment of the value of the patient's life'. Explaining that 'patients ask for treatment because this is how [the doctor-patient] relationship works', this physician demonstrated that treatment is the foundation of her relationship with patients. Another physician, meanwhile, argued that treatment is constitutive of her relationship with the patient and that withdrawing treatment [dialysis] 'is like stopping a close relationship with a patient' [F3/f/neph].

Regardless of whether or not physicians decide to withdraw futile treatment, it seems that the decision is based on the doctor's, rather than the patient's, viewpoint. Indeed, another physician confirmed that it is not always the patient's perspective that counts but that

> there are social rules . . . and we have to avoid that after three months people end up in a vegetative state. . . . That poses the question of how much will this cost the society. And, then we also have to ask what the emotional and social burden is for the family?
>
> [F1/m/intens]

Here, then, the consequences of inappropriate medical interventions are considered from a social perspective, rather than from an individual patient perspective.

Similarly, another physician thought that, rather than focusing on the patient's wish alone, it is often more important to

> reassure the patient, to explain that the staff is responsible for them, that it's our business to preserve their humanity, protect their dignity and to explain that we are the guarantors of their dignity. . . . What is important for us is the social guarantee we can give the patient because we are a country with social values.
>
> [F8/m/onc]

The values at stake are humanity, dignity and solidarity. This doctor wants his patients to feel that the medical profession acts according to social values and takes responsibility for patients in need.

A similar understanding of the patient as being part of and protected by the society is presented by another French physician, who thought that

> patients have not only rights, but also duties; the duty to consider the other. [. . .] It's pseudo-individualism [to only focus on the patient wish] and I think that the perversion of this is that the patient should be alone responsible for everything. But the decision is a collective one and is more global.
>
> [F14/m/neur]

This doctor refuses the primacy of individual autonomy and justifies his opinion by reference to a particular view of the individual, who is tied to the society through her duties towards others. The individual is not solely responsible for her decisions because these are 'collective' in a broader social sense. For this physician, 'collective' decisions do not seem to mean shared decision-making. Rather, he appears to be in line with the French National Ethics Committee (CCNE), which stated in 2000 that medical decisions should be in accordance with the society's values. More precisely, the Committee considered that the physician is a 'representative of the community' who 'defends and promotes the values of the society' (CCNE, 2000: 11).

When French doctors reflected on the participation of third parties in the decision-making process, they explained, similarly to the English physicians, that they do not want to rely too heavily on the family. One French physician explained that 'it will be too difficult and violent for [the family], and they might break down' [F13/m/neur] if they are expected to make decisions about treatment limitations. Like the English doctors, the French physicians want to ease the family's feelings of guilt. Yet, unlike the English doctors interviewed, none of the French physicians expressed concerns that the family might not be best able to brief them about the patient's values and preferences.

These interviews revealed, despite changing attitudes, a strong commitment among French physicians to intervening therapeutically in order to preserve life. The French doctors came to their decisions by taking a collective, social approach, rather than taking into account the perspective of the individual patient. In the French context, individual patient preferences are subordinated to collective values. This orientation aims to protect the vulnerable person and to guarantee their social integration. These values are defended by the medical body; therefore, physicians can make decisions on behalf of the individual.

9.5 Meaning, sense and (better) use of ADs

Doctors in both countries described having little experience with written directives and that those they had encountered tended to be written up by, in the words of one English participant, 'educated middle class people who are neither sick nor old, thus who do not really need an AD' [E2/m/neph] (see also Cicirelli, 1998). English physicians nevertheless acknowledged the fact that often patients make verbal advance statements instead.

9.5.1 English physicians' concern for the authenticity of ADs

Consistent with the importance that English physicians accord to patient preferences, all of these participants appreciated the idea of ADs and considered them to be completely binding if they are valid. The majority of doctors (8/14) explained that the main problem concerns the validity of the documents, because:

> they have to be very specific which is actually quite difficult to predict, because you can never cover every eventuality.
>
> [E4/m/ger]

So, 'how do you know that's genuine?' wondered one physician [E5/f/rheum] and another stated that 'the problem is, it's sort of time-bound, you know, it's only a snapshot of how someone is feeling at one point in their life . . . so, how sure can we be that this is the patient's wish?' [E6/m/onc].

As already stated, most physicians (10/14) considered that in-depth discussion would enable them to better understand the patient's wishes. However, four out of 14 physicians pointed out that it is in fact very difficult to introduce ADs into the discussion with patients because they could 'imagine that's quite scary for them' [E3/f/pall]. In order to address this difficulty, one doctor reflected on the possibility of introducing standard forms of ADs in the patient's medical file:

> [It would be] really, really helpful if we would have a page on treatment aims in our clerking booklet that we go through . . . I think that just advanced thinking about what their ceiling of care is going to be, would actually be really helpful. Just to have that more in the culture of thinking right at the start of coming in.
>
> [E5/f/rheum]

Another doctor objected, however, that 'making it bureaucratic, distancing it from the personal [aspects] makes it easier for the professional really, but it doesn't make it that much easier for the patient'. Therefore, he suggested that formalising ADs has to go hand-in-hand with more discussion and 'a greater acceptance that [advance care planning] is a normal part of what [doctors] do' [E4/m/ger].

The English physicians referred to the Liverpool Care Pathway (LCP) (2012), which, at the time the interviews were conducted, had been largely endorsed by professional bodies and implemented by hospital staff across the UK.[1] The LCP emphasises not only ADs, but also broader advance care planning and doctor-patient communication about end-of-life care. Advance care planning can help with identifying patients' general and specific preferences and it therefore aids assessment of the authenticity of a wish (Horn and ter Meulen, 2014). Yet, like ADs, advance care planning requires the physician to confront and communicate a bad prognosis which, in practice, makes physicians hesitant to implement either of these possibilities.

Concerns about the authenticity of previously expressed wishes echoes the ethical debate about ADs in the English speaking world. Whereas some authors defend the role of ADs in extending patient autonomy (Buchanan and Brock, 1990; Dworkin, 1993), other authors question the moral authority of previously expressed wishes. They doubt whether our (psychological) personal identity remains the same throughout life and argue that in fact our identity develops continually, depending on various external and psychological factors (Dresser, 1994; Parfit, 1984). Both arguments share a concern with 'true' patient autonomy. However, while acknowledging the importance of patient autonomy, in practice the wish to respect patient preferences is met with the reluctance of physicians to discuss the prognosis and future treatment options with the patient.

9.5.2 French physicians' scepticism regarding 'Anglo-Saxon' principlism

Whereas English physicians questioned ADs as a means of expressing the genuine will of the patient, French doctors dismissed the idea of an AD outright. Half of the physicians (7/14) interviewed believed that ADs do not have a place in French practice. One doctor pointed out that:

> ADs are Anglo-Saxon inventions; it's typical for them [the 'Anglo-Saxons'] to determine and respect all these principles . . . I draw a line between something that is Anglo-Saxon and something that is Latin because I want to give sense to a relationship . . . and do not want to resolve problems by signing a paper.
>
> [F3/f/neph]

Another French physician explained that 'Anglo-Saxon principlism' leads to the use of all kinds of 'protocols, ADs, do-not-resuscitate-orders, end-of-life protocols, etc.', without them helping doctors to make decisions. [F1] The arguments of these two doctors refer to the principlist approach in bioethics (Beauchamp and Childress, 2008) which, as Callahan points out, 'reflects the liberal, individualist culture from which it emerged' (Callahan, 2003: 288); this, as several French doctors noticed, does not fit with the idea that the physician should make decisions when caring for his or her patient.

When explaining that it is important to 'remain community-minded and make collective, rather than individual decisions', one French doctor even considered that 'it's not ethical to rely only on the patient [. . .]; it's ridiculous!' [F1/m/intens]. A minority of physicians (5/14) recognised, however, that although 'the idea [of ADs] comes from the Anglo-Saxon countries', such directives should also be accepted in France. Yet, they considered, in the words of one, that 'on a cultural level French people aren't there yet' [F5/f/pall]. Indeed, another physician explained that although

> the law of 2005 is a real reform and reorientation of medical practices . . . these changes are new and . . . the French National Medical Council only recently revised its paternalistic tradition. Prior to this, we learned not to embarrass patients with their illness but treated them in a way that we thought would be good for them.
>
> [F6/f/pall]

Before implementing ADs in France, another physician thought that

> it would be more important to accept the idea of palliative care, that is, of stopping treatment that has no benefit and to accept that this is not the end [of what physicians can do for a patient] – we have to change our technical, body centred thinking and learn to take into account the benefit, the comfort and the patient's wish.
>
> [F2/m/ger]

It appears that those French doctors who agreed that ADs could be beneficial saw ADs as having a particular meaning in France. Jean Leonetti, the author of the law of 2005, pointed out that the principal reason for introducing ADs was to 'ease doctors' feelings of guilt' when withdrawing life-sustaining treatment (Assemblée Nationale, 2008b: 237). Patient preferences appear to be secondary. The need to ease feelings of guilt shows how difficult it still is for many French doctors not to employ all means to cure a patient.

The interviews therefore revealed a long tradition of what is called *acharnement thérapeutique* or *obstination thérapeutique déraisonnable* in the French debate, which could best be translated by 'therapeutic determination or relentlessness' and 'unreasonable therapeutic stubbornness' (Horn, 2011). In such an environment, ADs are not understood in terms of enhancing patient autonomy, but remain an exotic idea, difficult to integrate in medical practice.

9.6 Conclusion

Drawing upon an analysis of interviews with French and English doctors, this study shows how patient preferences are taken into consideration in different social and cultural contexts and how these differences influence physicians' perspectives and attitudes towards ADs. Such an investigation demonstrates context-specific reasons for resistance towards the implementation of ADs, irrespective of whether or not the cultural and legal context favours respect for patient autonomy, and therefore ADs.

In England, a country with a strong libertarian tradition that values respect for individual wishes and beliefs, physicians consider ADs to be an important means of enhancing patient autonomy. The priority English physicians give to individual patient wishes points to a libertarian tradition which goes back to authors such as Locke (1993) or Mill (2005), as well as to the Protestant influence backing the right to make one's own decisions (Dickenson, 1999). Yet, the understanding of autonomy as an ideal according to which a person's wish is authentic and free of influences explains the reluctance of English physicians to implement ADs. The physicians only want to rely on an autonomous wish, meaning on a reflected decision made when the patient was competent and had understood the consequences of the decision. They believe, on the one hand, that the authenticity of an autonomous decision can be established through direct doctor-patient discussions, but, on the other hand, they appear to be reluctant to have such communication in the light of bad prognosis and death. In order to better understand the physicians' dilemmas in implementing values that are imbedded in their culture and law, it will be important to further investigate their practices. Such investigation should help to address problems related to the implementation of ADs within a context where patient preferences are valued.

By contrast, physicians in France focus on collective, social aspects rather than individual preferences. The French perspective alludes to Rousseau's (1954) understanding of the relationship between the individual and society.

According to Rousseau's idea of the social contract, every individual's opinions and preferences are subject to the general will, which represents the interests of the society as a whole (Rousseau, 1954). The general will needs to be guided by individuals who are concerned with the public interest and who want to promote social harmony and cooperation. As quoted above, in its 2000 report, the French National Ethics Committee attributed this role to physicians (CCNE, 2000). Such an understanding endorses the subordination of individual patient preferences to the professional opinion which relays social values (see also Horn, 2012; De Vries, Dingwall and Orfali, 2009). Such a hierarchical order is also supported by the Catholic tradition, whose impact on modern France cannot be denied (Willaime, 1996). In this context, ADs, which imply disclosure, communication and respect for individual wishes, are perceived as a foreign concept that does not match with the collective medical attitude (see also Meñaca et al., 2012; Evans et al., 2013). Yet, as the example of France shows, things are beginning to change and it will be interesting to observe whether physicians will gradually integrate the new libertarian emphasis on patient autonomy into their practice. Further research should also explore whether ADs can be useful in the French context or whether other forms of advance care planning, focusing on both patient wishes and physicians' responsibilities, could be more effective.

Physicians' reservations about the practical implementation of ADs vary depending on the role patient preferences play in a particular country. Contrary to what one might expect, problems associated with the use of ADs are not lesser in a context that emphasises respect for patient autonomy than in a context that does not regard patient autonomy to be the overriding principle. The problems perceived in each context are different and need to be addressed in specific ways. If, on the ground of respect for autonomy, policy-makers want to improve the implementation of ADs, measures should be taken to reassure English physicians about the authenticity of the patient's will. In France, doctors should be reassured that taking into account patients' wishes does not put into question their professional competency. In both countries, such measures could aim to enhance the recognition of 'the relational aspects of autonomy and central human needs for support and communication' (Krones and Bastami, 2014: 195). Understanding ADs as a means of opening a dynamic dialogue (Widdershoven and Berghmans, 2001) between physicians and patients could ease the tensions that emerged in each country: tensions between physicians' wishes to respect patients' preferences and the difficulty of initiating discussions about such preferences, as well as tensions between the value of therapeutic interventions and the emerging focus on patient participation.

This study suggests the importance of taking into account different cultural and social contexts in the ethical analysis of the importance of ADs, as well as the need to fine-tune policy-making. Understanding the differences between the physician-patient relationship and the role of patient preferences in England and France helps to inform the kind of policy and ethical guidance that should be developed.

Note

1 A recent independent review (Neuberger, 2013) identified problems with regard to the implementation of the LCP which led the Department of Health in England to recommend that the LCP is phased out (see Wrigley, 2014).

References

Assemblée Nationale (2008a) *Mission d'évaluation de la loi n° 2005-370 du 22 avril 2005 relative aux droits des malades et à la fin de vie n° 1287*. 1.

——— (2008b) *Mission d'évaluation de la loi n° 2005-370 du 22 avril 2005 relative aux droits des malades et à la fin de vie n° 1287*. 2.

Beauchamp, T.L. and Childress, J.F. (2008). *Principles of Biomedical Ethics*, 6th edn, New York: Oxford University Press.

Buchanan, A. and Brock, D. (1990) *Deciding for Others: The Ethics of Surrogate Decision-making*, New York: Cambridge University Press.

Callahan, D. (2003) 'Principlism and communitarianism', *Journal of Medical Ethics*, 29: 287–291.

Cartwright, C., Onwuteaka-Philipsen B.D. et al.; on behalf of the EURELD Consortium (2007) 'Physician discussions with terminally ill patients: A cross-national comparison', *Palliative Medicine*, 21(4): 295–303.

CCNE, Comité Consultatif National d'Ethique (2000) *Avis n° 63 fin de vie, arrêt de vie, euthanasie. Ethique et recherche biomédicale*.

Cicirelli, V.G. (1998) 'Views of elderly people concerning end-of-life decisions', *Journal of Applied Gerontology*, 17(2): 186–203.

Coggon, J. and Miola, J. (2011) 'Autonomy, liberty and medical decision making', *Cambridge Law Journal*, 70(3): 523–547.

Council of Europe (2009) *Recommendation of the Committee of Ministers to member states on principles concerning continuing powers of attorney and advance directives for incapacity*, December 9. Available HTTP: <https://wcd.coe.int/ViewDoc.jsp?id=1563397&Site=CM> (accessed 27 March 2014).

——— (2012) *Protecting human rights and dignity by taking into account previously expressed wishes of patients*, January 25. Available HTTP: <http://assembly.coe.int/main.asp?link=/documents/Adoptedtext/ta12/eres1859.htm> (accessed 27 March 2014).

De Vries, R. de, Dingwall, R. and Orfali, K. (2009) 'The moral organization of the professions: Bioethics in the United States and France', *Current Sociology*, 57(4): 555–579.

Dickenson, D. (1999) 'Cross-cultural issues in European bioethics', *Bioethics*, 13(3): 249–255.

Dresser, R. (1994) 'Missing persons: Legal perceptions of incompetent patients', *Rutgers Law Review*, 46: 624–630.

Dworkin, R. (1993) *Life's Dominion: An Argument about Abortion, Euthanasia, and Individual Freedom*, New York: Alfred A. Knopf.

Evans, N. et al. and EUROIMPACT (2013) 'End-of-life decisions: A cross-national study of treatment preference discussions and surrogate decision maker appointments', *PLoS One* 8(3): e57965.

Fagerlin, A. and Schneider, C.E. (2004) 'Enough: The failure of the living will', *Hastings Center Report*, 34: 30–42.

Feuillet Le-Mintier, B. (2011) 'Les directives anticipées en France, un indice de consentement à effets limités'. In S. Negri (Ed.). *Self-Determination, Dignity and End-of-life Care. Regulating Advance Directives in International and Comparative Perspective*, Leiden and Boston: Martinus Nijhoff Publishers, pp. 195–207.

General Medical Council (2008) *Consent: Patients and Doctors Making Decisions Together*, London: General Medical Council.
—––— (2010) *Treatment and Care towards the End of Life: Good Practices in Decision Making*, London: General Medical Council.
Hanson, L.C. and Rodgman E. (1996) 'The use of living wills at the end of life. A national survey', *Archives of Internal Medicine*, 156(9): 1018–1022.
Horn, R. (2011) 'Euthanasia and end-of-life practices in France and Germany. A comparative study', *Medicine, Health Care and Philosophy*, 16(2): 197–209.
—––— (2012) 'Advance directives in English and French law: Different concepts, different values, different societies', *Health Care Analysis*, 22(1): 59–72.
Horn, R. and ter Meulen, R. (2014) 'Advance directives in the context of limited resources for health care'. In N. Biller-Andorno, S. Brauer and P. Lack (Eds.), *Advance Directives: Ethical Issues from an International Perspective*, New York: International Library of Ethics, Law, and the New Medicine, Springer, pp. 181–192.
Kitzinger, J. and Kitzinger, C. (2012) 'The "window of opportunity" for death after severe brain injury: Family experiences', *Sociology of Health and Illness*, 35(7): 1095–1112.
Krones, T. and Bastami, S. (2014) 'From legal documents to patient-oriented processes'. In N. Biller-Andorno, S. Brauer and P. Lack (Eds.), *Advance Directives: Ethical Issues from an International Perspective*, New York: International Library of Ethics, Law, and the New Medicine, Springer, pp. 193–200.
Lautrette, A., Peigne, V., Watts, J., Souweine, B. and Azoulav, E. (2008) 'Surrogate decision makers for incompetent ICU patients: A European perspective', *Current Opinion in Critical Care*, 14(6): 714–719.
Liverpool Care Pathway for the Dying Patients (2012) 'Continuous quality improvement programme. The Marie Curie Palliative Care Institute'. Available HTTP: <http://www.mcpcil.org.uk/service-innovation-andimprovement-division/lcp.aspx> (accessed 27 March 2014).
Locke, J. (1993 [1690]) *The Two Treatises of Government*, London: Everyman.
Loi n° 2002-303 du 4 mars 2002 relative aux droits des malades et à la qualité du système de santé. *Journal Officiel*. 54. p. 4118.
Loi n° 2005-370 du 22 avril 2005 relative aux droits des malades et à la fin de vie. *Journal Officiel*. 95. p.7089.
Marie Curie Palliative Care Institute Liverpool (2012) *LCP Model Pathway – UK Core Documentation*. Online. Available HTTP: <http://www.sii-mcpcil.org.uk/media/10843/lcp%20core%20documentation.pdf> (accessed 11 June 2014).
Meñaca, A., Evans, N. et al. (2012) 'End-of-life care across Southern Europe: A critical review of cultural similarities and differences between Italy, Spain and Portugal', *Critical Review in Oncology Hematology*, 82(3): 387–401.
Mill, M.S. (2005 [1859]) *On Liberty*, New York: Cosimo classics.
Neuberger, J. (2013) *More Care Less Pathway: A Review of the Liverpool Care Pathway*, Crown Copyright. Online. Available HTTP: <https://www.gov.uk/government/uploads/system/uploads/attachment_data/file/212450/Liverpool_Care_Pathway.pdf> (accessed 11 June 2014).
Parfit, D. (1984) *Reasons and Persons*, Oxford: Clarendon Press.
Pennec, S., Monnier, A., Pontone, S. and Aubrey, R. (2012) 'End-of-life medical decisions in France: A death certificate follow-up survey 5 years after the 2005 Act of Parliament on patients' rights and end of life', *BMC Palliative Care*, 11(25): 25.
Rousseau, J.-J. (1954 [1762]). *The Social Contract*, Chicago: H. Regnery Co.
Schiff, R., Rajkumar, C. and Bulpitt, C. (2000) 'Views of elderly people on living wills: Interview study', *British Medical Journal*, 320: 1640–1641.

Seale, C. (2006a) 'National survey of end-of-life decisions made by UK medical practitioners', *Palliative Medicine*, 20: 3–10.

—— (2006b) 'Characteristics of end-of-life decisions: Survey of UK medical practitioners', *Palliative Medicine*, 20: 653–659.

Thouvenin, D. (2011) La loi n° 2005-370 du 22 avril 2005, dite loi Leonetti: la médicalisation de la fin de vie. In , J.-M. Ferry, *Fin(s) de vie – le débat*, Paris: Presses Universitaires de France, pp. 303–368.

Widdershoven, G. and Berghmans, R. (2001) 'Advance directives in dementia care: From instructions to instruments', *Patient Education and Counselling*, 44(2): 179–186.

Willaime, J.P. (1996) 'Laïcité et religion en France'. In G. Davie and D. Hervieu-Léger (Eds.), *Identités religieuses en Europe*, Paris: La Découverte, pp. 154–171.

Wrigley, A. (2014) 'Ethics and end of life care: The Liverpool Care Pathway and the Neuberger Review', *Journal of Medical Ethics*, Online first, May 21. Available HTTP: < http://jme.bmj.com/content/early/2014/04/21/medethics-2013–101780> (accessed 15 June 2014).

10 'You don't need proof when you've got instinct!': gut feelings and some limits to parental authority

Giles Birchley

10.1 Introduction

While, in Europe and beyond, decisions about children who lack competence to contribute to their treatment decisions are based upon their best interests, both the European Court of Human Rights and bioethical theorists consider that there must be substantial involvement of parents in these decisions. In the United Kingdom (UK), legal and clinical guidelines say that critically ill children's best interests must be agreed by their parents and doctors, or the courts, in a process of shared decision-making. There is widespread acceptance that there should be limitations on parental authority in shared decisions, yet parental authority is ill-defined, and without some agreement on the source of parental authority it is difficult to limit it either cogently or consistently.

This chapter presents results from an empirical ethics investigation into shared decision-making in the paediatric intensive care unit, a study that focused on critical decisions in which an infant child's treatment or non-treatment would be decided. While many of the parents involved expressed their views about their child's best interests as an intuition, this intuition was generally based on their knowledge, emotional intimacy and close proximity to their child. However, in some circumstances such intuition appeared to have no basis in fact or experience, and this was notably the case for the intuitions parents said they would rely upon to make critical decisions about treatment at the end of life. A combination of knowledge, emotional connection, intimacy and intuition also saw many parents actively contribute to decision-making and frequently request treatments for their child. I use intuition here to characterise an instinctive sense that something is the case – what is sometimes termed a 'gut instinct'.[1] Normative accounts of intuition, which I will discuss in this chapter, are divided about the basis and the value of intuitions, but not the definition; as McMahan puts it, moral intuition is a 'spontaneous moral judgement' (2000: 93).

The study results allow us to glimpse a rich picture of the sources of parental authority, and thus offer the cogent reasons we need in order to place consistent limits on the scope of parental authority in shared decisions.

I contend that parental authority can have a basis in intuition, which should be based upon tangible, intimate knowledge of their child, their child's therapy and their child's medical history; however I suggest that, without this basis, parental intuition alone should not be authoritative. I accept that requests for treatment may communicate such knowledge and thus be useful for raising the quality of care. However, I observe that such requests may also have a deleterious effect on other children within the clinical setting because of the physical limitations of resources and the varying abilities of parents as advocates. For these reasons, while I argue there are strong reasons to involve in decisions about their children parents who are (in ways I explore) close to their offspring, I suggest there are defensible, definable and consistent limits to the exercise of parental authority in shared decisions.

10.2 Parental authority in practice

Parents are widely considered to share decision-making authority with clinicians (Sullivan, Monagle and Gillam, 2014), all the more so in decisions about infants who are unable to express their own wishes. In the UK, clinical guidelines, including those from the General Medical Council (2010), the Nuffield Council on Bioethics (2007) and the Royal College of Paediatrics and Child Health (2004), suggest a parent-clinician partnership to serve the child's best interests. This clinical partnership is also recognised in common law in the leading case of *Re J (a minor) (wardship: medical treatment)* [1991] Fam 33, in which Lord Donaldson MR (at 41) characterised a parent's ability to refuse or consent to their child's treatment as part of a system of checks and balances on doctors or the courts.

There is, however, widespread agreement that there should be some limits to parental authority. For instance, parents have no authority to demand treatment under English law (Munby, 2013). Yet even this relatively clear legal boundary to parental authority relies on the best interests principle, which has been widely argued to be vague and indefinable (Bellieni and Buonocore, 2009; Baines, 2010). Clinical guidelines limit clinicians' authority to objective medical knowledge: for instance, the General Medical Council (2010: 47) says: 'You must not rely on your personal values when making best interests decisions [or] make judgements based on poorly informed or unfounded assumptions about the impact of a disability on a child'. However, guidelines suggest no similar boundaries to parental authority. Bioethicists like Schoeman have advocated for increased parental authority while limiting that authority by reference to somewhat platitudinous criteria, such as cases in which the child will come to 'extreme, irremediable and obvious harm' (Schoeman, 1985: 52). Others, such as Bailey (2001), have suggested that families' input ought to be based on subjective values because they act as a proxy for the subjective preferences of their relative. However, even if accepted without argument, such a criterion provides no scope for differentiating acceptable from unacceptable values. Moreover, by suggesting that, in the case of newborn babies, parents 'are often best placed to know what is in the interests of their child because of their closeness to him or her and the special bond that they enjoy', guidelines from the Nuffield Council on Bioethics (2007: 23) arguably suggest that parents' knowledge of their infant is intrinsic and intuitive – exceptionally difficult criteria on which to offer limits.

What all of the preceding criteria share is a failure to articulate clearly consistent boundaries to parental authority which can be applied in practice. The results from empirical ethics research into this issue, which I now present, suggest that to conceive parental knowledge as intrinsic or innately subjective fails to capture the rich and informative nature of this knowledge. While parents do claim intuitive knowledge of their infant's interests in critical medical situations, this is often based upon tangible factors. These factors, while not being entirely determinative, offer a platform from which to more clearly reflect on both the scope of parental authority and the limits we should place on our expectations of it in shared decision-making.

10.3 The BIPIC study

While European empirical studies have contributed to knowledge of a wide range of issues salient to the current topic, including the degree to which parental authority is determinative of children's treatment (Hagen et al., 2012) and the effect on parental wellbeing of sharing decisions (Caeymaex et al., 2013), the content of parental contributions to shared decisions is rarely examined (a rare example is a single case study from de Vos et al., 2015). Judging Best Interests in Paediatric Intensive Care (BIPIC) is a qualitative empirical ethics study funded by a Wellcome Trust Fellowship in Society and Ethics (grant number WT097725FR), which investigates the values and experiences of decision-makers in the paediatric intensive care unit, and thus examines parental contributions to decisions in detail.

10.3.1 Methodology

The study used a qualitative empirical ethics methodology[2] consisting of an empirical component followed by a process of reflective equilibrium, in which the empirical data was reconciled with ethical theory. The method of reflective equilibrium broadly followed that postulated by Daniels (1979). The empirical research drew participants from the four decision-making groups identified in guidelines from the Nuffield Council on Bioethics (2007), namely doctors, nurses, members of clinical ethics committees and parents. Only parent interviews are considered in this chapter, although their observations are corroborated by other groups. Parents were recruited through three paediatric intensive care units (PICU) and took part in in-depth face-to-face interviews about their experiences. Not all parents had direct experience of making a critical, life-or-death decision, although all had vivid memories of their child's critical illness and their own experiences relating to this.

Participants continued to be recruited and interviews conducted until no new themes emerged.

10.3.2 Recruitment method

The study was reviewed and approved by a local research ethics committee. To ensure the researcher had no access to confidential data, a senior clinician in each intensive care unit identified potential parent participants from clinical records. Parents were eligible to take part if their child had been a critically ill inpatient between one and two years prior to recruitment. Their child had to conform to the following criteria at the time of their admission: Paediatric Intensive Care Society critical illness level two or above (i.e. one or more organs supported); less than four years old or otherwise unable to contribute to decisions about their care; and a PICU stay of more than four days. Eligible parents were contacted by a letter from the senior clinician, and responded directly to the researcher if they were interested in participating. Parents were purposively recruited to reflect the range of outcomes expected nationally from a PICU admission, thus about 10 per cent had experienced a bereavement and another 30 per cent had children with ongoing morbidity.

10.3.3 Recruitment results

A total of 131 parents were approached by letter, of whom 17 responded and 14 subsequently took part in an interview (Table 10.1).

Parents were interviewed alone or in couples at a private location of their choosing, depending on their preference. Two parents brought friends or relatives to the interview for support, rather than a spouse. Parents provided written consent and were assigned code numbers to preserve their anonymity. Details of participant characteristics are given in Table 10.2.

10.3.4 Data collection

Interviews were semi-structured and followed a topic guide that was formulated from a literature review at the beginning of the project. Questions were modified as the study progressed in order to iteratively explore themes that emerged in prior interviews. Open questions encouraged participants to tell their story, and follow-up questions explored the experiences, values and

Table 10.1 Parent recruitment

Study Site	Approached	Responded	Consented	Interviewed	Total
Site 1	71	11	8	8	14
Site 2	40	3	3	3	
Site 3	20	3	3	3	

Table 10.2 Characteristics of BIPIC parent participants

Interview	Present at interview	Length of admission	Outcome of admission[a]
40	Both parents	210 days[b]	Ongoing morbidity
41	Both parents	61 days[b]	Death
42	Mother and relative	4 days	Death
45	Both parents	16 days	Ongoing morbidity
55	Mother	14 days[c]	Recovery
56	Both parents	5 days	Recovery
58	Mother	10 days	Ongoing morbidity
59	Both parents	4 days	Ongoing morbidity
60	Mother	12 days	Recovery
61	Mother	9 days	Ongoing morbidity
62	Mother	10 days	Recovery
63	Mother and friend	7 days	Recovery
64	Mother	5 days	Recovery
65	Both parents	10 days	Recovery

a *Recovery* is where child leaves PICU with an improvement in their admission baseline health, *Ongoing morbidity* is where the child leaves PICU with a deficit to their pre-admission baseline health.
b Includes time on ward due to multiple readmissions to PICU during hospital stay.
c Duration of ward plus PICU stay as times were unclear in the interview.

beliefs that underlay the participant's interpretations of children's best interests. Interviews lasted between 73 and 180 minutes. All participants agreed to have their interviews audio recorded.

10.3.5 Analysis

Interview recordings were transcribed by a professional transcriber. The transcripts were anonymised to remove identifying names and locations before being analysed, using thematic analysis (Braun and Clarke, 2006). This method was selected because it was iterative and did not require parents to participate in repeated interviews about a sensitive and potentially distressing topic. The analysis involved coding the interview data to identify key words, phrases and topics that participants used to express their experiences and beliefs. By analysing codes across all parent interviews, key themes emerged that offered insights into the parental role in decision-making.

10.4 Key findings

Parent participants (hereafter referred to simply as 'parents') felt they had a special understanding of their child's physiological and behavioural norms, as well as substantial clinical knowledge and expertise in their child's clinical history and clinical condition. Such understanding often took the form of an intuitive sense of the child's wellbeing, which apparently rested on this expertise and proximity. Where critical end-of-life decisions needed to be taken, most parents also thought that they would intuitively know what the right thing to do would be. Parents' knowledge and intuition also provided a platform from which to request treatments and advocate for their child; these requests included changing treatments, ensuring interventions were undertaken as planned and otherwise attempting to improve the quality of their child's care.

10.4.1 Parents' knowledge of their child

Parents recalled intuitive feelings of unease at the onset of their child's acute illness or if their child's clinical condition deteriorated. These feelings were driven by their knowledge of their child's normal appearance and behaviours, which resulted from a constant close proximity to their child. In a typical example, P41 describes becoming aware of her baby's sudden deterioration following an initial discharge from PICU:

> P41 (MOTHER): And I had not been apart from my baby ever, and I knew him, and I knew every colour on his face and every look that he gave me and every movement that he made, I knew it. So the minute that something changed, I knew it.

Parents also felt that their close proximity to their child throughout the hospital admission gave them a firm narrative of their child's medical history, and that this was sometimes more accurate than that of their doctors and nurses. For instance, one parent, by being present at shift changes, was both able to learn the clinical details and to correct mistakes or omissions in the clinical history. Others were familiar with earlier treatments or procedures and queried the accuracy of documentation:

> P40 (MOTHER): You've been in hospital with your child for several months, and you've seen like day in, day – 24 hours a day, you know what they've done. Like sometimes things might get written down, abbreviated to like what actually happened and you'll be like, 'Hang on a minute, that's not exactly what happened. This is what happened.'

This ability to keep an accurate narrative history was noted particularly where there were gaps in the medical narrative, such as when care was shared between more than one institution or where, as in the case of P59, the child had a long-term condition that was rarely seen by medical trainees:

> P59 (FATHER): ... not so much the regular nurses, but doctors that we don't see before, they're always asking us, because at the end of the day we

know more about her and her diagnosis than most of the doctors up there. It's only really the specialist for her that knows more than us.

Parents also brought a very particular perceptual knowledge of their child as an individual. While this sentiment was more often implied than expressed, P45, whose child had a relatively common congenital disability, was concerned this depersonalised her child to some clinicians:

> P45 (MOTHER): . . . because she's got [congenital condition] um she's treated in the same sort of way [as other infants with that condition]. So like well [certain symptoms] can be explained away because she's got [congenital condition], and you don't want that: you want them still to assess her as her and make sure that they don't make excuses or let things happen just because of that.

Parents were therefore able to bring a wide range of knowledge and connection with their child to discussions with healthcare professionals. Moreover, parents also related the ways they used this knowledge to advocate for particular directions to be taken in their child's treatment.

10.4.2 Parents' requests for treatment

Parents' knowledge of their child's medical norms and history meant they were able to interact with healthcare professionals to broaden and improve the medical narrative. Moreover, parents frequently intervened in their child's care and made requests for treatment. Examples included requesting extra laboratory tests on blood samples to match tests taken on prior occasions, challenging the method of a proposed surgery or, in this example, requesting that staff combine x-rays in order to reduce x-ray exposure:

> P65 (MOTHER): He was having some x-rays and they wanted to do two x-rays. I did question them and said, 'Why do you need to do two? Can you not just do one?' In the end, they just did one. But a bigger one. Because they wanted to take one of one area and one of another area. I said, 'Surely, he's only little, you can fit it into one,' and they did. I didn't want him to have more than he really needed.

Very often, these interjections were to remind staff of an intervention the parent had expected them to initiate, such as commencing their child's feed or complying with infection control measures. An example of this is P55's request that a central venous catheter be removed in line with local infection control policy, which she had discovered on the hospital's public website:

> P55 (MOTHER): A femoral line, he still had that in, and they came to take that out. 'Cos I complained, I said, 'He's not meant to have that in

there is he, after a certain amount of time?' And they said, 'Oh OK, we'll take that out,' you know, 'cos I knew you're not meant to have that in [from looking at the internet].

This data gives insights into tangible contributions parents made to the care of their child, and moreover shows these parents' requests for treatment could be based on competent assessments of technical criteria. However, there was one further strong driver of decision-making: intuition.

10.4.3 Intuitive knowledge

Some parents suggested their knowledge of what was best for their child was intuitive, and found it hard to believe that they would be able to act in a way that was contrary to their intuition. P61 talked of a 'gut feeling' that had played a role in her recognition that her child was becoming seriously ill, and because of this she felt parents would instinctively know when treatment was no longer in their child's best interests:

> P61 (MOTHER): I had that gut feeling, I knew [my child] wasn't right. It wasn't just a bug. It wasn't just give him [paracetamol] and [ibuprofen] and lots of fluid, and see how he was. That [. . .] morning was – he was lying on my bed – you knew there was something wrong. I suppose, maybe, as a parent, when you get to that point, again, you know that, yes, this is the end of the line. There's nothing more that can be done. No matter how hard it is, maybe you do that, that does kick in.

This projection of intuitive knowledge of their child from a situation they had experienced to an instance they had not was repeated by other parents; for example, P59, the mother of a life-limited child, said:

> P59 (MOTHER): I just think parents know the child's best interests. I don't think it even needs to take a doctor to say that. What kind of parent would put their child through something they didn't feel that they had to be put? No parent would. I think you just know.

Thus, while intuition was often underwritten by experiential knowledge of the child, this foundation caused parents to give credence to intuitions about more suppositional situations.

10.5 Discussion

Emergent themes from parent interviews suggest that parents' day-to-day intimacy with their child furnishes them with a practical knowledge of their child's wellbeing, which can be employed in a variety of clinical and non-clinical situations. This knowledge can be applied in clinical scenarios and at times can compete with clinicians' specialist knowledge. Practical knowledge gives parents a sense of intuition about their child's wellbeing, and this intuition can extend beyond familiar situations, for instance engendering the conviction that they will know the best interests of their child in a critical decision about treatment or non-treatment. Knowledge of their child as an individual may also provide a heightened degree of emotional sympathy, and, further, drive parents to request treatments that they consider to be in the child's interests. The interviews thus offer significant insights into the complex role of parents in the shared decision-making process, and allow some conclusions to be drawn. These conclusions focus particularly upon infants whose wishes and values, should they exist, we have no way of knowing.

The way parental knowledge is gathered suggests that a parent's intimacy with their child is profoundly important to their ability to contribute to a shared decision, an idea which has formed the mainstay of a number of influential theories of family authority. In the remainder of this chapter I shall use this information to set out some limits to parental authority. I will argue that it is parents' intimacy with their child which gives them familiarity with their child's medical course and this offers a credible basis for their role in the decision-making process. Such a basis, however, also implies a limitation where intimacy and familiarity are absent. While parents may form strong intuitions about their child's wellbeing, which, when driven by experience, are likely to be well-founded, intuitions that are not driven by experience (such as, often, decisions about whether treatment or non-treatment is in the child's interests) are of less practical value and must be viewed more cautiously in the decision-making process. While this implies a restriction, parental involvement in critical decisions may also be important because of the focus parents bring upon the child as an individual. Where a child suffers a common condition that may lead clinicians to depersonalise the child, parents' emotional sympathy may bring the focus back on to the individual and combat this depersonalisation. Finally, parents are strong advocates for their child and often request treatments. This phenomenon is particularly interesting, because it both highlights a reason for involving parents in shared decisions and a reason for limiting their authority, perhaps highlighting the difference between a 'request' and a 'demand'. This is because even valid requests for treatment may be a mechanism for raising the quality of care for their child, while conversely reducing equitability for those with less powerful advocates. Let us consider these conclusions in more detail.

10.5.1 Intimacy and knowledge

A parent's intimacy with, and proximity to, their child throughout their lives may lead to a detailed knowledge of their child's development and clinical history. Close proximity may also mean that parents develop a grasp of clinical facts about their child that is comparable to (or potentially greater than) that of attending clinicians. Constant presence at the child's bedside provides parents with a narrative that can be more coherent than a clinician who sees the child episodically due to the provision of their speciality, the fragmented nature of shift systems and so on. These observations suggest that intimacy is a key component in a parent's ability to contribute to decisions.

The importance of intimacy in parental decisions resonates with Hegel's theory that families are a unique and intimate community characterised by love (Hegel, 1851/1976: 110). Hegel argued that parents have a duty to imbue in their children a sense of individuality and self-worth, since this sense of individuality will lay the foundation for moral autonomy (Blustein, 1982: 90–95). In a similar position, Ross (1998: 20–38) and others (Schoeman, 1985; Downie and Randall, 1997; Erickson, 2010) have argued that parental authority in decision-making is drawn from the intimate nature of families. This intimacy distinguishes them from other collections of individuals since they know each other best, share each other's goals, their wellbeing is intertwined and the boundary between the interests of their members is blurred. For Ross, these interconnected interests mean that families should make unfettered decisions about their members, and controversial decisions such as those based on the quality of a child's life should remain within the family's ambit. Other thinkers argue that parental authority in medical decisions rests upon parents' exposure to grief (McHaffie, 2001:393–415) or the burden of care they will carry if their child has a disability (Harrison, 2008). While they may have merit, because these arguments rest on reducing burdens for the parents rather than the child, they are inherently controversial.

Other theorists are wary of involving parents in decisions. For instance, Dare (2009) contends that parental perceptions of best interests may be mistaken, and that mere possession of a beneficent motivation does not single parents out from doctors or other well-motivated carers; indeed, as Archard (2004: 137–149) observes, it is dangerous to assume parental beneficence. Dare also suggests that parental knowledge may be plausible in some circumstances, but that the family has no intrinsic knowledge of the needs or motivations of an infant, nor does the burden of care which falls upon families reasonably entitle them to disregard medical facts and likely prognoses.

Responses from BIPIC give us a lens through which to consider these theoretical contributions. It seems that Ross is correct to identify the importance of intimacy to parental decision-making, however, this is not because parents share the child's interests, but because intimacy is a source of knowledge about (and, as I will consider later, emotional connection with) children's best interests. The value of this claim rests on important presumptions. The first is that the parent is actually an intimate with their child; clearly a parent who has had little contact with their child (such as an absent father) will have no intimate knowledge. Secondly, the parent must be competent to both remember and report the clinical narrative. This will often be the case but, as parents have a range of abilities, there will be instances where parents will not be able to meet the intellectual or emotional demands that this involves. However, assuming these caveats are met, intimacy, and especially intimate knowledge, is a credible criterion on which to found parental authority in shared decision-making.

10.5.2 Intuition

In BIPIC, intimacy also gave parents a strong sense of intuition about their child's best interests, and the contributions to shared decisions that parents reported relied strongly upon their intuitions. In many cases these intuitions were derived from their intimacy with their children, and the knowledge that this gave rise to. Thus parents were used to the way their child looked and behaved when they were well, and this drove their intuitions that their child was becoming sick. Crediting this type of 'gut feeling' with authority seems reasonable, since it is based on the knowledge that will be gained from close association. But parental intuitions were not limited to areas about which they had intimate knowledge. Intuitions about whether treatment or non-treatment was in the best interests of their infant were not based upon parents' past knowledge of their child; and infants could not have communicated their wishes about the length and intensity of efforts to continue their lives, even if they had had such thoughts.

In these circumstances it is helpful to consider how intuitions have been perceived in moral philosophy. In metaethics, the study of the nature of right and wrong, intuition has been considered at length. G.E. Moore (1903) regarded intuition as the only way of *directly* appreciating what is fundamentally morally right (in other words, we could not find secondary reasons for moral approval without also possessing an intuition); a century later, Audi (1998) wrote that intuition was epistemically equal to inference in detecting fundamental moral principles. Yet, in the realm of clinical ethics, since we are uncertain about what is fundamentally morally right, moral intuitions are given less status than in metaethics, being seen instead as playing a part in moral behaviour, without alone being regarded as sufficient to make moral decisions. Such a view is espoused by McMahan (2000), who does not disregard intuitions (since he believes they may harbour deeply important beliefs that are essential to humanity), yet he rejects the idea that intuitions alone can provide moral answers. McMahan instead argues that moral intuitions are important because they offer us somewhere to start our moral inquiries. Our intuitions let us take a guess at the correct answer, from which we can try to reason using the knowledge, observations and arguments at our disposal. I therefore contend that parental intuitions about critical treatment decisions may lead to the discovery of important, hitherto unarticulated, reasons that may influence the final decision. Such intuitions should prompt further inquiry. Yet these intuitions cannot form the sole basis on which to continue or discontinue treatment. Knowledge, rather than intuition, must be the bedrock of parental authority.

Intuition does, however, have a further role to play. As I noted above, parents are not just a source of knowledge about their infant, but also a source of intuitive emotional connection. A parent who appreciates their child as an individual is expressing a fundamental tenet of parenthood. While this may have no bearing on the validity of their opinions, it may nevertheless be an important reason for involving families in decision-making. In the emotivist ethical framework of David Hume (1998/1751), emotional sympathies, rather than rationality and argumentation, are the *source* of moral feeling. Hume argued that, while rationality can provide us with moral answers, it is emotional sympathy that gives us the moral questions – for example, it is because we emotionally value human life that bioethics debates how to promote this value.[3] In practice this means a parent's intimate emotional connection to their infant may make them emotional catalysts who can ensure that 'rational' clinicians focus on what is valuable about the infant. For instance, parents may draw attention to the value of their child when clinicians have submerged that concern in a multitude of others, or have written off a child as a 'futile' case. Thus parents may offer an antidote to prejudice, emotional fatigue or overwork amongst staff. Because this emotional sympathy does not need to be informed, while a powerful reason for considering parents' views about the child's treatment, it should not represent grounds for parental authority on its own.

10.5.3 Requests for treatment

Parental intimacy, knowledge, intuition and emotional connection come together when parents request treatments in the belief that they will improve the quality of their child's care. Parents may fight for what they perceive as the interests of their child with stamina that exceeds any other party. A parent, as a child's advocate, can literally demand the attention of doctors and nurses, and such behaviour may advance their child's care in a way that will be effective in a large, busy hospital. For instance, a clinician may be encouraged to give extra pain relief, to expedite an important test result or to seek a second opinion, where these steps may otherwise not be undertaken. This is an important consideration, for if we wish to do what is best for children, a strong advocate is an important asset. Thus, while English law tells us parental *demands* are not determinative, some, perhaps many, parent *requests* for treatment actively improve the quality of their child's care, an undeniably important role.

The benefits of these requests must be tempered with a recognition that advocacy is a two-edged sword. Parents may also request treatments that work *against* the benefit of the child and are at best a distraction, and at worst impede clinicians from doing their best for the child. Even if we assume such instances are rare and the usual outcome of a treatment request is to do good to the child concerned, parental inclination is to maximise their own child's opportunity, which may clash with another important clinical motive, that of treating patients equitably. This equitability is based on inherent limitations of resources, such as the finite time clinicians have to spend at the patient's bedside. Parents who demand a larger share of these resources for their child deprive others whose parents are quieter or less effective at making their case, not to mention those children who have no parent to advocate for them. Although this phenomenon has not been studied in a hospital setting, a recent review offers compelling evidence that articulate, middle-class public service users are adept at vocalising and advancing their needs (Matthews and Hastings, 2013).[4] This underlines international evidence from primary care settings indicating that patients from wealthier, more articulate social groups receive longer consultations (Deveugele et al., 2002; Furler et al., 2002; Mercer and Watt, 2007). Although not directly analogous to the sort of micro-allocation that takes place between patients at the ward level, there are clear parallels.

There is thus a mixed picture of the effects of parental requests for treatment which adds more nuance to the legal position, and helps us tease out the difference between a *demand* and a *request* for treatment. Some additional perspective can be gained by considering phenomena related to the family more generally. Rawls (1971/1999) argued that, since families vary in wealth and ability and are motivated to use what resources they possess to benefit their children, they are basic drivers against social equality. Such observations go back at least as far as Plato's *Republic* and have led to utopian experiments with collectivised child-rearing in various modern societies, such as Maoist China, Israel and Soviet Russia (Archard, 2004: 213–215). Because of this patchy history, Blustein (1982: 212–214 and passim) concludes that we must respond to Rawls' critique, yet we have no convincing model that improves upon the family itself as a nurturing environment for children. Instead, if we wish to benefit children at large, individual families must be restrained in their ability to advantage their members. These observations are important because they clarify the basic conflict between a parental desire to benefit their child and the clinician's desire to offer care fairly and equitably. Parental requests for treatment as a means of achieving a good quality of care must therefore be divided from a presumptive right of families to benefit their child at disproportionate cost to others, and the latter, which we could label treatment *demands*, should be beyond the limits of family authority.

10.6 Conclusion

Throughout Europe, decisions about children, and in particular children who lack the capacity to express their wishes, are made in their best interests. These are broadly conceived as arising from a shared decision between doctors and parents, but, while clinical roles in a shared decision are clearly defined, the scope of parental authority in shared decision-making is ill-defined. This is equally true of bioethical accounts and, in the UK at least, clinical guidelines and the law. Clinical guidance in some cases appears to consider parental input to be based on intrinsic knowledge of the child's best interests, while bioethical accounts lack detailed or consistent criteria for placing limitations on parental authority. Even the lack of authority to demand treatment within the law lacks clarity since it relies on the vagaries of the best interest test.

Interviews with parents about their own contributions to shared decisions reveal contributions in several related areas. Parents' intimacy with their child may make them sensitive to their child's health and behavioural norms. Their close proximity to their child throughout their clinical stay may give them access to an unbroken clinical narrative, and their emotional intimacy may lead them to communicate the unique value of their child to others. This intimacy may be felt as an intuition, although parents may also have strong intuitions in areas where they have no underlying experience. Proximity, intimacy and intuition may also make parents powerful advocates for their child's cause, requesting treatments to improve the quality of their child's care and making sure their interests are heard by clinicians amongst the demands of others.

Such contributions provide powerful reasons to include parents in shared decisions, but they also give us criteria to demarcate some consistent limits to parental authority: Parents must have intimate contact with their child and the capacity to use this knowledge. Parental intuitions that are grounded in intimacy and knowledge appear more authoritative than those ungrounded intuitions that are more suppositional. We must be wary of giving both types of intuition the same status, and when parents are in new and unfamiliar situations their intuitions may represent the beginning rather than the end of a moral inquiry. Parental requests for treatment are in many cases reasonable and likely to benefit their child, yet the authority of these requests must be bound by reference to the needs of others. Articulate parents must not be afforded benefits for their children to the detriment of others with less effective advocates.

While offering robust theoretical criteria, the scope of parental authority offered here is intended to help guide consistency and transparency in practical cases. While shared decision-making between doctors and parents represents a significant area of consensus, we risk inconsistency if we share decisions without inquiring into why parental views may be authoritative. By analysing the contributions that parents make to shared decisions in practice, we can bring clarity to an area where authority is too often assumed to be self-evident.

Notes

1 The quotation in the title is from the character Joe Cabot in the 1992 film *Reservoir Dogs* (dir. Tarantino).
2 The degree to which empirical data should cause the re-evaluation of normative theory is a controversial topic in bioethics. Although I, along with many others, suggest empirical data makes a valid contribution to these problems, I shall leave it to others, such as de Vries and van Leeuwen (2010), to make these arguments.

3 Such arguments are gaining renewed traction through social intuitionist explanations of the psychological sources of moral thinking (Haidt, 2001), which suggests our thought processes produce intuitive moral judgements before we embark on rational moral reasoning.
4 It is notable that this review suggests there is no evidence that articulate parents and families create broader uplift of standards from which there is a more general benefit, as is sometimes claimed.

References

Archard, D. (2004) *Children: Rights and Childhood*, 2nd edn, Abingdon, Oxon: Routledge.
Audi, R. (1998) 'Moderate intuitionism and the epistemology of moral judgement', *Ethical Theory and Moral Practice*, 1(1): 15–44.
Bailey, S. (2001) 'In whose interests? The best interests principle under ethical scrutiny', *Australian Critical Care*, 14(4): 161–164.
Baines, P. (2010) 'Death and best interests: a response to the legal challenge', *Clinical Ethics*, 5(4): 195–200.
Bellieni, C.V. and Buonocore, G. (2009) 'Flaws in the assessment of the best interests of the newborn', *Acta Paediatrica*, 98(4): 613–617.
Blustein, J. (1982) *Parents and Children: The Ethics of the Family*, Oxford: Oxford University Press.
Braun, V. and Clarke, V. (2006) 'Using thematic analysis in psychology', *Qualitative Research in Psychology*, 3(2): 77–101.
Caeymaex, L., Jousselme, C., Vasilescu, C., Danan, C., Falissard, B., Bourrat, M.M., Garel, M. and Speranza, M. (2013) 'Perceived role in end-of-life decision making in the NICU affects long-term parental grief response', *Archives of Disease in Childhood: Fetal and Neonatal Edition*, 98(1): F26–F31.
Daniels, N. (1979) 'Wide reflective equilibrium and theory acceptance in ethics', *The Journal of Philosophy*, 76(5): 256–282.
Dare, T.I.M. (2009) 'Parental rights and medical decisions', *Pediatric Anesthesia*, 19(10): 947–952.
Deveugele, M., Derese, A., van den Brink-Muinen, A., Bensing, J. and De Maeseneer, J. (2002) 'Consultation length in general practice: cross sectional study in six European countries', *British Medical Journal*, 325(7362): 472–477.
de Vos, M.A., Seeber, A.A., Gevers, S.K., Bos, A.P., Gevers, F. and Willems, D.L. (2014) 'Parents who wish no further treatment for their child' *Journal of Medical Ethics* 41(2), 195–200.
de Vries, M. and van Leeuwen, E. (2010) 'Reflective equilibrium and empirical data: third person moral experiences in empirical medical ethics', *Bioethics*, 24(9): 490–498.
Downie, R.S. and Randall, F. (1997) 'Parenting and the best interests of minors', *Journal of Medicine and Philosophy*, 22(3): 219–231.
Erickson, S.A. (2010) 'The wrong of rights: the moral authority of the family', *Journal of Medicine and Philosophy*, 35(5): 600–616.
Furler, J.S., Harris, E., Chondros, P., Powell Davies, P.G., Harris, M.F. and Young, D.Y. (2002) 'The inverse care law revisited: impact of disadvantaged location on accessing longer GP consultation times', *Medical Journal of Australia*, 177(2): 80–83.
General Medical Council (2010) *Treatment and Care towards the End of Life: Good Practice in Decision Making*, London: General Medical Council.
Hagen, E.M., Therkelsen, Ø.B., Førde, R., Aasland, O., Janvier, A. and Hansen, T.W.R. (2012) 'Challenges in reconciling best interest and parental exercise of autonomy in pediatric life-or-death situations', *The Journal of Pediatrics*, 161(1): 146–151.
Haidt, J. (2001) 'The emotional dog and its rational tail: a social intuitionist approach to moral judgment', *Psychological Review*, 108(4): 814–834.

Harrison, H. (2008) 'The offer they can't refuse: parents and perinatal treatment decisions', *Seminars in Fetal and Neonatal Medicine*, 13(5): 329–334.

Hegel, G.F. (1976 [1821]) *Philosophy of Right*, Trans: Knox, T.M, Oxford: Oxford University Press.

Hume, D. (1998 [1751]) *An Enquiry Concerning the Principles of Morals*, Oxford: Oxford University Press.

Matthews, P. and Hastings, A. (2013),' Middle-class political activism and middle-class advantage in relation to public services: a realist synthesis of the evidence base', *Social Policy and Administration*, 47(1): 72–92.

McHaffie, H.E. (2001) *Crucial Decisions at the Beginning of Life: Parents' Experiences of Treatment Withdrawal from Infants*, Abingdon, Oxon: Radcliffe Medical Press.

McMahan, J. (2000) 'Moral intuition'. In: *The Blackwell Guide to Ethical Theory*. H. LaFollette (ed.), Oxford: Blackwell Publishing Ltd., 103–120.

Mercer, S.W. and Watt, G. (2007) 'The inverse care law: clinical primary care encounters in deprived and affluent areas of Scotland', *Annals of Family Medicine*, 5(6): 503–510.

Moore, G.E. (1903) *Principia Ethica*, Cambridge: Cambridge University Press.

Munby, J. (2013) 'The right to demand treatment or death', In: *A Good Death? Law and Ethics in Practice*. L. Hagger and S. Woods (eds), Farnham, Surrey: Ashgate Publishing Ltd, 9–22.

Nuffield Council on Bioethics (2007) *Critical Care Decisions in Fetal and Neonatal Medicine: Ethical Issues*, London: Nuffield Council on Bioethics.

Rawls, J. (1999 [1971]) *A Theory of Justice*, Revised edn, Cambridge, MA: Harvard University Press.

Ross, L.F. (1998) *Children, Families, and Health Care Decision Making*, Oxford: Oxford University Press.

Royal College of Paediatrics and Child Health (2004) *Withholding and Withdrawing Life Saving Treatment in Children: A Framework for Practice*, 2nd edn, London: Royal College of Paediatrics and Child Health.

Schoeman, F. (1985) 'Parental discretion and children's rights: background and implications for medical decision making', *Journal of Medicine and Philosophy*, 10(1): 45–61.

Sullivan, J., Monagle, P. and Gillam, L. (2014) 'What parents want from doctors in end-of-life decision-making for children', *Archives of Disease in Childhood*, 99(3): 216–220.

11 Beyond listening or telling: moral case deliberation as a hermeneutic approach to clinical ethics support

Suzanne Metselaar, Margreet Stolper and Guy Widdershoven

11.1 Introduction

The role of the ethicist in clinical ethics consultation has long been the object of debate.[1] The central question governing this debate is: *Should the clinical ethicist listen or tell?* (Zaner, 1996). In line with the two options distinguished by Zaner, Edwards and Liaschenko describe two models of clinical ethics (Edwards and Liaschenko, 2003). In the 'modest' model, the clinical ethicist is primarily seen as a *mediator* who does not provide direct answers but helps people to focus on important issues and facilitates a dialogue between health care professionals. By contrast, the 'immodest model' sees the ethicist as an *expert* who gives answers and provides solutions. In our view, both models are problematic.

A mediator, as described in the 'modest' model, needs many skills, such as enabling everyone to be listened to, resolving conflicts and encouraging people to reach consensus, but he or she does not necessarily need any particular philosophical or moral skills. In that case, a mediator does not need to be an ethicist.

The 'immodest' model is vigorously defended by Peter Singer (1972: 116–117), who states:

> Someone familiar with moral concepts and with moral arguments, who has ample time to gather information and think about it, may reasonably be expected to reach a soundly based conclusion more often than someone who is unfamiliar with moral concepts and moral arguments and has little time.

Against this view, it can be argued that nowadays, at least in Western societies, it is not that straightforward what a 'sound' conclusion is, which concepts are relevant and which arguments are valid in bioethics (Abma et al., 2010). Western societies are characterized by (cultural) diversity, plurality and fragmentation, in which neither an uncontested foundation for moral truth nor a shared moral framework between patients and (among) health care professionals can be presupposed (Engelhardt, 2011). Accordingly, it may be doubted that an individual ethicist, no matter how much training and time he or she has, will be able to find definite solutions to moral dilemmas in medical practice which do justice to everyone involved.

Hence, it seems that both models are unfit to provide a basis for clinical ethics support in present-day health care. The 'modest' model puts too little demands on the activities of the ethicist, whereas the 'immodest' model asks too much. Does this render the clinical ethicist – or even clinical ethics support as such – obsolete? Since caregivers regularly deal with difficult moral dilemmas in medical practice – for instance, whether to provide treatment or not – that cannot simply be postponed or left undecided upon, clinical ethics support does seem to be worthwhile. The question is then what this support, and the accompanying role of the clinical ethicist, would look like.

In the present chapter, we defend a *hermeneutic approach* to clinical ethics support as an answer to this question. In our practice as clinical ethicists, moral case deliberation is a prominent form of this hermeneutic approach. We will first give an outline of the procedure of moral case deliberation. Next, we will present a case example. After that, we will go into the philosophical background of moral case deliberation by elaborating on the principles of hermeneutic ethics. Finally, we will reflect on the role of the clinical ethicist, and argue that facilitating moral case deliberation requires a specific kind of moral expertise: he or she needs to be in possession of what we would like to call *hermeneutic skills*.[2]

11.2 What is moral case deliberation?

Moral case deliberation is a methodically structured joint reflection among a – preferably multi-disciplinary – group of health care professionals (nurses, physicians, psychologists, social workers, pastoral workers, etc.) on a real case that is experienced as morally troublesome. The moral case deliberation is facilitated by an ethicist (or a health care professional who has received intensive training, such as we provide at our institution (Plantinga et al., 2012)). There are several methods to structure the reflection, such as the Socratic dialogue and the dilemma method, which proceeds from and revolves around a concrete moral dilemma that people struggle with in medical practice (Stolper et al., 2012). In this section, we will shortly elaborate on the subsequent steps taken in the dilemma method, so as to give an example of the way in which a moral case deliberation can be structured.

First, the case is introduced by one of the health care professionals, who has to have first-hand experience of the case. The case can pertain to either a situation in the past or a current situation, in which a course of action has yet to be decided upon.

Next, by asking questions, the situation is reconstructed on the basis of the experience of the health care professional who introduced the case. This concerns a purely *descriptive* analysis: What exactly happened? Who was involved? What was the sequence of events? How did people (including the case presenter) respond? Which courses of action were suggested? After the case is presented, the group defines the moral question in the case. The focus is on the moral dilemma experienced by the case presenter.

This is followed by an analysis of various *normative* perspectives on the case. These can be both the perspectives of stakeholders in the case and those of the participants in the moral case deliberation meeting – on many occasions, these two groups overlap to a large extent. This step entails an exercise in putting oneself in someone else's shoes to allow oneself to see or experience something from someone else's point of view. For instance, the participants seek to establish what is important for the patient in the case. On the basis of what they know of the patient, they investigate crucial *values* of the patient in the situation. This exploration of different moral perspectives does not aim at a fully reliable or objective reconstruction of the views and experiences of others (either present or not), but entails a joint interpretation of the views of others, based on the experience of the participants who are familiar with the perspective under consideration.

In the next step, an individual moral weighing takes place. The participants reflect on what they themselves would choose and which moral value(s) is (are) absolutely crucial to them in dealing with this moral dilemma. They are encouraged to relate this to concrete courses of actions, from which viable alternatives to deal with the dilemma can emerge that were not considered before. Furthermore, the participants consider the disadvantages of their choice – given that a dilemma always offers a choice between 'two evils' – and how to take responsibility for repairing the damage done.

Finally, by sharing and jointly examining the individual choices and values, the participants engage in a dialogue in which differences and similarities are explored. The aim of this phase is to investigate each other's normative viewpoint in relation to the case. In what sense are the values mentioned by other participants relevant to oneself? Individually, the result is a growth in understanding of the normative considerations of others, and a wider perspective on the case. For the group, this entails a joint deliberation on the most relevant values, and possible courses of action, in a search for *consensus*, i.e. a common ground from which to proceed. However, although the group deliberation aims at agreement, while acknowledging and doing justice to diverging views, this does not imply taking over the decision of the health care professional who is responsible. Rather, this process provides the person responsible for the decision with a wider and more balanced set of values and possible actions.

The objective of a moral case deliberation is the clarification of a specific moral dilemma and the accompanying moral considerations, so that the participants are well aware of the consequences following from their actions. It renders explicit values, norms, customs, and perspectives that until then were implicit and unarticulated (Widdershoven and Metselaar, 2012). Furthermore, especially when it concerns a medical team which is to make a decision that affects all team members, the aim is to find a shared moral perspective, notwithstanding individual differences, and a consensus, to some extent, on what is the right thing to do in the situation at hand.

On a more general level, moral case deliberation aims to enhance the moral competences of the participants, and to promote the exchange of expertise and responsibility within a group of health care professionals. On an organizational level, moral case deliberation can support the development of ward or hospital identity by exploring and defining core values. Moreover, it can contribute by translating core values into policy and concrete actions (and vice versa) (Abma et al., 2009). For instance: What does 'patient confidentiality' mean in the daily work of a doctor or nurse? Or what policy has to be developed when a team continuously experiences dilemmas with patients of different cultural backgrounds?

Finally, moral case deliberation can contribute in providing support for health care professionals, as it may create a space for exploring the source of emotions, such as frustration or (moral) distress, and encourage the view that the moral dilemmas people encounter in their work are the shared responsibility of the team (Weidema et al., 2013).

11.3 A case example

We will illustrate the procedure of moral case deliberation with an example from a neonatology ward. In this case, it will become particularly clear how, in a moral case deliberation (culturally), divergent perspectives on 'good care' can be made the object of a fruitful dialogue.

The staff of a neonatology ward (physicians, nurses, social workers, pastoral workers) meets once a month for a moral case deliberation, guided by an ethicist. On one occasion, the case of Aziz was presented (the patient is anonymized by changing the patient's name and details). Aziz was born after a caesarean section at 32 weeks, and was not doing well. He had symptoms of a neurogenetic condition (two of his siblings died of the same condition), was intubated because of respiratory problems after an intestinal operation and had a very poor prognosis. His parents were religious Muslims. They were aware of the severity of the situation and accepted that Aziz had a genetic disease. His father, however, argued: 'As long as there is life, there is hope'. The dilemma the staff struggled with was: Do we operate again if necessary? Or do we opt for palliative treatment?

After the presentation and clarification of the case, the group investigated the values and norms relevant to the participants in the case. Which values motivated their actions and concerns? How could these values be translated into concrete norms for action? The ethicist helped the group to articulate these values and norms. In moral case deliberation, this is not done by explaining the theoretical concepts on a *general* level, but rather by asking further questions, aiming to articulate *personal* experience, such as: In what sense is this value important for you? How would you like to promote it in the given situation? In this case, the staff brought forward *comfort* for Aziz as an important value, which they translated in the norm 'keep interventions to a minimum'. They also made clear that *respect* for Aziz's parents was important to them, which they related to telling the truth, even in the case of a poor prognosis. Placing themselves in the position of the parents, based on the information they had about them, they recognized the value *hope* to be crucial for the parents, and reasoned that this would concretely mean that the physician should not give up hope and abstain from intervening. Furthermore, *transparency* was brought up, as the physician should mention the facts as they are. The importance of *time* was also mentioned, as Aziz's parents needed time to cope with the situation. Finally, the importance of *home* to the parents was stressed, as they wished to take Aziz home.

Through the elaboration of values, the staff came to understand that several values were important to the parents, the relations between which needed further examination. Some participants experienced a contradiction between the value of transparency and that of hope, indicating that being open about the prognosis would entail the message that hope was futile. After a question for further elucidation by the ethicist, the imam present at the deliberation suggested that the values of transparency and hope do not necessarily conflict, as medical facts, however serious, do not prescribe how one should appreciate the situation and give meaning to it. Given that the parents knew that the child would not survive, the value of hope was probably not related to a belief in miracles, but to the possibility of dealing with the situation in a meaningful way, based on religious interpretations of life and death. This perspective was an eye-opener for many participants in the deliberation, as they thought that hope, which the parents kept mentioning to the nursing staff, could only relate to the possibility of a cure, and that this indicated that the parents did not want to accept the severity of Aziz's condition.

The ethicist then invited the group to consider these values in the context of medical care at the end of life, such as the value of comfort, which had been identified as important for them. This lead to a conversation about basic values in end-of-life care, and the conclusion that spiritual elements, such as hope, are indeed crucial to good palliative care. This enabled the staff to decide for palliative care, not against the parents' wishes, but rather as a way to do justice to their point of view. Considering the fact that Aziz could not go home, they decided to create a homelike environment with the possibility of privacy for the family. Also, palliative treatment would give the parents the time they valued so much. As a team, they learned from this dialogue that in palliative care, hope, time and home are important values, and that hope does not necessarily have to pertain to the possibility of a cure.

11.4 The philosophical background of moral case deliberation

Moral case deliberation, such as the deliberation on the case of Aziz, implies a *hermeneutic approach* to clinical ethics support. Although he himself was not an ethicist, the principles of hermeneutic ethics can be found in the work of

Hans-Georg Gadamer, primarily in his 1960 work, *Truth and Method*. In the present section, we will elaborate on the *principles* of moral case deliberation.

Moral case deliberation proceeds from the idea that 'good care' cannot be defined without taking into account the specific context of a moral dilemma and the people that are involved in it (Molewijk et al., 2008; Widdershoven and Molewijk, 2010). Therefore, moral case deliberation is based on the presupposition that moral questions, values and norms are always to be understood in their *application* to a concrete case. There is no fixed 'yardstick' or universal rule for action that can be used in a plurality of particular situations (Gadamer, 2004: 17). Although theoretical concepts and general lines of ethical argumentation can be elucidating or inspiring, in a moral case deliberation, only the *contextual meaning* of concepts and arguments, that is, the way in which they relate to the case at stake and to the personal experiences of the people involved, is seen as truly valuable (Widdershoven, Abma and Molewijk, 2009).

Thus, moral case deliberation does not focus on abstract principles, but aims at elucidating specific values, rules and principles that are important to the stakeholders in a specific situation. This makes moral case deliberation *radically concrete*. The outcome of a moral case deliberation about a specific case cannot be directly applied to another, more or less similar, situation; moral dilemmas emerging in different contexts, with different narratives and experiences, require new reflection and deliberation (Stolper et al., 2012).

In *Nicomachean Ethics*, Aristotle observed that moral or practical wisdom (*phronêsis*) is different from objective, theoretical wisdom (*sofia*). In the case of *phronêsis*, the subject is not a distant observer, but directly affected by what he or she sees, and morality is something he or she has to *do*. Moreover, *phronêsis* is always *judgement informed by experience*: one might be born with the potential to become ethically virtuous and practically wise, but these only become actual qualities through experience (Aristotle, *Nicomachean Ethics*, 1144b14–17). Similarly, Gadamer argues that moral knowledge 'embraces in a curious way both means and end and hence differs from technical knowledge. That is why it is pointless to distinguish here between knowledge and experience . . ., moral knowledge must be a kind of experience' (Gadamer, 2004: 288).

Taking this approach of moral knowledge as a point of departure, in moral case deliberation, the experience of health care professionals is regarded to be the principal source of moral knowledge as well as the decisive point of reference. As they are the experts of their own professional world, and involved in a situation they themselves experience to be morally troublesome, and as they are the ones responsible for making decisions and taking action, they are supposed to develop the answers to their moral questions in interaction with each other (Abma et al., 2010).[3]

As such, moral case deliberation is always a *dialogue* in which viewpoints, values and answers to moral questions are shared and investigated. Participants are encouraged to put their moral understandings into words, to listen actively, to open up to the other, to postpone their judgements and conclusions and to put their prejudices into play (Molewijk et al., 2008). A crucial element of moral case deliberation is therefore the Socratic art of asking the right questions, accompanied by the strategic attitude of *agnosia* – 'not-knowing'.

Gadamer praises this method as an art that primarily consists of two elements: (1) the persistence in *questioning*, and (2) an orientation towards *openness* (Gadamer, 2004: 330). With regard to this first element, he speaks of 'the priority of the question' in understanding and agreement through dialogue. By asking questions, one continuously challenges the speaker until the truth of what is under discussion finally emerges (Gadamer, 2004: 331). This does not mean an aggressive and suspicious inquisition; rather, Gadamer argues, it is characteristic of every true conversation that each interlocutor practises openness, which means to truly accept the other's point of view as worthy of consideration and looks to grasp what the other means, so as to come to an agreement (Gadamer, 2004: 347). The openness that is required for a genuine dialogue includes postponing one's prejudices to replace them by new ones, belonging to more profound insights.

Accordingly, moral case deliberation fosters *moral learning* of health care practitioners. If practitioners would merely follow the expert judgement of the ethicist, it is unlikely that this would result in further development of their own moral knowledge and their own ability to deal with a complex situation and its ambivalences. In a moral case deliberation in which the ethicist is first and foremost a *facilitator* of the reflection, practitioners can morally 'cultivate' themselves. This cultivation is referred to by Gadamer as *Bildung* (Gadamer, 2004: 10), which can be defined as *'trained receptivity towards otherness'* (Gadamer, 2004: 17). Gadamer argues that a successful dialogue establishes the transformation of the interlocutors involved, because

> to reach an understanding with one's partner in a dialogue is not merely a matter of total self-expression and the successful assertion of one's own point of view, but a transformation into a communion, in which we do not remain what we were.
>
> (Gadamer, 2004: 341)

Hence, moral case deliberation offers a platform for an ongoing learning process which improves normative professionalism, or 'moral craftmanship': the commitment to do the moral part of a job well by criticizing, reflecting upon, understanding and deliberating on the moral aspects of the job (Parker, 2012).

11.5 The role of the ethicist in moral case deliberation

Let us return to the question raised at the beginning of this chapter, pertaining to the role of the clinical ethicist. From the explanation of the practice of, and the philosophy behind, moral case deliberation, it may have become clear that it refrains from an 'immodest' view on the role of the ethicist. In moral case deliberation, the ethicist is not there to stipulate what needs to be done, nor in possession of the best line of argumentation, specification or weighing of principles. However, this does not mean that the role of the ethicist as a facilitator of moral case deliberation is that of a mere mediator of the communication process. Indeed, the ethicist fosters the joint reflection process by monitoring, guiding and structuring the conversation, but there is more to it than that. In the present section, we will set out what skills we consider to be necessary to properly facilitate a moral case deliberation, and we will point out that these are philosophical and ethical skills. To be more precise, as moral case deliberation represents a hermeneutic perspective to clinical ethics support, we like to designate these skills as 'hermeneutic skills'.

First, the facilitator of a moral case deliberation needs to be able to help the participants to formulate a moral question. Often, health care professionals have a bad feeling about a complex situation, but have difficulty in pointing out what exactly makes the case morally troublesome, or which moral issues are under pressure. Based on both earlier experience and training in moral concepts and theory, the ethicist then has to guide the participants in discovering, articulating and fine-tuning the major moral dilemma and the moral questions at stake (see also Zoloth-Dorman and Rubin, 1997; Huxtable, 2012). In our case at the neonatology ward, however, this was not a problem, since the group was experienced in doing moral case deliberations, and had learned to recognize and articulate ethical issues themselves.

Second, the facilitator of a moral case deliberation should be able to guide the analysis of a case. This entails the ability to distinguish the descriptive from the normative, and assist the participants in making this distinction. It also means helping participants to consider various perspectives on the case, and to describe the different values that, from these perspectives, are important to the case. Thus, the ethicist in the case at the neonatology ward invited the staff to make explicit their own values, but also to venture into those of the family. In doing so, the ethicist had to take care that the professionals did not present their own values as superior to those of the patient or the family. This requires creating an awareness of the epistemic status of values: they always concern a perspective, and thus a partial truth, which it is important for the participants to be reminded of when objectivity is claimed, or when a perspective is argued to be incontestable. Thus, the family's values, such as 'hope', 'time' and 'home', should be regarded as equally worthy of investigation as the professional values that were brought forward, such as 'comfort' and 'respect'.

Third, as asking questions is central to moral case deliberation, the facilitator should master the art of *maieutics*, and be able to encourage the participants to question, rather than to state or argue. The facilitator needs to be 'a person skilled in the art of questioning . . . who can prevent questions from being suppressed by the dominant opinion' (Gadamer, 2004: 361). By raising questions, the facilitator provides an example to the group, and shows the participants that it is more important to ask questions about the perspective of the other, than to argue for one's own point of view. In the moral case deliberation at the neonatology ward, the ethicist asked for an elucidation of the contradiction between transparency and hope, which led to a further inquiry by the group into possible ways to see these two values as not being mutually exclusive.

Fourth, the facilitator of a moral case deliberation should foster the hermeneutic process, i.e. encourage the participants to engage in a dialogue and to try to understand what is unfamiliar, or even what may seem incomprehensible to them at first. Therefore, the ethicist should be able to help participants comprehend their own position, to disclose the presuppositions that shape their understanding and to encourage an open attitude – an attitude of not-knowing – towards the other perspectives presented. This also involves realizing the importance of differences in moral perspectives, as they may bring about a richer and deepened understanding when investigated through dialogue. In the moral case deliberation at the neonatology ward, the ethicist helped by identifying the differences between the views of the staff and those of the parents, but also fostered a fusion of horizons by stimulating the participants to learn that the family's need to retain hope was not at odds with medical values, especially with values that pertain to palliative care.

Fifth, the facilitator should guide the professionals in finding and articulating the moral values at stake in the case, and in developing more systematic moral knowledge. This can, but need not necessarily, entail introducing some theory or theoretical concepts (Molewijk, Slowther and Aulisio, 2011). The ethicist might also, based on his or her experience, ask a question which has not been raised yet, and thus add a consideration to the deliberation that has not yet been taken into account – which would be adding to the plurality of perspectives of the participants, rather than overruling them. In our case, the ethicist asked the group to relate the family's value of hope to the value of comfort in the medical context of end-of-life care, as she thought – and had learned from experience – that in good palliative care, hope, in this case of an end-of-life situation that does justice to the family's religious values and beliefs, and comfort, which in this case meant relieving the suffering of Aziz and creating an environment as comfortable as possible for both patient and parents, could be reconciled.

Finally, the facilitator of a moral case deliberation should be able to apply method in a sensible and sensitive way. A structured method can help the participants to distinguish various steps in the deliberation, and retain the results of each step. Yet, a conversation method should be adapted to the specific needs of the situation and the participants, and not become a 'disciplinary practice' that constrains the dialogue and joint investigation. Rather, the facilitator has to provide the participants with the freedom to focus on the case itself, while trusting that someone else looks after the optimal conditions for the dialogue and takes care that all important elements of the deliberation are accounted for. Therefore, the facilitator needs to have a knowledge of methodologies of case analysis and how to use these instruments in a skilled and thoughtful way.

In sum, facilitating a moral case deliberation entails much more than merely being a mediator. Many of the skills that are needed are philosophical or ethical in nature. In fact, they are hermeneutic skills, as they are directed at helping the participants to interpret their experience in moral terms, to render explicit values related to various perspectives on a case and to broaden their horizon through dialogue.

11.6 Conclusions

In this chapter we presented moral case deliberation as a favourable approach to clinical ethics support. We elaborated on the principles of moral case deliberation, which are found in hermeneutic ethics. According to hermeneutic ethics, dialogue is the basis of any moral deliberation. Central to this dialogue are the exchange and understanding of the moral perspectives and considerations of people involved in a case that is perceived as morally troublesome, as well as the search for a common ground, or a 'shared horizon'. We have shown that this approach to clinical ethics support is particularly fruitful in a context of (cultural) diversity, which is prominent in present-day health care.

Finally, we return to our initial question: *Should the ethicist listen or tell?* From a hermeneutic perspective, listening is more fundamental than telling. Yet, listening – and fostering listening of participants in moral case deliberation meetings – requires specific expertise from the ethicist. The ethicist should be able to assist participants in formulating (moral) questions, to encourage openness and mutual understanding, to help them in articulating their own values, norms and arguments, and relating them to those of others, and to foster the dialogue and reflection through the skilful use of method. To do so, the ethicist is a crafts(wo)man who needs hermeneutic skills, as we have argued. In applying these skills, the ethicist goes *beyond* the dichotomy of either listening or telling. He or she supports the group in doing so as well, as moral case deliberation is neither an empathic assimilation of the others' point of view, nor a superior stating of one's own arguments and conclusions, but rather, a joint process that aims to establish a shared perspective on the moral issue at hand – while appreciating differences – and to see a moral situation in a new way.

Notes

1 See for example the following publications: Weinstein, 1994; Agich, 1995; Casarett, Daskal and Lantos, 1998; Yoder, 1998; Cowley, 2005; Crossthwaite, 2005; Smith and Weise, 2007; Gesang, 2010; Archard, 2011; Rasmussen, 2011; Cowley, 2012; Adams, 2013; Priaulx, 2013.
2 We owe the use of the term 'hermeneutic skills' in this context to Giulia Inguaggiato.
3 As to whether patients and their moral experiences should be involved in moral case deliberation, see Weidema et al. (2011).

References

Abma, T.A, Baur, V.E., Molewijk, B., and Widdershoven, G.A.M. (2010) 'Inter-ethics: Towards an interactive and interdependent bioethics', *Bioethics*, 24(5): 242–255.

Abma, T.A., Molewijk, B., and Widdershoven, G.A.M. (2009) 'Good care in ongoing dialogue. Improving the quality of care through moral deliberation and responsive evaluation', *Health Care Analysis*, 17(3): 217–235.

Adams, D.M. (2013) 'Ethics expertise and moral authority: Is there a difference?', *The American Journal of Bioethics*, 13(2): 27–28.

Agich, G. J. (1995) 'Authority in ethics consultation', *Journal of Law, Medicine, and Ethics*, 23: 273–283.

Archard, D. (2011) 'Why moral philosophers are not and should not be moral experts', *Bioethics*, 25: 119–127.

Aristotle. (1947) 'Nicomachean ethics'. Trans. by W.D. Ross. In R. McKeown, *Introduction to Aristotle*, New York: The Modern Library, pp. 308–543.

Casarett D.J., Daskal F., and Lantos J., (1998) 'The authority of the clinical ethicist', *Hastings Center Report*, 28(6): 6–11.

Cowley, C. (2005) 'A new rejection of moral expertise', *Medicine, Health Care and Philosophy*, 8: 273–279.

——— (2012) 'Expertise, wisdom and moral philosophers: A response to Gesang', *Bioethics*, 26(6): 337–342.

Crossthwaite, J. (2005) 'In defence of ethicists. A commentary on Christopher Cowley's paper', *Medicine, Health Care and Philosophy*, 8: 281–283.

Edwards, S., and Liaschenko, J. (2003) 'Editorial', *Nursing Philosophy*, 4(3): 177–178.

Engelhardt, H.T. (2011) 'Confronting moral pluralism in posttraditional Western societies: Bioethics critically reassessed', *Journal of Medicine and Philosophy*, 36(3): 243–260.

Gadamer, H.-G. (2004 [1960]) *Truth and Method*, London: Continuum.

Gesang, B. (2010) 'Are moral philosophers moral experts?', *Bioethics*, 24(4): 153.

Huxtable, R. (2012) *Law, Ethics and Compromise at the Limits of Life: To Treat or not to Treat?*, Abingdon, Oxon: Routledge.

Molewijk, A.C., Abma, T., Stolper, M., and Widdershoven, G. (2008) 'Teaching ethics in the clinic. The theory and practice of moral case deliberation', *Journal of Medical Ethics*, 34(2): 120–124.

Molewijk, B., Slowther, A., and Aulisio, M. (2011) 'The practical importance of theory in clinical ethics support services', *Bioethics*, 25(7): ii–iii.

Parker, M. (2012) *Ethical Problems and Genetics Practice*, Cambridge: Cambridge University Press.

Plantinga, M., Molewijk, B., de Bree, M., Moraal, M., Verkerk, M., and Widdershoven, G. (2012) 'Training healthcare professionals as moral case deliberation facilitators: Evaluation of a Dutch training programme', *Journal of Medical Ethics*, 38: 630–635.

Priaulx, N. (2013) 'The troubled identity of the bioethicist', *Health Care Analysis*, 21(1): 6–19.

Rasmussen, L.M. (2011) 'An ethics expertise for clinical ethics consultation', *Journal of Law, Medicine and Ethics*, 39(4): 649–661.

Singer, P. (1972) 'Moral experts', *Analysis*, 32(4): 115–117.

Smith, M.L., and Weise, K.L. (2007) 'The goals of ethics consultation: Rejecting the role of "ethics police"', *American Journal of Bioethics*, 7(2): 42–44.

Stolper, M., Metselaar, S., Molewijk, B., and Widdershoven, G. (2012) 'Moral case deliberation in an academic hospital in the Netherlands. Tensions between theory and practice', *Journal International de Bioéthique*, (3–4): 53–66.

Weidema, F.C., Abma, T.A, Widdershoven, G.A.M., and Molewijk, B.A.C. (2011) 'Client participation in moral case deliberation: A precarious relational balance', *HealthCare Ethics Committee Forum*, 23(3): 207–224.

Weidema, F.C., Molewijk, B.A.C., Kamsteeg, F., and Widdershoven, G. (2013) 'Aims and harvest of moral case deliberation', *Nursing Ethics*, 20(6): 617–631.
Weinstein, B. (1994) 'The possibility of ethical expertise', *Theoretical Medicine*, 15(1): 61–75.
Widdershoven, G., Abma, T., and Molewijk, B. (2009) 'Empirical ethics as dialogical practice', *Bioethics*, 23(4): 236–248.
Widdershoven, G., and Metselaar, S. (2012) 'Gadamer's truth and method and moral case deliberation in clinical ethics.' In M. Kasten, H. Paul, and R. Sneller (eds.), *Hermeneutics and the Humanities: Dialogues with Hans-Georg Gadamer/Hermeneutik und die Geisteswissenschaften: Im Dialog mit Hans-Georg Gadamer*, Dordrecht: Leiden University Press, pp. 287–305.
Widdershoven, G., and Molewijk, B. (2010) 'Philosophical foundations of clinical ethics: A hermeneutic perspective'. In J. Schildmann, J. Gordon and J. Vollmann (eds.), *Clinical Ethics Consultation. Theories and Methods, Implementation, Evaluation*, Farnham, Surrey: Ashgate, pp. 37–51.
Yoder, S. (1998) 'The nature of ethical expertise', *Hastings Center Report*, 28(6): 11–19.
Zaner, R.M. (1996) 'Listening or telling? Thoughts on responsibility in clinical ethics consultation', *Theoretical Medicine and Bioethics*, 17(3): 255–277.
Zoloth-Dorfman, L., and Rubin, S.B. (1997) 'Navigators and captains: Expertise in clinical ethics consultation', *Theoretical Medicine and Bioethics*, 18(4): 421–432.

12 Authority, markets and society: three possible foundations for European bioethics

Angus Dawson

12.1 Introduction

In this chapter I discuss three possible 'models' to use as a way to ground and discuss how we could approach thinking about bioethics in Europe. By a 'model' I mean something that helps us to understand the world, with a primary role in providing an explanation for why things are as they are (Dawson, 2009a). Models are commonly linked to particular sets of values, and so in turn link to normative and justificatory issues. Each of my three proposed models is based around a single key concept as follows: authority, markets and society. Of course, although I refer to each by the name of a single concept, they are each really a web or family of related concepts. The three models can be, roughly, thought of in a historical sequence as representing the past, present and what I hope is the future.

I welcome the opportunity to talk about European bioethics, not just because this chapter is part of a European project, through the European Association of Centres for Medical Ethics (EACME), but also because I think there is a danger that when we think about bioethics, or more narrowly medical ethics, we may miss our own European traditions and values. Bioethics, wherever the term might have originated, really found its voice in the United States in the 1970s. As a result, there is a risk that the particular values and the rankings of the values of one country dominate global discussion. There is a real danger that strong European traditions of seeing solidarity and equity as being central to debates about health are lost in an unthinking and automatic reaching for autonomy, seeing it as being the most important value and at the heart of the solution to every problem. This point does not necessarily entail any kind of commitment to relativism, as I believe that values such as solidarity and equity are also crucial to debates in US bioethics, despite what might be claimed by those from that country (Dawson and Jennings, 2012).

My focus in this chapter is on individual clinician-patient encounters, with a particular focus on the issue of consent; although, I will suggest later that all issues in bioethics, including those in clinical medicine, ought to be approached from the perspective of a more societal ethics. To provide an introduction to the three models I will sketch three different true 'stories'. This is not because I'm a convert or advocate for narrative ethics, but that this is an excellent way to capture key issues and complexity in a quick and vivid manner. Most of this chapter will be taken up with articulating and exploring the values that animate the three different models that I've outlined. What values can we see at work in each model? What are the advantages and disadvantages of each model? What kind of health care and society do we, ultimately, want? My argument is that we have made some gains through many of the broad societal changes that occurred over the last fifty years, but we need to take care not to remove key aspects of what makes our lives go well together in our rush to provide answers to pressing moral problems.

12.2 Authority

My first story is derived from the English legal case of *Hatcher v Black* (*The Times*, 2 July 1954). In this case a female broadcaster who worked for the BBC specifically asked if an operation recommended for a throat condition could possibly damage her voice. She was assured that this was not a possibility, but damage did occur and she did not broadcast again. It was held in the case that the doctor had deliberately lied to the patient, with the intention of ensuring that she underwent the procedure, an operation that he believed was in her best interests. It was noted by the judge that no doctor called as a witness in the case disagreed with this professional behaviour. The views expressed in this case seem clearly dated and problematic. We can see a set of deeply embedded assumptions about both the role of patient and professional. The doctor is permitted, even expected, to decide what should be done according to his own expert judgement and his own conception of what is best for the patient. The relationship between professional and patient is one that places trust at the centre of the clinical relationship. The doctor is a figure of authority and the patient has little if any role in decision-making about what should be done.

This kind of behaviour would surely now be condemned as unethical. The doctor has not taken the patient's wishes into account, has overridden her autonomy and not gained an informed consent to an operation that carries some risks. In addition, the patient has explicitly brought a particular concern to the attention of the doctor, because her livelihood depends upon it, but this has been ignored. There was no discussion of what options for treatment might be available taking that concern into account, including the option of doing nothing. From the perspective of contemporary medical ethics, this is an easy case to deal with. The doctor fails in his duty to respect the patient and is paternalistic, even arrogant. Even though the contemporary ethical and legal analysis of this case is straightforward, we can ask whether there is anything to be said for supporting the doctor's actions in this case? Perhaps, in this particular case, the doctor's behaviour is indeed straightforwardly wrong, but we should be careful not to infer general rules from this case. For example, it does not follow that action where the patient's view is sometimes overridden or where the patient is not given access to information relating to all risks is always wrong. It may well be justifiable to act in the patient's best interests, where the patient makes a poor or irrational choice. In such a case the idea of beneficence may take priority over respect for autonomy. To believe otherwise is to hold that, say, autonomy should always take priority over beneficence (Gillon, 2003), and this may produce parallel problems to always prioritising autonomy (Dawson and Garrard, 2006). We generally see trust in one's doctor as being a good thing, and there does not seem anything wrong in a doctor accepting such trust and acting without explicit consent when he or she knows that this is what the patient prefers. This might be justified by appeal to autonomy, but it is hardly supportive of the kind of robust informed consent that many enthusiasts for autonomy would require. Support for respecting such a trust-based approach to medical care may well appeal to beneficence as much as autonomy. The patient is better off, from his or her perspective, not to be involved in all the bothersome and anxiety-inducing details about a procedure. The doctor knows this, and proceeds on this basis. This can be accepted even if the *Hatcher* case is seen as problematic. The difference is that in that case, a specific concern was brought to the attention of the doctor, but the patient's explicit concern was ignored.

12.3 Markets

There has been a general shift in social attitudes, and many people now see the 'authority' model as problematic. It is not, perhaps, too much of an exaggeration to say that much of the history of bioethics over the last forty years has been focused on criticism of such views, both reflecting and driving such changes, with an increasing appeal to individual patient autonomy, rights and choices as the dominant theoretical position. In turn, such a theoretical or principled position is then used to support a consistent call for such things as privacy and informed consent. As I have suggested elsewhere, this is perhaps the dominant voice in contemporary bioethics (Dawson, 2010). Has the victory for individual choice and autonomy been won? Is patient autonomy to be accepted as the preeminent, dominant value, as 'first amongst equals' (Gillon, 2003; Dawson and Garrard, 2006)? One of the implications of an autonomy-first model is that the patient is ultimately responsible for what happens. We are in the marketplace because the patient is required to accept the principle of *caveat emptor*. Should the individual patient be left as the sole and final decision-maker in the free market of choice? My second story may give grounds for questioning such an idea.

A member of my family was recently diagnosed with early stage prostate cancer. He went along to see his general practitioner (GP) to talk about the options for treatment. His GP was in his late twenties, not long out of medical school. He suggested there were three different treatment options (surgery, hormone treatment and radiotherapy, watchful waiting). He described them in some detail and then invited the patient to choose one of the three options. The patient understood very clearly the facts as given about the choices before him, but he asked his GP for some help in making a choice, as it was not obvious which was the best option for him. The GP briefly outlined the choices again, and then once again invited the patient to make a decision. Despite repeated requests for assistance, the GP refused to offer advice about which option he thought might be best. He said, presumably appealing to the ethical principles he had learnt in medical school, that 'it is your choice and it is not my business to influence your decision'. The patient left feeling confused, anxious and angry.

This case can be considered as the antithesis of the *Hatcher* case, described above. Here, the dangers of deciding for the patient have been learnt to such an extent that it is felt that no opinion can be offered, despite the fact that the patient is asking for help in making a decision. One interpretation of the story is that the GP is misapplying his medical ethics. He is not listening to what this patient wants; he is not respecting this patient's autonomous choice. Instead, the GP has decided that his duty is not merely to respect autonomy but to promote it. He insists that the patient takes responsibility for his choice about the treatment option and his own health. The doctor's role is seen as an information provider, but not as a chooser or even a helper in such a difficult choice. The patient is the expert and ought to make his own choice. I presume that I am not the only one that thinks that something has gone wrong here. The focus of this clinical encounter has become autonomous choice not care. The GP's actions are rather cold, rational and legalistic. The background assumption is that we exist in a marketplace where free and equal individual parties rely on 'contractual' notions of inter-personal conduct. On this view, once the asymmetry in information about the three options has been addressed, the obligations upon the GP are exhausted. The responsibility of choice is imposed on an unwilling patient, and this seems needlessly cruel. Seeing autonomy as a presumptive value carries the risk that other values such as beneficence and non-maleficence are marginalised.

12.4 Society

My third story is my own. The last time I was in hospital I was admitted through Accident and Emergency (A&E) to a general orthopaedic ward. I had suffered with back pain for a few months, and the condition of my prolapsed disc had deteriorated, to the point that I was in constant pain and could not sit or stand for long periods. One day I realised that my bladder was not working, and I had been warned in advance by my GP that if this ever happened it was a sign that something was seriously wrong. In A&E it was decided that the disc was pressing on the nerves controlling my bladder function and that surgical intervention was necessary. I was admitted to a small ward with six beds, but as it was now late on a Friday afternoon it was decided that no surgery would be performed before Monday. I had come to terms with having a boring weekend, I had exchanged superficial pleasantries with the other four people on the ward, and settled down to re-read *Pride and Prejudice*, one of my favourite books. However, in the early evening a new patient arrived and was placed in the sixth bed. He had a broken leg, but it quickly became apparent that he had other problems. He seemed confused, and kept trying to get out of bed, apparently wanting to go and have a smoke. He shouted and screamed and was aggressive towards the care staff, and this went on all weekend. On the first night, he was told by his other family members that his son (a soldier) was going to come and see him. I was in the bed next to him, and he was so confused that he thought I was his son. He kept up a one-sided 'conversation' by shouting things at me all night. This all meant that I and the other members of the ward had virtually no sleep all weekend. Even when nodding off during the brief lulls in the noise, other things would interrupt sleep such as the lights being switched on in the ward at 6.00am when the new nursing shift began. The routine of hospital life is a succession of interruptions, through the recording of patient observations, drugs rounds and inedible meals. Not even the pleasure of reading about Mr Darcy and the Miss Bennetts was adequate compensation. On Monday morning the fracture patient was moved into a private room, although we could still hear him screaming in pain. We later found out that he was in the last stages of lung cancer, with metastases in his leg (hence the fracture) and the brain (hence the confusion). Why he was on an orthopaedic ward, rather than somewhere where his complex and palliative needs could be cared for, was never explained. He died a few days later. Just after he had been moved, the surgeon arrived to 'consent' me for my operation. I was in severe pain, and suffering from severe sleep deprivation. Luckily, there was little choice for me, as something had to be done about my disc and surgery was presented as the only option. There was no discussion of any alternative procedures or any risks, except for the risk of permanent paralysis from the operation. That risk was mentioned, but marginalised, only because I asked about it. All I wanted was to have my pain removed and to sleep. I was very far from the state of the patient as the perfect consumer of information, rationally weighing different options, and then making an informed choice. In retrospect I am still glad that there was little pretence that I could participate in any meaningful dialogue about what was best for me.

Why do I think this story is important? I presume that this tale of being a patient and going an entire weekend without any sleep in hospital is an extreme one. But I do think that the reality of the experience of being a patient is often forgotten in academic bioethics. Being a patient means entering into a specific role. Patients are not, in general, the hyper-rational, maximising deliberators that many philosophers and lawyers tend to assume that they are when they discuss issues such as informed consent. Often patients are in pain, they are afraid, they have a health condition that they want to escape, they are quickly institutionalised and they have had too little sleep. In general, their focus is on being cured, not on receiving and understanding information about every single remote risk that might occur. Of course, some people may want to know every such detail, but I think that they are rare. It is surprising how few discussions of informed consent focus on the reality of being a patient and what patients actually want. Other aspects of this story are also relevant for our discussion. For example, it is often the case that patients are isolated, even if they are on a ward with others. They are in a very strange environment, surrounded by strangers and away from their everyday and meaningful social relationships with family and friends. The lack of the familiar and routine social contact with others can be unsettling and increase feelings of dislocation and confusion.

I have called the third model a societal model, because of what is missing from this third story (Dawson, 2013). I'm using this term to call attention to two important aspects of this case. First, we should note the importance of understanding the social reality of patient-professional interactions (and thereby the importance of social science to bioethics). Generally speaking, doctors in the 1950s, such as those in the *Hatcher* case, would and could assume that patients would trust them. The rise of autonomy since that time can offer protection to patients, but it can also result in the extreme isolation experienced by the patient in the prostate case, burdened with the responsibility of making medical decisions alone. My own experience brings home powerfully, at least to me, that there is something valuable in trusting relationships between doctors and patients at a time of crisis. As bioethicists we need to understand in more detail what patients really want at their time of need and not just assume that they want maximal autonomy and endless pieces of information about their condition, treatment options and what might go wrong in the course of their treatment. Second, in calling attention to a societal model I am also pointing to the fact that humans are biological and social creatures (and this is relevant, perhaps even key, to our normative commitments). A European bioethics that is focused on thinking about ethics in a societal context can appeal to 'embedded' values that have not been discussed in much normative work (Dawson, 2013). Such values will include things such as equity, solidarity, needs, trust, reciprocity and common goods (Dawson, 2011). Such values are relevant even in cases of individual clinical care. There is, of course, some work on all of these concepts and their application, but perhaps it is time for them to be seen as being much closer to the core and to the future of bioethics than has been the case in recent years (Dawson, 2010). There is most discussion of such value within the context of public health, but such values are directly relevant to all health care (Dawson, 2010). Autonomy is an important value, but it is not the only important value. In clinical care, my hypothesis would be that most patients want to be part of a conversation about their care, they want to be respected, but their priority is ultimately to be cared for.

In this chapter I have focused on telling stories to try and illustrate general theoretical points. I generally prefer to focus on arguments and evidence in my work. I have in the past been critical of the place of informed consent within bioethics, particularly in research ethics (Dawson, 2009b). However, even in such work there is an appeal to the empirical evidence we have for the problems that patients and research subjects have in understanding information that is given to them. I find it surprising that so many of my colleagues in bioethics do not engage with such empirical evidence and do not see how it is directly relevant to more normative argument. Is informed consent really going to be the solution to so many issues in bioethics if in reality so many people find it difficult to understand information within a clinical context? Indeed, if as a patient it is not information that is my priority, why do you insist on giving it to me?

12.5 Conclusions

In future European bioethics, there should be a focus on thinking about ethics in health care from the perspective of the lived reality of being a patient. We should not just assume that patients are hyper-rational, self-interested deliberators. They are social and biological beings and we need to think about how this is relevant to thinking about ethics. This will result in more subtle normative discussions, with a greater tendency to appeal to the discussion of more 'social' values. Each of the three models that I outlined above, through discussion of my three stories, has its advantages and disadvantages. However, I have suggested that the societal model is to be preferred. We have left the authority model behind, and we currently live according to the market model with all its problems, but it is the societal model that provides the best fit with what it is to live a meaningful life. Future work in clinical ethics, medical ethics and bioethics in general should take this into account.

References

Dawson, A. (2009a) 'Theory and Practice in Public Health Ethics: A Complex Relationship' in Peckham, S. and Hann, A. (eds.) *Public Health Ethics and Practice*. London: Policy Press, pp. 191–209.

———— (2009b) 'The Normative Status of the Requirement to Gain an Informed Consent in Clinical Trials: Comprehension, Obligations and Empirical Evidence' in Corrigan, O., Liddell, K., McMillan, J., Richards, M. and Weijer, C. (eds.) *The Limits of Consent: A Socio-legal Approach to Human Subject Research in Medicine*. Oxford: Oxford University Press, pp. 99–113.

———— (2010) 'The Future of Bioethics: Three Dogmas and a Cup of Hemlock', *Bioethics*, 24 (5): 218–225.

———— (2011) 'Resetting the Parameters: Public Health as the Foundation for Public Health Ethics' in Dawson, A. (ed.) *Public Health Ethics: Key Concepts and Issues in Policy and Practice*. Cambridge: Cambridge University Press. pp. 1–19.

———— (2013) 'Presidential Address: Contextual, Social, Critical: How We Ought to Think about the Future of Bioethics', *Bioethics*, 27(6): 291–297.

Dawson, A. and Garrard, E. (2006) 'In Defence of Moral Imperialism: Four Equal and Universal Prima Facie Duties', *Journal of Medical Ethics*, 32(4): 200–204.

Dawson, A. and Jennings, B. (2012) 'The Place of Solidarity in Public Health Ethics', *Public Health Reviews*, 34: 1. Available HTTP: <http://www.publichealthreviews.eu/upload/pdf_files/11/07_Dawson.pdf> (accessed 24 October 2014).

Gillon, R. (2003) 'Ethics Needs Principles—Four Can Encompass the Rest—and Respect for Autonomy Should Be "First among Equals"', *Journal of Medical Ethics*, 29: 307–312.

Part IV
European bioethics in academic rooms

13 Medical ethics in medical classrooms: from theory to practice

Wing May Kong

13.1 Introduction

Taking medical ethics into medical classrooms, be they undergraduate lecture theatres, hospital wards or clinic rooms in primary care, brings a range of challenges. Few students or doctors will have chosen medicine primarily because of an interest in medical ethics and there will be a small minority who consider medical ethics teaching an unnecessary waste of time. In Europe and the United States (US) medical ethics teaching in medical schools has received increasing attention over the past four decades (Goldie, 2000; Eckles et al., 2005). Since 1993, medical ethics has been a required part of the undergraduate medical curriculum (GMC, 1993) in UK medical schools and, in 1999, the World Medical Association (WMA) recommended that all medical schools should teach medical ethics (WMA, 1999). However, medical ethics remains a relatively small discipline within medical schools and teaching is often delivered by lone academics without a natural home in either a clinical or academic department (Mattick and Bligh, 2006). Reviews of medical ethics teaching in Europe and the US have identified common challenges around resources for teaching and the method and aims of medical ethics teaching (Goldie, 2000; Claudot et al., 2007).

There has been an ongoing debate as to whether the aim of medical ethics teaching should be to provide future doctors with the skills and competencies to practise in an ethical manner or whether, in addition, teaching should nurture and develop a doctor's moral character. Whilst there has been increasing interest in virtue ethics, the language of virtues does not sit easily with the educational language of learning outcomes and competencies. Section 2 of this chapter will reflect on the aims of medical ethics teaching and in particular whether the development of the virtuous doctor is a legitimate teaching aim. Section 3 will consider organisational challenges specific to the UK as well as the more general challenges of resources and teaching expertise, role modelling, assessment and the translation of ethical thinking into ethical practice. Section 4 will consider how these challenges can be addressed, drawing on curriculum development and delivery within the author's UK teaching institution (Imperial College, London), new teaching technologies and the wider educational literature. Section 5 will return to the notion of the good doctor and consider, in the light of the preceding discussions, whether we can nurture virtuous doctors. A case will be made for expanding the role of humanities teaching to complement and enhance medical ethics. Section 6 will conclude that whilst there are considerable challenges there are also great opportunities for medical ethics to engage with a wider community of teachers to enable better translation of ethical thinking into ethical practice in ways that encourage the development of virtuous doctors.

13.2 What are the aims of teaching medical ethics?

13.2.1 Ethical reasoning

In its 1999 resolution, the WMA asserted that 'Medical Ethics and Human Rights form an integral part of the work and culture of the medical profession' and that medical ethics teaching should be obligatory in medical schools worldwide (WMA, 1999). The overarching aim of bringing ethics into the medical curriculum must be to make 'better' doctors, but what is meant by 'better' needs some unpicking.

There is a general consensus that doing the right thing in medicine requires more than good medical knowledge and technical skills. Doctors need the ability to recognise the ethical dimension present in every medical encounter, analyse those ethical issues effectively and act on this ethical analysis. In the recently published, widely endorsed core content of learning drawn up by the medical education working group of the Institute of Medical Ethics (IME), the authors outline the core knowledge and competencies identified through consensus working groups of UK medical ethics teachers (Stirrat et al., 2010). The document was drawn up through an extensive consultative process including workshops in which 29 of the 32 UK medical schools were represented.

As well as identifying the core topic areas of learning, such as 'Confidentiality' and 'Justice and Public Health', the document lists eight overarching aims for undergraduate teaching:[1]

1. Aspire to and be equipped for a lifetime of good practice and learning
2. Understand and respect the strengths and weaknesses of views different from their own while maintaining personal integrity
3. Develop an awareness and understanding of ethical, legal and professional responsibilities required of them as students and doctors
4. Think about and reflect critically on ethical, legal and professional issues
5. Acquire knowledge to facilitate ethical decision-making and clinical judgement that is morally, legally and professionally justifiable
6. Acknowledge and respond appropriately to clinical and ethical uncertainty

7   Respond appropriately to new challenges in medical practice as a result of scientific advances (e.g. in genetics) and social changes
8   Integrate the necessary knowledge, skills, attitudes and behaviours into medical and professional practice.

(Stirrat et al., 2010: 57)

Aims 3–8 largely relate to skills and observable behaviours (aims 3, 4 and 5 can be seen as knowledge and skill-based aims encompassing ethical reasoning and knowledge of the legal and professional framework of clinical practice; aims 6, 7 and 8 emphasise the importance of translating ethical knowledge and skills into appropriate actions in clinical practice). The first two aims are concerned with the development of moral character and personal integrity and, as such, pose some educational challenges; I will return to these two aims at the end of this section.

The document describes a spiral model of learning in which students progressively develop their ethical reasoning and integrate this with their clinical learning. In years 1 and 2 students should have a 'recognition and understanding of core ethical and legal concepts' and be able to apply 'common ethical arguments . . . [to] constructed case scenarios'. In years 3 and 4 students should be able 'to apply common ethical arguments to actual clinical encounters . . . and public health interventions' and be able to reflect on the 'ethical practice of self, peers and teachers'. In years 5 and 6 students should be able to 'integrate ethical analysis of actual clinical encounters with clinical knowledge and skills and legal obligations' and 'propose action/decision based on this synthesis' (Stirrat et al., 2010: 59). This spiral model requires medical ethics to be embedded both vertically and horizontally within the medical school curriculum.

It is worth recognising that skills in ethical reasoning and discussion are likely to be of benefit in many areas of medicine including those seemingly far removed from medical ethics. Sheehan et al. assessed moral reasoning in 350 recently qualified doctors in the US and found a high correlation between moral reasoning and independently related clinical performance (Sheehan et al., 1980). Negotiations with colleagues and patients, development of healthcare strategy and healthcare business case proposals all benefit from the ability to recognise and analyse values and communicate those analyses effectively. In addition, medical ethics teaching is increasingly leading to students and doctors pursuing medical ethics research and policy development.

13.2.2 The relationship between medical law and medical ethics

Whilst the law and professional codes of practice may be seen as separate from medical ethics, ethical practice requires a sound knowledge and understanding of the legal and professional framework within which medicine is practised. Doctors need to act in ways which fulfil their professional and legal obligations and also be able to reflect on them. In addition, medical ethics has contributed significantly to the development of law and professional guidance.

Furthermore, the advocacy role of doctors requires an understanding of the legal rights of individuals as well as the ethical obligations of doctors.

Medical students may initially feel that the law offers more certainty; a set of rules in contrast to the perceived woolliness of medical ethics. However, without an understanding of the normative basis of law, medical students run into difficulties when they are required to apply the law in clinical practice. In a cross-sectional study, over 1,100 first and final year medical students at two UK medical schools were surveyed regarding their perceptions of medical law (Preston-Shoot et al., 2011). While confidence with key areas of medical law (confidentiality, consent, capacity and human rights) was greater for final year students, less than 50 per cent of students felt confident in any one area of law. Amongst final year students only 8 per cent felt confident in applying the law in clinical practice and only 19 per cent felt confident in managing the relationship between the law, professional obligations and ethics.

These figures, in part, reflect a wider anxiety about the transition from student to junior doctor (Brennan et al., 2010). However, a recent survey has shown that formal law teaching takes place largely in the first half of undergraduate medical teaching (Preston-Shoot and McKimm, 2010) and this is further compounded by the fact that, as with medical ethics, most senior doctors will have had no systematic training in medical law. This may explain the finding by one study of first year doctors in a UK medical school who reported that undergraduate learning in medical law was commonly eroded by their seniors (Schildmann et al., 2005).

These findings provide support for the argument that medical law teaching needs to be better integrated through the undergraduate curriculum. By ensuring that medical law teaching is explicitly taught as part of clinical teaching, rich opportunities will be provided to examine the relationship and tensions raised between medical ethics and medical law in clinical practice.

13.2.3 Developing the virtuous doctor?

A more controversial question is whether we should (or indeed whether we can) be trying to make good doctors in the sense of good people. In the UK, surveys have consistently shown medical doctors to be amongst the most trusted professional group in society suggesting a societal expectation that doctors are good people (Ipsos MORI, 2013). Several authors have emphasised that, in addition to the skills of ethical reasoning, attention must be paid to the development of moral character, which is needed to 'enable [doctors] to do the right thing', to recognise ingrained injustice and unacceptable cultural norms (Campbell, Chin and Voo, 2007; Bryan and Babelay, 2009; Stirrat et al., 2010). In the UK, the recent Mid Staffordshire Inquiry exposed shocking failures in healthcare. One of the problems identified in the Inquiry report was that doctors accepted poor practice as the inevitable norm (Francis, 2013). However, while we may want our doctors to be kind, compassionate, honest and fair, we have no way of reliably assessing whether our doctors do indeed possess these qualities (as opposed to simply behaving as though they do). This is not necessarily a reason not to try to nurture these virtues through teaching. However, in a teaching environment dominated by competencies and measurable outcomes, a persuasive case will need to be made that nurturing virtues is both possible and desirable.

Even if we could agree that nurturing virtues was a valid teaching aim, we would need to agree how good a doctor a good doctor should be. Carlo Urbani was the infectious disease specialist who led the initial assessment and World Health Organisation (WHO) response to the first case of SARS (severe acute respiratory syndrome) in Vietnam. Urbani was instrumental in the WHO pandemic alert, isolation of the affected hospital and clinical care of the first SARS patients. Soon after this Dr Urbani contracted SARS and died leaving his wife and three children. Among the first 60 people to die of SARS, almost half were healthcare workers, many of whom had chosen to isolate themselves from their families to prevent spread of the infection. Such self-sacrifice, dedication and compassion are admirable but, most would agree, supererogatory. Setting the character standard so high would be unreasonable and would leave us with few individuals eligible for the profession. Furthermore, it could be argued that for doctors to understand the foibles, anxieties and suffering that form the messy jigsaw of human illness, they themselves should be less than ideal.

Accepting that our aims must be reasonable, what virtues can and should ethics education try to nurture? The seven classical virtues of wisdom, temperance, justice, courage, faith, hope and love are not specific to medicine and it is arguably not the role of medical education to take on wholesale responsibility for ensuring doctors are virtuous citizens. Nonetheless, there are virtues or aspects of character that do appear particularly relevant to good medicine.

Kumagi has proposed that there are three different types of knowledge in medicine: technical (validated through basic science and clinical research), practical (embracing standards of clinical practice, clinical competencies) and critical (Kumagi, 2014). Critical knowledge links learning with human needs, such as freedom from suffering and injustice, and is central to medical ethics. This critical knowledge requires a deep understanding of human needs, their social context and one's own moral agency. Kumagi suggests that this critical knowledge can be understood as the Aristotolian virtue of *phronesis* (Aristotle, 2009) or practical wisdom. This practical wisdom requires the lifelong habit of reflection and discussion to enable understanding of oneself and the needs of others and how to fairly respond to those needs.

The virtue of justice (which encompasses honesty, advocacy and fairness) is of particular relevance to medical practice, if we accept that modern day healthcare is a matter of justice (Walzer, 1983). Doctors' responsibilities include priority setting and resource allocation in healthcare and advocacy for the vulnerable. A good doctor needs to understand the needs of the patient in front of him or her but also balance these against the needs of other patients and the wider population.

There remains the difficulty of reconciling the development of virtues with the dominant competency-based model for medical education. Within this model, teaching and learning are evaluated against the acquisition of specific competencies. The educator needs to identify what a doctor needs to be able to do to fulfil his or her role and then define learning outcomes or competencies based on this analysis. However, there has been criticism in medical education generally (Talbot, 2004) and specifically in medical ethics (Hafferty and Franks, 1994; Goldie, 2000) of the increasing reliance on this approach. A comptency model cannot capture critical knowledge and the understanding integral to this knowledge. Arguably however, critical knowledge and the virtue of practical wisdom are central to good medical practice. Additionally, a competency approach assumes learning can be reduced to defined learning outcomes that can be completed and passed. In contrast, the acquisition of the virtues of practical wisdom and justice is an ongoing project, nurtured and developed through lifelong practice and reflection.

There is general agreement that medical ethics teaching should provide medical students with the knowledge and skills for ethical reasoning and should enable students and doctors to translate their ethical reasoning into ethical practice. In addition, an argument has been made here that medical ethics teaching should also address the development of the virtues of practical wisdom and justice. In the next section I will consider the challenges to achieving these aims.

13.3 Teaching medical ethics: a big mountain to climb?

Anyone who has been involved in developing or setting up medical ethics teaching in a medical school will appreciate the multiple obstacles that need to be negotiated. It may be some consolation to know that similar obstacles are faced by colleagues teaching in more traditional disciplines as well (e.g. anatomy, physiology) (Souba et al., 2011) and that teaching here is also all too often perceived as the poor relation to research. Some of these challenges reflect the fact that medical ethics is a relatively new addition to the medical curriculum. Others relate to translating medical ethics in the classroom into ethical practice at the bedside. This section will end by considering the challenge of the 'hidden curriculum' (Hafferty and Franks, 1994; Coulehan and Williams, 2001): what students and junior doctors learn through observation of unprofessional behaviour by other health professionals, including their seniors, and from the organisational culture in which they study.

13.3.1 Institutional and infrastructure challenges

Non-clinical medical ethics teachers can feel isolated both from clinical teachers and from university colleagues in law and philosophy. In the UK, medical ethics does not have its own cognate assessment panel and, anecdotally, medical school teaching leads have reported that their research has been excluded from the 2013 Research Excellence Framework[2] assessment (Kong et al., 2011). Medical ethics teachers are often single-handed (Mattick and Bligh, 2006) with a heavy teaching load. Thus, academics may feel that taking on a teaching post will leave them academically isolated with little time for research and potentially compromising a future academic career outside of the medical school.

Funding is an issue for all higher education institutions but medicine in the UK has the additional complication of the SIFT (Service Increment for Teaching) system for funding clinical undergraduate teaching. SIFT equates to £20–30K per student in clinical training. For hospital based teaching SIFT money goes directly from the Department of Health to NHS Trusts[3] where it becomes part of each Trust's overall budget. Therefore, for the majority of NHS hospitals, there is no direct link between teaching activity and SIFT payments (Clack, Bevan and Eddleston, 2002). Consequently, medical schools have little effective influence on how this money is used. This funding model can create huge difficulties when medical schools want to introduce new teaching methods and harmonise the teaching of newer disciplines, such as medical ethics, across multiple hospitals.

Since the General Medical Council's (GMC) publication of *Tomorrow's Doctors 1993* (GMC, 1993), medical ethics has received increasing attention within medical education and training. Today undergraduate and postgraduate curricula in medicine include competencies in medical ethics and law. Defining these has helped prioritise medical ethics teaching but, as the scandals at Mid Staffordshire NHS Trust (Francis, 2013) and elsewhere in the UK (Keogh, 2013) have shown us, a doctor who has achieved her ethical competencies is not necessarily an ethical doctor (Kong and Vernon, 2013). As discussed in section 2, concerns have been raised that the focus on competencies detracts from other vital aspects of medical education and the development of professional identity (Bryan and Babelay, 2009; Kumagi, 2014).

13.3.2 Bringing ethics teaching to the bedside

There is general consensus that medical ethics teaching benefits from the opportunity for small group discussion and time for personal reflection. Bringing ethical discussion to ward rounds, outpatient clinics and primary care consultations provides rich opportunities for small group teaching and integrating ethical and clinical reasoning. Engaging senior clinicians in medical ethics teaching is necessary if students and doctors are to see medical ethics as an integral part of everyday clinical practice. In its consensus statement, the Institute of Medical Ethics working group states that medical ethics teaching should be an obligation of all teachers and not the sole responsibility of designated teachers (Stirrat et al., 2010). However, many UK medical schools have intakes of often over 300 students per year and content heavy curricula. Thus small group teaching integrated across other areas of clinical teaching raises many practical difficulties in terms of recruiting sufficient numbers of teachers, effectively engaging, organising and communicating with clinician teachers across multiple, geographically distinct teaching sites and ensuring the quality of teachers and quality of teaching in a normative discipline such as ethics.

13.3.3 Clinicians as educators

Medical ethics was only identified as a core component of the undergraduate medical curriculum in 1993 (GMC, 1993). The Institute of Medical Ethics issued its original consensus statement on undergraduate medical ethics teaching in 1998 (Consensus statement by teachers of medical law and ethics in UK medical schools, 1998) but a survey of UK medical schools in 2006 found that its recommendations had still not been fully implemented (Mattick and Bligh, 2006). Thus, most senior clinicians will have had no formal medical ethics training. Furthermore, clinicians may find the normative discourse of ethics inaccessible and imprecise and assessment unreliable. At the author's institution clinician teachers were often anxious that they had had less training in medical ethics than their students. While senior clinicians may lack training in moral philosophy they have a wealth of professional experience and many years of reflective practice which they can bring to teaching sessions. Nonetheless, they are likely to need appropriate teaching support to give them the confidence and skills to bring ethical discussions into their usual bedside teaching.

At a practical level, only a minority of senior clinicians will have sessions in their job plans specifically allocated for undergraduate teaching. Whilst many clinicians enjoy teaching, it is also seen as creating time pressures and reducing productivity (Sturman, Rego and Dick, 2011). In the current climate of austerity with increasing demands on clinical productivity, senior clinicians may feel reluctant to take on new teaching initiatives particularly in unfamiliar areas such as ethics where additional teacher training and support may be needed. Therefore, to succeed, teaching initiatives to engage clinicians as educators in medical ethics need to be sensitive to these professional and practical issues.

13.3.4 Vertical and horizontal integration of ethics and law

Doctors need to develop ethical sensitivity as well as skills in ethical reasoning (Campbell et al., 2007). They need to be able to articulate and analyse these issues, integrate their ethical reasoning with their clinical assessment and from this respond in an ethical and effective manner. Vertical integration is needed to help students build on their learning and clinical experience as they progress through medical school. Horizontal integration encourages students to move away from a silo approach to learning and to recognise the ethical issues that arise in everyday clinical practice. With robust horizontal integration, senior clinicians should feel as comfortable and confident to discuss ethical issues that arise at the bedside, in a consultation or in an operating theatre as they would to discuss diagnoses, surgical procedures or management options. Indeed the ethical discourse would form a seamless part of these clinical discussions.

Ethics is part of virtually every clinical encounter but ethics teaching often draws on constructed case scenarios which have been written to bring out specific ethical issues, focusing on 'big' ethical dilemmas. It is therefore perhaps unsurprising that students and doctors can find it difficult to recognise the ethical issues that arise in their everyday practice. However bringing ethics teaching into everyday clinical practice presents challenges. A recent study examined case-based discussions between trainee physicians and their supervisors in a medical outpatients setting. The researchers identified significant ethical issues in 81 per cent of the 139 observed case discussions. However ethical issues were explicitly identified and discussed by clinician supervisors in only 12 per cent of the cases (Carrese et al., 2011).

In the above study, the authors suggest that the paucity of explicit identification and discussion of ethical issues may reflect the perceived time pressures and competition with other areas of learning, a lack of confidence about teaching ethics or that the teachers have not recognised the ethical issues. Active collaboration with clinicians is essential if ethics teaching is to be embedded in clinical practice. Simply passing the teaching baton to interested clinical colleagues risks patchy, unsustainable uptake by the core of ethics enthusiasts. If horizontal integration is to succeed, academic institutions must ensure that ethics leads have the time and resources to work with clinicians in the development and delivery of an integrated ethics teaching strategy.

13.3.5 The hidden curriculum

Well-developed ethical awareness and reasoning will have little healthcare benefit if these are not translated into clinical practice (Campbell et al., 2007). Various studies have found that around two-thirds of medical students report observing what they perceive as unethical behaviour by other health professionals. However, only a minority of these students reported taking any action (Feudtner, Christakis and Christakis, 1994; Rennie and Crosby, 2002).

One barrier to aligning values to action is the hidden curriculum (Hafferty, 1998). This is what students learn from observation of their teachers, other health professionals and the institutional culture. This curriculum is not acknowledged in formal or informal education but may have a greater influence on ethical reasoning and practice than formal teaching (Coulehan and Williams, 2001). In addition, students and junior doctors often feel powerless to act when they witness unethical behaviour (Parker, Watts and Scicluna, 2012) or even obliged to act unethically because of pressure from their seniors (Schildmann et al., 2005).

Providing students and junior doctors with a safe environment to discuss the hidden curriculum and its impact on ethical practice is valued by students but alone does not seem to be enough to change student behaviour (Parker et al., 2012). McDougall has argued that medical students and junior doctors need to acquire the skills to 'speak up' if they are to successfully translate their ethical reasoning into action (McDougall, 2008).

Despite these challenges to medical ethics teaching, there are many opportunities to innovate and improve. These will be considered in the following section.

13.4 Medical ethics teaching: rising to the challenge

In the previous section I have argued that firmly embedded vertical and horizontal integration of medical ethics is essential if ethics teaching is to translate into ethical behaviour in practice. This requires the engagement and support of a large number of senior clinicians, often across multiple teaching sites. Assessment is a major driver for learning, particularly amongst undergraduate students. An effective response to the challenges of teaching medical ethics must consider how assessment can be best used to promote appropriate learning. Whilst I have argued that the aims of ethics teaching cannot all be reduced to measurable learning outcomes, there are specific skills and behaviours that can be validly assessed. In this section I will draw on experience from the institution in which I teach, the use of new learning technologies and the wider educational literature to address the challenges of vertical and horizontal integration, assessment and the hidden curriculum.

13.4.1 Embedding vertical and horizontal integration

Within our medical school we have been developing a vertically and horizontally integrated teaching programme for ethics and law. To deliver this we have recruited around 100 clinicians who tutor across the undergraduate curriculum. These clinicians are based in primary care and our 8 secondary care teaching campuses. We started from the assumption that most doctors practise ethically and professionally but may lack the skills, confidence or habit to articulate their ethical reasoning to their students. Only a minority of our tutors have completed any form of external training in medical ethics: mainly short courses (1 week or a series of weekends) in medical ethics. The medical ethics teaching is part of an undergraduate curriculum which is largely non-clinical in years 1 and 2 and then clinical in years 3, 5 and 6 (in year 4, students all undertake an intercalated programme, in subjects such as neuroscience, reproductive health, global health, which leads to a BSc qualification[4]).

Core knowledge and skills (reflection, small group discussion, ethical theory and reasoning) are introduced in years 1 and 2. In year 3 our students have to submit a series of short reflections on significant events[5] encountered during each of their clinical rotations and produce a group presentation based on the ethical analysis of one of these. They also give formatively assessed group presentations on self-selected current resource allocation issues.

The ethics teaching in the first 3 years is centrally organised. In year 5 we worked very closely with our colleagues in psychiatry, primary care, obstetrics and gynaecology and paediatrics to develop student assignments that are organised and delivered by each speciality. The assignments take the form of case-based discussions or significant event analyses undertaken either individually or as small groups. The assignments are based on events (involving patients or staff or both) identified by the students on their clinical rotations. Whilst there is a focus on ethical and/or legal issues, the students are explicitly required to integrate their ethical and legal analysis with their clinical learning.

We carried out a small pilot study to look at the impact of our integrated year 5 teaching, interviewing year 5 students (n = 6) who had recently completed obstetrics and gynaecology and Foundation Year doctors (n = 10) who had completed their obstetrics and gynaecology ethics group presentation (a significant event analysis) 2 years previously. Questions were designed to map to specific competencies in the GMC's *Tomorrow's Doctors* document (GMC, 2009). We found that 60 per cent of respondents reported that the assignment had helped them relate ethical areas in the curriculum to their clinical practice, 94 per cent that it had increased their awareness of ethical and legal issues and 87 per cent that it had improved their skills in tackling these issues in practice.

Our teaching in years 3 and 5 is aimed at increasing ethical sensitivity as well as improving ethical reasoning and discussion. In year 3, the case/issue identified for discussion for the significant event analysis and resource allocation sessions is left entirely to the students. Given this remit, students have identified an impressively wide range of encounters and events for ethical discussion, many of which would not be found in textbook ethical scenarios, e.g. student examination of patients with dementia, allowing health professionals to jump the queue in outpatient clinics, access to palliative care for patients not entitled to NHS treatment, incentivising breast feeding and geographical variation in NHS funding.

13.4.2 Clinicians as educators

A key aspect of our educational strategy is to develop our clinicians as educators. Developing and supporting clinicians in this role provides a large potential teaching resource and is essential to successful horizontal and vertical integration of ethics. However it requires considerable investment in resources to ensure that teaching quality and consistency are maintained and that clinicians feel confident to teach in this field. We appointed a teaching lead whose main remit is tutor support through local training sessions and highly popular teaching away days. Tutor support focuses as much on generic teaching skills, e.g. facilitation, giving feedback and small group dynamics, as on ethical theory and legal knowledge. The hope is that this approach, as well increasing formal teaching of medical ethics in clinical practice, will also encourage ethical discourse beyond timetabled teaching sessions and into everyday practice going some way to combatting the hidden curriculum.

To support this horizontal and vertical teaching programme we have worked with professional e-learning technologists to create a series of on-line, virtual learning objects (interactive e-learning modules) covering the core knowledge and ethical theory. These virtual learning objects contain self-evaluation exercises and prompts for reflection.

The original driver for the e-learning modules was to support vertical integration by our year 5 students. The modules enabled students to refresh themselves on their previous year 2 and year 3 learning as part of the preparation for their year 5 assignments. By making these virtual learning objects accessible to teachers as well as students we can ensure that teachers are up to speed and confident with what students have been taught. Our course guides for students and teaching include a range of essays and papers in medical ethics chosen for their relevance and accessibility. These, together with the virtual learning objects, can help teachers to structure their own ethical thinking.

In designing new teaching sessions we were conscious of the need to minimise the assessment burden on already busy clinicians. The assignments in years 3 and 5 are formatively assessed across 5 domains: 1) defining the problem, 2) identifying additional information (e.g. psychological and social aspects of the case, empirical evidence), 3) ethical and legal reflection and analysis, 4) integrating information and analysis, and 5) involving other parties (e.g. other health professionals, healthcare networks). Domain 4 requires students to propose a way forward for the case and to justify this proposal in terms of their ethical and legal analysis and the other relevant information/evidence. Domains 1, 2, 4 and 5 are generic domains for case-based discussions used in postgraduate assessment in the UK and therefore familiar to our clinician tutors. The formative assessments also use similar assessment criteria to those used in postgraduate assessments: 'above expectations', 'meets expectations', 'below expectations'. Our aim was to 'demystify' the ethical and legal analysis by embedding it within a familiar teaching and assessment structure which can also easily be transferred to their postgraduate teaching and supervision.

13.4.3 Assessment

The pressure to perform well throughout medical school has increased with the centralised application system for Foundation Year[6] jobs in the UK. Allocation of Foundation Year posts is determined by a student's ranking in his or her final year application. Undergraduate exam results are a major determining factor in this ranking process. Medical students have a content-heavy curriculum and understandably prioritise areas that are assessed. If medical ethics is to be given due weight, satisfactory performance in at least one assessment of medical ethics should be a requirement for progression at medical school and ethics and law should continue to be assessed throughout the undergraduate curriculum.

As with other areas of medicine, use of a variety of assessment methods, both formative and summative, is needed to assess the range of learning outcomes in medical ethics. Assessments should be designed to assess the learning outcomes of the teaching. For instance, if one of the learning outcomes is the ability to read, reflect and apply ethical arguments, an open book summative assessment for which students have set preparatory reading might be a valid assessment method. Incorporation of ethical and legal domains into practical assessments such as OSCES (objective structured clinical examination skills) (Smee, 2003) and PACES (practical assessment of clinical examination skills) provides a way of assessing ethical behaviour and reinforcing the importance of integrated learning (Fenwick et al., 2012).

Typically within a PACES assessment station, students will be faced with an actor taking on the role of a patient in a specific clinical scenario. The student is assessed according to a series of specific skills, e.g. history taking, abdominal examination, management planning. Ethics can be one of the skills that is assessed but it is important that a clear description is given of the ethical skill being assessed. For instance, a station might involve a patient being treated with insulin for their diabetes who has not informed the DVLA of their clinical condition. The ethical skills being assessed might include demonstrating respect for patient autonomy and confidentiality and demonstrating awareness of ethical obligations owed to the wider public. To ensure reliability, assessors should be given clear guidance as to what would be expected for a student to achieve a pass for these skills. An assessment rubric with 'communications and ethics' or 'professionalism and ethics' as an assessment domain, but with no additional description or guidance, is unlikely to provide a meaningful assessment of ethical skills.

These summative assessment methods, however, risk reinforcing the idea that the ethical doctor can be reduced to a series of standardised, assessable competencies. In previous sections I have argued that a competency-based approach alone is insufficient for teaching and learning in medical ethics. It is therefore important that summative assessments are complemented by other forms of assessment and teaching. A recurring theme in the literature has been the development of professional and moral identity (Hafferty and Franks, 1994; Goldie, 2000; Bryan and Babelay, 2009). Kumagi has suggested that the formation of professional identity requires the doctor to acquire virtues such as integrity, compassion and practical wisdom but also to incorporate these into his or her personal identity (shaped by personal background, values, experiences and beliefs). This, he proposes, can be achieved through teaching that encompasses reflection, discourse and imagination (Kumagi, 2014).

The majority of our teaching is delivered through small group teaching which explicitly emphasises the importance of discourse and reflection.

Attendance at these sessions is compulsory. Participation in small group formative assignments is a requirement for sign off for the relevant speciality rotations. At our teacher training sessions we have provided workshops on giving feedback and time for verbal and written feedback is specifically timetabled into lesson plans. We have also recently introduced peer moderated marking for our year 3 formative assessment in which students rate other group members on their contribution to the group presentation. The group as a whole receives a mark for their presentation and this is moderated by each student's peer marks to give a final individual mark for each student. These initiatives are intended to encourage constructive group discussion and team working.

13.4.4 Aligning values with action: overcoming the hidden curriculum

In section 3 I noted that medical students commonly observe what they perceive to be unethical behaviour (Parker et al., 2012). However there is also evidence that, for various reasons, senior clinicians often fail to explicitly discuss ethical issues when they arise in practice (Carrese et al., 2011). As a result students may mistakenly misinterpret behaviour of their seniors as unprofessional or unethical. For instance a consultant's seemingly off-hand response to being told by a junior doctor that one of her patient's has died may reflect the need of the consultant to prioritise her other patients, or to display outward strength to her team despite her sadness, or frustration that the patient died despite much time and emotional energy (unseen by the student) devoted to that patient. However without explicit reflection, the student (and perhaps her team) may be left assuming that compassion has little value in practice.

For our integrated year 5 ethics teaching discussed in section 3, teaching leads are encouraged to incorporate the student discussions and presentations into regular departmental meetings. These meetings encourage engagement of clinicians not formally involved in ethics teaching and have been well received. They provide an opportunity for students to see senior clinicians actively involved in ethical discussions and addressing uncertainty. The departmental format encourages explicit reflection as senior clinicians openly discuss how they might do things better and reflect on the barriers to doing so. In this way the discussions support clinicians as positive role models for ethics and law in clinical practice and help counter some of the negative impact of the hidden curriculum.

Evidence suggests that the discordance between what we should do and what we actually do is not restricted to clinical practice. The moral imperative to do no harm is deeply embedded in society. FeldmannHall et al. found that while there was a strong refusal to inflict harm for personal gain (delivering electric shocks to a known individual in return for monetary gain) in a hypothetical situation, the same individuals behaved in the opposite manner in the real life situation where the monetary gain was real (FeldmanHall et al., 2012).

Arguably, therefore, ethics education needs to address the potential incentives (e.g. career advancement, avoiding emotional exposure, clinical expediency) for unethical behaviour.

13.5 Nurturing virtuous doctors

The approach to ethics teaching in the UK is to focus on ethical reasoning and awareness rather than teaching students what to think (Stirrat et al., 2010). However, as argued in section 2 there are virtues that we might want our students to aspire to. The development of moral identity as an ongoing process has been discussed in earlier sections. Most would surely agree that Kumagi's description of the physician with a 'deep and abiding personal engagement with medicine as a social and moral activity' is one to be aspired to (Kumagi, 2014: 982). However, what is open to debate is whether this aspiration should fall within the remit of medical ethics teaching.

While we can, with reasonable reliability and validity, assess how a doctor or student reasons and what they do in practice, we can only guess at the attitudes and values that underpin this behaviour. One immediate problem in trying to teach people to be good is that we cannot reliably or validly assess the attitudes of others and therefore we cannot assess whether our teaching is achieving the desired outcomes. Nonetheless, it would be a sad day if we felt that only those areas that can be assessed should be the concern of education.

Arguably, we can assess institutional attitudes. If we accept the influence of the hidden curriculum, then we should ensure that our medical schools and clinical institutions are underpinned by virtues such as honesty, justice, wisdom and compassion. A medical learning environment that does not promote these values is unlikely to nurture these values in its students and doctors (Benbassat, 2012). However the organisation of medical schools and universities may make it difficult to challenge situations in which these virtues are not clearly demonstrated by the institution (Souba et al., 2011).

Evidence suggests that the habit of reflection is associated with greater insight into personal competency and a reduced likelihood of formal complaints about professional behaviour (Rogers and Ballantyne, 2012). There are therefore grounds for thinking that encouraging the habit of reflection may lead to students and doctors having greater insight into their personal values and attitudes. Appreciation of differing perspectives is important to the process of reflection and the use of well-facilitated small group discussion has been advocated as a way to promote this. Reflection should not be restricted to formal teaching sessions. Senior clinicians could be encouraged to include students in debriefs and discussions of clinical incidents and significant events.

The constraints of large year group sizes, however, mean that small group teaching can be an unaffordable luxury. Classroom response systems such as clickers provide a way of bringing some of the benefits of small group teaching to the lecture theatre. Students each have a handheld device which allows them to answer or vote in response to a question posed by the lecturer on an electronic presentation. Earlier systems could be cumbersome and the software difficult to navigate, but, more recently, relatively cheap smartphone-based devices have become available.

We have used clickers in large (over 300 students) lecture-based teaching as a way to help students appreciate the differing viewpoints amongst their peers and provide a starting point for further reflection. Immediately following their first visit to the dissecting room and encounter with a human cadaver, students were asked, in a lecture theatre setting, to respond using clickers to questions about their response to seeing the cadaver and to cadaveric organ donation. Their responses are limited to the range of response options given, but have the advantage of anonymity. When asked 'How did you feel when the body was uncovered?' 57 per cent responded 'Comfortable, I was interested to see what it looked like', 30 per cent responded 'A bit nervous, unsure how I would react' and 8 per cent 'Uncomfortable, but I felt it was something I needed to do'. When asked if they would donate their body for anatomical dissection 16 per cent responded 'almost definitely' and 25 per cent 'almost definitely not'. The clicker responses are automatically converted to a graphical form demonstrating for both teacher and students the range of viewpoints amongst the students. Within the session we wanted to introduce students to the retained organ controversy that arose from the Bristol Royal Infirmary Inquiry into paediatric deaths following cardiac surgery (Kennedy, 2001). We began by encouraging students to reflect on their personal views on anatomical donation, asking them 'How would you feel if parts of your dead body could be used for research/education without your permission or your family's?'; 14 per cent said 'It would be OK – I'd be dead', 14.8 per cent 'It would be OK – it's for a good cause', 30 per cent 'Angry/unhappy – it would be distressing for my family', 22 per cent 'Angry/unhappy – it's my body' and 8 per cent 'Angry/unhappy – I don't know why'. This provided a powerful way of engaging students (Finlay and Fawzy, 2001) with the ethical debate that arose from the retained organ controversy.

In addition to the habit of reflection, Kumagi advocates teaching approaches that incorporate imagination and discourse to enable students to develop and refine their understanding of self, others and the world around them. This understanding is integral to the development of professional and moral identity (Kumagi, 2014). This seems particularly pertinent given that there is evidence to suggest that students' ability to empathise with the pain and suffering of others is eroded as they progress through their clinical training (Hojat et al., 2009).

When students enter the clinical classroom they find themselves exposed to emotionally challenging situations. Within their first years they will experience, second-hand, more human tragedy than most people are exposed to in a lifetime. Usually in their early twenties, their personal exposure to tragedy and emotional turmoil is likely to be limited. This may limit their ability to respond constructively to the tragedies that unfold in the medical arena. Added to this are the challenges of the hidden curriculum and the pressure to conform to the behavioural norms of doctors (Finlay and Fawzy, 2001).

It has been suggested that humanities teaching can improve empathy amongst students and young doctors, help them retain their moral identity and create a learning environment which acknowledges and accepts uncertainty (Rosenthal et al., 2011). As part of our intercalated BSc programme[7] we offer students a 10 week ethics module which focuses on death and the dead body. For this teaching we have developed some collaborative teaching sessions with our colleagues in medical humanities.[8] These include film viewing sessions exploring death, the dead body, grief and dying (*Departures* (Takita, 2009) and *Dark Victory* (Goulding, 1939)) and a guided tour of the National Gallery in London focusing on representations of the dead body in art. We also developed an innovative teaching initiative: in response to the retained organ controversy (Kennedy, 2001; Redfern, 2001), students from the ethics and medical humanities BSc modules were assigned to mixed groups and invited to draw on preparatory teaching from their respective courses, on topics like 'the body as property' (Campbell, 2009) and 'the medical gaze' (Foucault, 2003), to produce a creative response to the testimonies given by parents and doctors to the Kennedy (Kennedy, 2001) and Redfern Inquiries (Redfern, 2001).

The resulting presentations were reflexive, imaginative and ethically sensitive. Students have used a range of expressive modes including theatre, video, art and poetry in their responses. One group produced a series of haiku (Davies, 2012):

> *Heart, valves and organs*
> *A free-for-all, pick-and-mix,*
> *These are my children*
>
> *Standard procedure*
> *As hollow an excuse as*
> *'following orders'*

Subsequently one student has reflected that 'Through the reflections of the parents' statements [she] felt [she] was better equipped to understand and empathise with family members' when faced with parental distress on her paediatric placement and that, by working with humanities students, she was able to appreciate 'the emotional effects and how these can inspire creative responses'.

There is therefore evidence to suggest that humanities teaching has the potential to preserve empathy, promote reflection and respond to emotional distress in a way that does not require emotional hardening. This teaching may help students in their understanding of self and others and their development of moral identity. It is however disappointing that, while there is growing evidence demonstrating the value of medical humanities in medical education (Rosenthal et al., 2011), there is no reference to medical humanities in the latest edition of the GMC's *Tomorrow's Doctors* (GMC, 2009).

13.6 Conclusion

In this chapter, I have reflected on the challenges and opportunities when medical ethics moves into clinical classrooms. With its normative basis and requirement for logical consistency and reasoned argument, medical ethics forms a natural bridge between the science and the art of medicine. The opportunity to educate doctors rather than philosophers puts medical ethics in action where it can challenge practitioners and be itself challenged. Greater engagement of students and doctors widens the academic community, facilitates the translation of theory into practice and increases the practical relevance of medical ethics.

The clinical community provides a major and largely untapped teaching resource for medical ethics. Engaging clinicians as educators promotes vertical and horizontal education and encourages clinicians to embed medical ethics into everyday clinical discourse. This engagement requires support and resources from ethics leads and their academic institutions if it is to be successful. Judicious use of newer teaching technologies can enhance learning opportunities. Virtual learning objects provide versatile and accessible learning resources for teachers and students. Interactive teaching tools such as clickers can facilitate reflection and discussion in large lecture based teaching. Summative assessment is a major driver of learning. Well-designed assessments can help ensure that students prioritise ethics learning and the acquisition of specific skills and behaviours. Making small group sessions compulsory and emphasising the importance of feedback in teaching and formative assessment can help students understand ethics learning as an ongoing process of development.

Whether teaching can or should be trying to make good doctors in a moral sense is a subject for debate. I have argued that practical wisdom and justice are virtues of particular relevance to medicine. Nurturing these virtues should fall within the remit of ethics education even if it does not lend itself to a competency-based model of medical education. There are grounds for optimism that greater use of the humanities in medical education and an increasing focus on reflection and discourse can help students and doctors develop their moral identity, a key component of nurturing the good doctor.

Notes

1 The order of these aims has been changed for the purpose of the discussion in this chapter.
2 The Research Excellence Framework assessment was introduced by the Higher Education Funding Council in England as a method for assessing the research of British higher education institutions and a means of distributing funding to these institutions based on research excellence.
3 An NHS Trust is an organisation within the National Health Service (NHS) which provides healthcare services. For the purposes of medical education these will be acute hospitals (Acute Trusts).

4 A BSc is a Bachelor of Science degree and is usually obtained from a 3-year undergraduate degree course. Within most UK medical schools students can intercalate by completing an additional 1-year course separate from their medical course. Successful completion of the 1-year intercalated programme in addition to their first 2 undergraduate years qualifies the student for a BSc in addition to their medical degree.
5 Significant events are events or encounters that had a significant emotional impact on the individual. The impact may be positive or negative. Significant event analyses are a well-established learning and reflection method in postgraduate training.
6 In the UK, after qualifying from medical school doctors must successfully complete a Foundation Year to become fully registered medical doctors.
7 See note 4.
8 As part of their intercalated BSc programme students can undertake a 10 week medical humanities course in which students explore and examine the relationship between art, literature, film and poetry and medical practice.

References

Aristotle. (2009). *The Nicomachean Ethics*. (W. D. Ross, Trans.) New York: Oxford University Press.
Benbassat, J. (2012). Undesirable features of the medical learning environment: a narrative review of the literature. *Advances in Health Sciences Education* 18(3), doi: 10.1007/s10459-012-9389-5.
Brennan, N., Corrigan, O., Allard, J., Archer, J., Barnes, R., Bleakley, A., Collett, T. and de Bere, S. R. (2010). The transition from medical student to junior doctor: today's experiences of Tomorrow's Doctors. *Medical Education* 44(5): 449–458.
Bryan, C. S., and Babelay, A. M. (2009, September). Building character: a model for reflective practice. *Academic Medicine* 89: 1283–1288.
Campbell, A. V. (2009). *The Body in Bioethics*. Abingdon, Oxon: Routledge.
Campbell, A., Chin, J., and Voo, T. (2007). How can we know that ethics education produces ethical doctors? *Medical Teacher* 29(5): 431–436.
Carrese, J., McDonald, E. L., Moon, M., Taylor, H., Khaira, K., Catherine Beach, M., and Hughes, M. (2011). Everyday ethics in internal medicine resident clinic: an opportunity to teach. *Medical Education* 45(7): 712–721.
Clack, G., Bevan, G., and Eddleston, A. (2002). Service increment for teaching (SIFT): a review of its origins, development and current role in supporting undergraduate medical education in England and Wales. *Medical Education* 33(5): 350–358.
Claudot, F., Alla, F., Xavier, D., and Coudane, H. (2007). Teaching ethics in Europe. *Journal of Medical Ethics* 33: 491–495.
Consensus statement by teachers of medical law and ethics in UK medical schools. (1998). Teaching medical ethics and law within UK medical education: a model for the UK core curriculum. *Journal of Medical Ethics* 24: 188–192.
Coulehan, J., and Williams, P. (2001). Vanquishing virtue: the impact of medical education. *Academic Medicine* 76(6): 598–605.
Davies, R. (2012, April). *Haiku in Response to the Retained Organ Controversy*. Imperial College, London.
Eckles, R. E., Meslin, E. M., Gaffney, M., and Helft, P. R. (2005). Medical ethics education: Where are we? Where should we be going? A review. *Academic Medicine* 80(12): 1143–1152.
FeldmanHall, O., Mobbs, D., Evans, D., Hiscox, L., and Navrady, L. (2012). What we say and what we do: the relationship between real and hypothetical moral choices. *Cognition* 123(3): 434–441.
Fenwick, A., Johnston, C., Knight, R., Testa, G., and Tillyard, A. (2012). *Medical Ethics and Law: A Practical Guide to the Assessment of the Core Content of Learning*. Merseyside: Institute of Medical Ethics.
Feudtner, G., Christakis, D., and Christakis, N. (1994). Do clinical clerks suffer ethical erosion? *Academic Medicine* 69(8): 670–679.

Finlay, S. E., and Fawzy, M. (2001). Becoming a doctor. *Medical Humanitites* 27(2): 90–92.
Foucault, M. (2003). *The Birth of the Clinic*. Abingdon, Oxon: Routledge.
Francis, R. (2013). *Report of the Mid Staffordshire NHS Foundation Trust Public Inquiry*. London: The Stationery Office.
General Medical Council (GMC). (1993). *Tomorrow's Doctors*. London: GMC.
––––––– (2009). *Tomorrow's Doctors*. London: GMC.
Goldie, J. (2000). Review of ethics curricula in undergraduate medical education. *Academic Medicine* 38: 108–119.
Goulding, E. (Director). (1939). *Dark Victory* [Motion Picture].
Hafferty, F. (1998). Beyond curriculum reform: confronting medicine's hidden curriculum. *Academic Medicine* 73(4): 403–407.
Hafferty, F. W., and Franks, R. (1994, November). The hidden curriculum, ethics teaching and the structure of medical education. *Academic Medicine* 69: 861–871.
Hojat, M., Vergare, M., Maxwell, K., Brainard, G., Herrine, S., Isenberg, G., et al. (2009). The devil is in the third year: a longitudinal study of erosion of empathy in medical school. *Academic Medicine* 84(9): 1182–1191.
Ipsos MORI. (2013, February 15). *Ipsos MORI Trust Poll*. Retrieved 9 May 2014, from Ipsos MORI: http://www.ipsos-mori.com/Assets/Docs/Polls/Feb2013_Trust_Topline.PDF
Kennedy, I. (2001, July 18). *The report of the public inquiry into children's heart surgery at the Bristol Royal Infirmary 1984–1995: learning from Bristol*. Retrieved 27 May 2014, from National Archives: http://webarchive.nationalarchives.gov.uk/20130107105354/http://www.dh.gov.uk/en/Publicationsandstatistics/Publications/PublicationsPolicyAndGuidance/DH_4002859
Keogh, B. (2013). *Review into the Quality of Care and Treatment Provided by 14 Hospital Trusts in England: Overview Report*. London: Department of Health.
Kong, W. M., Boyd, K., Gillon, R., Farsides, B., and Stirrat, G. (2011). Include medical ethics in the research excellence framework. *British Medical Journal* 343: d3968. doi: 10.1136/bmj.d3968
Kong, W. M., and Vernon, B. (2013). Harnessing the LMG legacy: the IME's vision for the future. *Journal of Medical Ethics* 39(11): 669–671.
Kumagi, A. K. (2014). From competencies to human interests:ways of knowing and understanding in medical education. *Academic Medicine* 89(7): 978–983.
Mattick, K., and Bligh, J. (2006). Undergraduate ethics teaching: revisiting the consensus statement. *Medical Education* 40: 329–332.
McDougall, R. (2008). Combating junior doctors' '4am logic': a challenge for medical ethics education. *Journal of Medical Ethics* 35(3): 203–206.
Parker, L., Watts, L., and Scicluna, H. (2012). Clinical ethics ward rounds: building on the core curriculum. *Journal of Medical Ethics* 38(8): 501–505.
Preston-Shoot, M., and McKimm, J. (2010). Prepared for practice? Law teaching and assessment in UK medical schools. *Journal of Medical Ethics* 36(11): 694–699.
Preston-Shoot, M., McKimm, J., Kong, W., and Smith, S. (2011). Readiness for legally literate medical practice? Student perceptions of their medico-legal undergraduate education. *Journal of Medical Ethics* 37(10): 616–622.
Redfern, M. (2001). *The Royal Liverpool Children's Inquiry: Report*. Norwich: The Stationery Office.
Rennie, S., and Crosby, J. (2002). Students' perceptions of whistle-blowing: implications for self regulation. A questionnaire and focus group survey. *Medical Education* 36(2): 176–179.
Rogers, W., and Ballantyne, A. (2012). Towards a practical definition of professional behaviour. *Journal of Medical Ethics* 36(4): 250–254.

Rosenthal, S., Howard, B., Schlussel, Y., Herrigel, D., Smolarz, B., Gable, B., et al. (2011). Humanism at heart: preserving empathy in third-year medical students. *Academic Medicine* 86(3): 350–358.

Schildmann, J., Cushing, A., Doyal, L., and Vollmann, J. (2005). Informed consent in clinical practice: pre-registration house officers' knowledge, difficulties and the need for postgraduate training. *Medical Teacher* 27(7): 649–651.

Sheehan, T., Husted, S., Candee, D., Cook, C., and Bargen, M. (1980). Moral judgement as a predictor of clinical performance. *Evaluation and the Health Professional* 3: 394–404.

Smee, S. (2003). Skills based assessment. *British Medical Journal* 326: 703–706.

Souba, W., Way, D., Lucey, C., Sedmark, D., and Notestine, M. (2011). Elephants in academic medicine. *Academic Medicine* 86(12): 1492–1499.

Stirrat, G., Johnston, C., Gillon, R., and Boyd, K. (2010). Medical ethics and law for doctors of tomorrow: the 1998 Consensus Statement updated. *Journal of Medical Ethics* 36(1): 55–60.

Sturman, N., Rego, P., and Dick, L. (2011). Rewards, costs and challenges: the general practitioner's experience of teaching medical students. *Medical Education* 45(7): 722–730.

Takita, Y. (Director). (2009). *Departures* [Motion Picture].

Talbot, M. (2004). Monkey see, Monkey Do: a critique of the Competency Model in graduate medical education. *Medical Education* 38: 587–592.

Walzer, M. (1983). *Spheres of Justice*. Oxford: Martin Robertson and Company Ltd.

World Medical Association (WMA) (1999, October) *WMA Resolution on the Inclusion of Medical Ethics and Human Rights in the Curriculum of Medical Schools World-Wide*. Retrieved 9 May 2014, from World Medical Association: http://www.wma.net/en/30publications/10policies/e8

14 Teaching medical students: more room for an ethical 'differential analysis', please?

Rouven Porz and Andreas E. Stuck

> [The newly learned] 'ethics tools' make it clear that the medical profession is not a power game and that I will not necessarily be able to impose what I have learnt or what I consider right. Everyone has different moral values, which may not coincide with mine.
>
> (Medical student, Jenny Amsler, in her Ethics Essay, Bern 2012)

The annual European Association of Centres of Medical Ethics (EACME) Conference in 2006 was held in Leuven, Belgium, with the theme and title *New Pathways for European Bioethics*. Contributions to the conference were collected in a book, and the editors proposed four thematic areas as having key roles in the future of European bioethics (Gastmans et al., 2007: 1). First, the relatively new relationship of the discipline of bioethics to the social sciences, a meeting point which had become known conceptually as 'empirical ethics'. Second, the relationship of bioethics to law and politics. Third, bioethical reflection on new technologies; and, finally – the area that plays an important role in his chapter – the approach of care ethics, which can be viewed as a correcting or supplementary element to the often dominant four principles approach postulated by Tom Beauchamp and James Childress (Nortvedt, 2007; Vanlaere and Gastmans, 2007; Verkerk, 2007; Beauchamp and Childress, 2008).

This chapter concerns care ethics in the context of academic teaching, where we believe that care ethics must be given more room. This applies not just to care ethics, but also to virtue ethics, hermeneutical, and other ethical approaches that are frequently linked to one another, and differentiated from, or used to supplement, the four principles approach. In our own teaching we use the different approaches as different tools with which to analyse difficult clinical or everyday situations. We deliberately speak of ethical 'tools' or ethical 'instruments'. In our teaching in Bern, Switzerland, we also like to use the metaphor of different 'lenses' or 'glasses'. You see a different world depending on the glasses you wear. With the ethical 'glasses' of the four principles approach, a pregnant woman who wishes to abort her child may be seen only as an autonomous woman whose decision must simply be respected. With the 'glasses' of care ethics, one might also see a vulnerable young woman who is caught up in power relationships, whose personal environment does not allow her to take on responsibility for a baby, and so forth. The use of such different lenses leads, in our view, to an important learning goal of medical ethics: a change of perspective. Our students should be in a position not just to develop their own moral perspective, but also to be able to empathise with other perspectives. This is clear from the opening quotation, for example, which was written by the Bern medical student Jenny Amsler, after she had attended the ethics seminars: 'Everyone has different moral values, which may not coincide with mine.' This sounds simple, but as a realisation it is anything but trivial. If she then recognises her 'power' as a doctor, and states that her future profession should not be a 'power game', this is a reflection on power relationships that indicates we have reached the core topic of feminist care ethics. From a lecturer's point of view, such reflection is important, particularly to transmit to our students that their future professional role must not consist solely of knowledge and methods, but also of a certain professional attitude.

The students we refer to here are studying human medicine in the Medical Faculty in Bern, Switzerland. Andreas E. Stuck, professor of and consultant in geriatrics in Bern, the second author of this text, is responsible for embedding ethical content in the teaching of human medicine. The first author, Rouven Porz, who was trained as a high school teacher, teaches the medical students how to wear the different 'glasses'.

We understand our contribution here in the following terms: we not only want to talk *about* our teaching and our students, we also want *to give voice* to some of the students and *open up* the doors of our academic classrooms to the reader. To do this, we refer to the 2011–2012 academic year, and particularly to the 'ethics essays' written by the medical students in 2012, the theme of which was to address one's own moral uncertainties with elderly patients. The aim of putting this into words was, first, to challenge the students to trace their own moral intuitions; and, second, to interpret these intuitions from the viewpoint of the different ethical tools or glasses. It is not a matter of developing possible solutions or making decisions. In the first section, we show how the educational focus lay in the guided reflection on one's own unease in a geriatric environment. In the second section, we select two of these essays to illustrate two moral intuitions and the students' interpretations of them. These examples are not intended as a way of 'evaluating' the students' intuitions and interpretations ethically. They should rather serve as a basis for the reader to be able to consider whether it is worth enlivening the academic room of bioethics with different ethical theories.

In the final section, we attempt to place our teaching in a European perspective. If there is anything resembling a 'European' perspective, then in our view this has most to do with the value placed on different ethical approaches in bioethics. Put provocatively: the representatives of the four principles approach do not have a greater claim to power in the interpretation of medically difficult situations than the representatives of other theories. A European bioethics could be characterised as one which accords the same weight to different ethical approaches in bioethics. We want therefore to plead for a European bioethics that deliberately gives voice to, and creates rooms for, differing professional theories and knowledge. Of course, this goal is more about creating and shaping 'moral attitudes' among bioethicists and health care professionals than about applying ethical knowledge or ethical methods.

14.1 Essays in ethics: using theories as tools

The ethics essays in the 2011–2012 academic year to which we refer here are a didactic development of the essays set in previous years. Up to 2011, the essays used an objective ethical question as a starting point. However, when evaluated from a pedagogical point of view, it was clear that ethical amateurs (medical students) found it almost impossible to formulate a precise 'ethical' question without prior knowledge (Porz, 2013). The new essays thus pursued a two-stage learning goal. One was to get the approximately 160 students to articulate their own moral uncertainty about a situation they had experienced as part of one of their clinical rotations. (We talk about the fifth-year medical students here, of a total of six years of study. Those fifth-year medical students are thus at the end of their university studies and are assigned to six one-month clinical rotations in internal medicine, gynaecology and obstetrics, paediatrics, surgery, primary care, and psychiatry.) For this, they were instructed to identify, in one of their placements, a situation involving an elderly patient that they found personally challenging and in which they had a bad 'gut feeling', and to write it up as follows: a brief description of the situation; a note about why they felt it to be special; and a list of the principal questions within it that preoccupied them. This presentation of their 'gut feeling' was then supposed to be followed by a more objective ethical interpretation of their unease, in particular when viewed through the different pairs of 'lenses' (Sherwin, 1999).

The preceding lecture therefore (briefly) taught the students four ethical approaches. The first pair of glasses/tools taught the students to understand their future professional role in difficult situations from the viewpoint of the four principles approach (Schöne Seifert, 2005; Beauchamp and Childress, 2008), for example, through questions such as: In this situation, did I respect the patient's capacity for autonomy? Did I seek to promote the patient's welfare? Was I able to prevent further harm? Did I behave justly? The second pair of glasses taught the students to analyse the situation from a feminist approach to care ethics, with a conceptual focus on relational autonomy, context, dependencies, responsibilities, vulnerability, power relationships (Tong, 1997; Feder-Kittay, 2005; Scully, 2005; Walker, 2007). These concepts were then additionally simplified and 'translated' into questions the medical students could use, such as: What is the particular context of this situation?

In what relationship do the actors stand to one another? Who is dependent on whom? Which voice is heard the least? Who carries the moral responsibility? What is the worst thing that can happen? The third pair of glasses introduced an explicitly hermeneutically oriented perspective, inspired by the hermeneutics of Hans-Georg Gadamer (1960). Hermeneutics is the art of interpretation. A hermeneutical approach to clinical ethics calls for an understanding of human beings and how they make meaning of the situations they encounter, acknowledges that this understanding is mediated by language, words and concepts, and fosters the articulation of the experiences of those who are affected, all of which results in a merging of perspectives (Porz and Widdershoven, 2010). The basic idea of this pair of glasses can be expressed in questions such as: How does the patient perceive this situation? Can I think myself into this perspective? Am I able to fuse this new perspective with my own? The fourth and final pair of glasses introduced the students to a virtue ethics approach to one's own action in the situation, for example: Was I clever, courageous, considerate (Aristotle, 2006)? Did I behave with integrity, conscientious empathy, etc. (Beauchamp and Childress, 2008: 30ff)?

Although this was not pursued further, the medical students were also briefly told that care ethics is understood by some authors as a form of virtue ethics, and that narrative and hermeneutic elements are also characteristic concepts in most care ethical approaches (Feder-Kittay, 2005). In addition to the lecture, the students received a text summarising the content and background of the four different pairs of 'glasses' (Porz and Stuck, 2013).

For the present text, we provide two essays as examples. The opening description of the bad 'gut feeling' in each case is extensive (both patients and doctors are anonymised, and the students gave explicit permission for the use of their work in this context). We then use quotations from these essays to present the students' application of the ethics tools in a comprehensible way. Methodologically speaking, our procedure does not have an objective or representational goal. On the contrary, we aim to give the individual student a chance to speak. We are, of course, aware that it is we who are writing here, not the two students, and so this procedure always contains the methodological risk (and the – maybe – unbalanced power-relationship) that our own interpretations will overshadow those of the students.

14.2 Giving voice to our students: emergency paternalism and the driving licence

The first description is of a situation in the Accident and Emergency Department (A&E) of a hospital where the medical student was doing an internship. The second relates to a student's placement in a GP's practice. We first present the two case descriptions by the two students, then provide a few quotations from their essays to show which 'glasses' the two students used to reflect on these situations. Finally, we make our own comments on their essay stories.

14.2.1 Emergency paternalism

> A 76-year-old patient presented early in the morning to A&E complaining of severe pain in his left foot, which he had had since a long walk on the previous day... The junior doctor responsible discussed the case with the consultant, who remarked that the X-ray showed no pathological findings except for arthritis. The consultant examined the patient again and recommended conservative treatment, with analgesia and resting the foot. The patient however insisted on further imaging diagnostics, as he had never before felt such severe pain. The consultant explained to him that this was unnecessary, but that if his pain continued, he should return to the foot pain clinic...
>
> In a subsequent discussion with the junior doctor, the consultant said that the vague description of the pain was typical of a psychiatric diagnosis. From her experience, she immediately recognised patients who were just seeking attention, and she believed a further scan would have simply been a waste of money.
>
> What makes this situation so special for me? The senior doctor bases her decision on her intuition and dismisses the patient's pain as psychosomatic... What specifically preoccupies me as a student? Rushed decisions can mean important details are missed. In this context I ask myself how far even an older and experienced doctor can rely on their own intuition. If a patient explicitly asks for a scan, are we allowed to refuse it on the basis of our assessment of his mental health?
>
> (Medical student, description of situation, Ethics Essay, Bern 2012)

From this description of the situation, and the questions the student poses, it is clear that the professional manner of the consultant causes her some discomfort. Of course, at this point we do not have the voice of the consultant herself. Did things really happen the way the student described them? What would the consultant say about it? But we are not concerned here with discovering the 'truth', or even with the medical question of how the 76-year-old could best have been helped. We are more interested in the pedagogical learning goal of giving the student the possibility, through writing this essay, of being able to reflect from an ethical point of view. First she tries using the four principles:

> From the point of view of the four principles, respect for the patient's autonomy in the sense of self-determination was not observed. The patient was refused a further investigation that he had explicitly asked for.

Then she approaches the situation by examining the virtues of the consultant. Here she sees that the 'virtue of empathy' was injured:

> In relation to the basic virtues of a physician, it is not the doctor's discernment that I question, but the virtue of empathy... Stating a possible

psychological component as the only reason [for the foot pain] is in my eyes not empathy but a premature decision.

The student continues using the glasses of care ethics:

> The glasses of care ethics provide a better explanation of the relationships: in my view, a situation develops in which the patient is completely dependent on the doctor's decisions . . . Believing that she knows more about the patient's condition than he does himself, she sets herself a couple of steps higher than the rest of the actors.

Then the student attempts to place herself in relation to the situation she has experienced. Retrospectively, she empathises with the patient, considering – perhaps even a little ironically – whether she should have stepped out of her role as a student who 'doesn't yet know everything' and convinced her consultant to think through other possible differential diagnoses:

> As a student, I did not take on more than the role of bystander in this scenario. Real intervention in the situation would also have been inappropriate. Nevertheless I could have scrutinised the consultant's decisions. For example, as the student who doesn't yet know everything often gets a brief explanation of the procedure, I could have taken on the role of the patient's mouthpiece and asked questions in his presence about tentative diagnoses.

For a hermeneutic change of perspective, she writes further about her role as bystander:

> The position from which one observes a scenario like this is also important; as an active participant my view might have been quite different from that of a passive bystander.

From our viewpoint as lecturers, we have found that it is worth presenting different ethical concepts as different glasses. Medical students in particular are used to thinking in terms of different differential diagnoses. How else could they classify the symptoms of a potential disease? And which other disease could it be? Throughout their studies they are trained in this mode of critical and wide-ranging thinking. Why should they then have to assume only one intellectual approach in ethics? Why use only the four principles in the teaching of medical ethics? Medical students in particular should find it easy to learn different and sometimes mutually exclusive approaches to ethical diagnosis. Our pedagogic view is confirmed by the student herself. She concludes in her essay:

> The different ethical tools helped me in each case to split the situation up into its constituent parts and thus place them under scrutiny. The tool

of change of perspective in particular unfolds the different aspects and views brought by the various actors, and this precisely is what helps us to recognise why an ethically difficult situation arose in the first place.

In addition to these points we offer the following thoughts on the student's presentation from our point of view as lecturers. The student's essay starts with an ethical unease, but goes on to show that in a case like this there are also overlapping legal and medical questions to answer. From a legal point of view, a patient does not have the right to get an investigation from a doctor if this investigation is not indicated medically. On the other hand, a doctor would commit a serious error refusing to prescribe a medically necessary investigation. In our case this background generates a precise medical question: How did the consultant ascertain that a further investigation of the foot was *not* indicated? From a medical perspective, the case description does not give sufficient details to answer whether the consultant's decision not to conduct further imaging diagnostics was medically correct or not. Thus, one key learning objective of this ethics essay is to teach this medical student to understand the legal context and to formulate a precise medical question. In this situation, the student should have insisted on getting a satisfactory medical answer from the consultant on why she concluded that further imaging of the foot was not indicated. We are not, of course, concerned primarily with answering this question, but we want to indicate that the ethically oriented essays also throw up new perspectives for the students in legal and medical terms. In addition, there are also challenging power relationships at play here. It is far from easy for a medical student to question a decision or a treatment plan of a senior physician. As such, learning how to adequately (and, if necessary, persistently) address a relevant question to a senior colleague was an important additional learning objective of the teaching module. This objective was a central component of an additional subsequent ethics seminar, in which we discussed the students' experiences with the cases in groups of approximately 25 students.

14.2.2 The driving licence

The following description relates to a student's placement in a general practitioner's (GP) practice:

> An 81-year-old woman came to her GP's practice. I was on a student placement with the GP. The question was whether the woman could keep her driving licence. She is retired . . . and lives alone on an isolated farm . . . (To be able to reach her nearest shop, which was a long way away, she depended on her car.) Six months previously she had had an accident . . . She had recovered well and was soon able to return home. A short time after she was hospitalised again: she had caused a minor car

accident and her confusion had attracted attention... As a consequence, she was not allowed to drive for 3 months, because of an increased risk of epileptic fits.

At the GP's practice it was a case of deciding whether she could now drive a car again. The medical test results were borderline; there were certainly some reasons for the GP to ensure that her driving licence was not renewed. Finally the GP came to the conclusion that the old woman should be allowed to continue driving.

What makes this situation so special for me? The doctor is making a decision here that is not only about the medical situation, but also about the woman's private and social life . . . What specifically preoccupies me? . . . How far may a doctor intervene in a patient's private life? . . . And is the GP the right person here to make this decision?

(Medical student, description of situation, Ethics Essay, Bern 2012)

From the viewpoint of the four principles, the student sees her experience in the GP's practice as a conflict between respect for patient autonomy and non-maleficence. On this second principle, she says:

[It's about] avoiding harm. It's central to this case: if the patient continues to drive, even though this might not be medically recommended, there is a risk that she may injure herself, her passengers or others. Handing in her driving licence early could contribute here to non-maleficence.

She also recognises that respect for patient autonomy cannot mean that the doctor simply accepts the patient's wishes. The patient wants to go on driving. This appears clear. But the doctor also has a legal obligation:

In the case described, the doctor is legally obliged to decide, independently, whether the patient should be given the permission to drive again. The patient has little control over this. Here, *respect* for autonomy can be maintained in the decision but not *autonomy itself* (the decision is transparent to the patient, but is not negotiable).

The student here obviously acknowledges that legal rules are not 'negotiable'. In this context, the GP is obliged to act according to the juridical rules of his country. The patient would have to accept a negative decision: the legal obligation trumps the personal autonomy of the patient. However, the student noted that the doctor in the situation she experienced did nevertheless decide in favour of the old woman's wish to carry on driving. She reflects:

From a purely principlist point of view, one could imagine that the doctor is abdicating the responsibility he actually has in making this decision.

In her essay, she then switches to the glasses of care ethics:

> The principlist point of view may place too little value on the relationship and mutual influence of the actors . . . This is a longstanding doctor-patient relationship . . . Here, the GP may not necessarily be the right person to make this decision. He knows the patient and her social situation too well to be able to decide purely based on facts . . . The decision should be a relatively objective one for all road users: those who fulfil the criteria are allowed to drive.

From the point of view of care ethics arises the possibility that the GP may not be the right person in this context to make a decision about fitness to drive; instead, perhaps a neutral individual should make this decision. The student justifies her reasoning:

> In making this decision, the doctor carries a great moral responsibility . . . It is possible that in this situation the doctor tends to think too much about the patient and not enough about other road users.

The student thus appears to disagree with the GP's decision. She was surprised that the old woman will be allowed to continue to drive – in any case, she felt enough unease about the whole situation that she decided to write her ethics essay on it. Nevertheless, she attempts to place herself into the perspective of the GP:

> But in the end it is the patient who is sitting at the doctor's desk and not all other road users – therefore it is understandable that the focus of attention is on her.

Finally, donning the glasses of hermeneutics, the student attempts to present the symbolic value of driving in the life of the elderly woman. She understands driving to have an 'emotional' significance:

> The huge emphasis on the car is understandable in the context of the patient's situation. Because she lives in the country, without a car . . . shopping and outings would no longer be possible. It is understandable that the car not only has a material significance for the patient, but also an emotional one.

Of course it is intellectually tempting in this case to decide what would be right and what would be wrong here. Did the doctor make the right decision? How could he have made a better decision? But it is precisely this hasty move – which most of us tend to make intuitively in daily clinical life – that we wanted to avoid through the didactic construction of the ethics essays. The students were supposed to express their moral unease, classify it from the viewpoint of the different glasses – but then stop. This slowing down of the ethical analysis was a further important learning goal for the ethics essays. And, as mentioned before, some weeks after the completion of all the essays, the students had the opportunity to think through their individual cases in a guided way in small seminar groups. The discussion of this essay showed, for example, that analysing this case required hardly any actual knowledge of ethics, but primarily the recognition of the doctor's conflict of interest: in this case it is particularly important to know, from a purely medical point of view, on what grounds a doctor can reliably determine whether a patient is fit to drive or not. And it is important to know whether I, as a doctor, can make this decision for a patient with whom I already have a longstanding relationship (and therefore there may be a potential conflict of interest). This essay thus opens up questions of medical *professionalism* rather than purely ethical knowledge. Looking at their own future profession through different lenses, and thus internalising different (and often differing) perspectives might also help students to reflect upon the professionalism of their role to come. Furthermore, in evaluating the essays we have often encountered that what appears to be an *ethical* issue at first sight (from the students' perspective) is often based on an uncertainty in specialist *medical* or *juridical* knowledge. Nevertheless – or perhaps precisely because of this – we are convinced that our differentiated approach to teaching students about ethics tools makes it easier for the students to stop viewing such cases as just black-and-white issues, or even staying fixed on their own moral opinion. The differentiated change of perspective can help in determining whether their moral unease really does highlight a genuine ethical problem, or whether more medical or legal expertise could help. Our teaching therefore always starts from the assumption that ethics, law and medicine must supplement or complement each other in a triangular relationship.

14.3 Teaching counts in shaping moral attitudes

Bioethics could be said to have developed over the last 25–30 years into an independent academic discipline. To be able to work in bioethics, one must follow the rules of the academic world: publishing, acquiring research funding, obtaining research findings and publishing again. Such is the life-cycle of the academic. Unfortunately, within academia, teaching is rarely given the same emphasis. This applies to most disciplines, including bioethics and medical ethics. This is particularly the case for the teaching of medical students, nursing staff and other health care professionals, rather than more advanced training in bioethics itself. There are now several different Master's programmes providing training in bioethics or clinical ethics in Europe, the most well-known of which is the Erasmus Mundus Master of Bioethics, run by the Universities of Leuven, Padua and Nijmegen, and organised by Paul Schotsmans and Pascal Borry (EMMB, 2013).

There are, however, very few possibilities for bioethicists to exchange information about their own academic teaching. One recent innovation is the International Association for Ethics Education (IAEE, 2012), which was initiated by Henk ten Have. In 2012, an international conference was held in

Pittsburgh, USA, focusing for the first time on the teaching of bioethics and medical ethics. In this chapter we have tried to show that academic teaching in bioethics can be an exciting challenge, particularly if students are given an opportunity to learn about different ethical theories. To illustrate this we have used our teaching in the Medical Faculty in Bern. In concluding, we would like briefly to address three topics: first, our criticism of the four principles; secondly, the narrative context of our ethics essays; and, finally, the European perspective of our contribution.

First, at various points in our text we have emphasised that we find the four principles approach to be too dominant in biomedical teaching. We do not see the four principles approach problematic in itself, at least not as presented by Beauchamp and Childress, who point out very clearly that knowledge of different theories is required (2008: 333ff), including an understanding of care ethics (2008: 36ff) and a knowledge of the moral virtues that determine the attitude of health care professionals (2008: 38ff). However, it appears to us that this background knowledge to which Beauchamp and Childress refer is rarely treated in any depth, so that effectively only the four principles – lacking context and theoretical superstructure – remain. In this respect our demand for more thorough and wide-ranging teaching of ethics relates not to a criticism of principlism, but rather to our (perhaps provocative) suspicion that many lecturers who teach the four principles have themselves never actually read Beauchamp and Childress.

Secondly, the didactical focus of our ethics essays should make it clear that we emphasise the narrative element of these essays in two ways. First, we expressly asked the students to write their essay in a narrative form. Second, the primary use of their narratives provides us with illustrations of our teaching. In recent years, narrative has received increasing attention in biomedical ethics. Sometimes we even speak of 'narrative ethics' (Widdershoven, 1996; Porz, 2008), understood as an approach that gives particular attention to the value systems and norms of personal stories. For the present context – ethics teaching for medical students in relation to elderly patients – this therefore means we need to pay more attention to the students' stories. Considering the two ethics essays above from this angle, the narratives highlight situations in which future doctors are brought into a relationship with patients and their relatives. Even more importantly, the narratives also show how these future doctors retrospectively put such moments of relationship into words, what appears to them to be ethically important in the situations and what they view as questionable (cf. Porz and Stuck, 2013).

Finally, a European bioethics could aim to accord the same weight to different ethical approaches in bioethics. Of course, this goal is more about creating and shaping 'moral attitudes' among bioethicists and health care professionals than only applying ethical knowledge or ethical methods. However, from our point of view we would like, therefore, to plead for a bioethics that deliberately gives voice to, and creates rooms for, a more nuanced and differential ethics case analysis, using a wider range of 'lenses' and 'glasses'.

References

Aristotle. (2006) *Nikomachische Ethik*, Stuttgart: Reclam.
Beauchamp, T. and Childress, J. (2008) *Principles of Biomedical Ethics*, 6th Edition, Oxford: Oxford University Press.
EMMB (2013) 'Contact', https://med.kuleuven.be/eng/erasmus-mundus-bioethics/contact (acc. 14 Oct 2013).
Feder-Kittay, E. (2005) 'The concept of care ethics in biomedicine', in Christoph Rehmann-Sutter et al. (eds) *Bioethics in Cultural Contexts*, Dordrecht: Springer, 319–340.
Gastmans, C., Dierickx, K., Nys, H. and Schotsmans, P. (eds) (2007) *New Pathways for European Bioethics*, Antwerpen: Intersentia.
Gadamer, H.-G. (1960) *Wahrheit und Methode*, Tübingen: Mohr.
IAEE (2012) 'International Association for Education in Ethics'. Available HTTP: http://www.duq.edu/academics/schools/liberal-arts/centers/center-for-healthcare-ethics/international-association-for-education-in-ethics (acc. 02 May 2014).
Nortvedt, P. (2007) 'Care sensivity and the "moral point of view"', in C. Gastmans et al. (eds) *New Pathways for European Bioethics*, Antwerpen: Intersentia, 81–98.
Porz, R. (2008) *Zwischen Entscheidung und Entfremdung*, Paderborn: Mentis.
—— (2013) 'Zur Wahrnehmung von Recht und Ethik bei Medizin-Studierenden', *Schweizerische Ärztezeitung*, 94(11): 441–442.
Porz, R. and Stuck, A. (2013) 'Zur impliziten Normativität im Denken von Medizinstudiereden – am Beispiel Würde', in T. Meireis (ed.) *Altern in Würde. Das Konzept der Würde im vierten Lebensalter*, Zurich: Theologischer Verlag Zürich, 123–136.
Porz, R. and Widdershoven, G. (2010) 'Verstehen und Dialog als Ausgangspunkt einer praktischen Ethik', *Bioethica Forum*, 3(1), 8–12.
Schöne-Seifert, B. (2005) 'Danger and merits of principlism: meta-theoretical reflections on the Beauchamp/Childress-approach to biomedical ethics', in C. Rehmann-Sutter, M. Düwell and D. Mieth (eds) (2006) *Bioethics in Cultural Contexts*, Dordrecht: Springer, 109–120.
Scully, J.L. (2005) 'Disability embodiment and an ethics of care' in C. Rehmann-Sutter, M. Düwell and D. Mieth (eds) *Bioethics in Cultural Contexts*, Dordrecht: Springer, 247–261.
Sherwin, S. (1999) 'Foundations, frameworks, lenses: the role of theories in bioethics', *Bioethics*, 13(3/4), 199–205.
Tong, R. (1997) *Feminist Approaches to Bioethics*, Boulder, CO: Westview Press.
Vanlaere L. and Gastmans, C. (2007) 'A normative approach to care ethics', in C. Gastmans et al. (eds) *New Pathways for European Bioethics*, Antwerpen: Intersentia, 99–120.
Verkerk, M. (2007) 'Care ethics as feminist perspectives on bioethics', in C. Gastmans et al. (eds) *New Pathways for European Bioethics*, Antwerpen: Intersentia, 65–80.
Walker, M.U. (2007) *Moral Understandings: A Feminist Study in Ethics*. Oxford: Oxford University Press.
Widdershoven, G. and Smits, M.-J. (1996) 'Ethics and narratives', *The Narrative Study of Lives*, 4, 275–287.

15 Bioethics in academic rooms: hearing other voices, living in other rooms

Raymond G. de Vries

> 'Shoot, boy, the country's just fulla folks what knows everything, and don't understand nothing, just full of em.'
>
> (Capote, 2004: 46)

15.1 Introduction: the twilight of autonomy

Bioethics, born in the twentieth century, has been consumed with autonomy. Seen in its historical context, the occupation with autonomy makes sense. Bioethics began as an effort to 'speak truth to power' – it was a part of the 'rights movements' of the 1960s and 1970s (civil rights, the women's health movement, animal rights), with a desire to make a strong statement that the medical-industrial complex must not be allowed to run roughshod over the best interests of research subjects and patients. In the wake of atrocities committed on individuals in the name of science – the Nazi experiments, Tuskegee, the Willowbrook State School, the Jewish Chronic Disease Hospital, and abuses brought to light by Beecher and Pappworth (Rothman, 1992) – this emphasis on autonomy was fitting.

Although challenges to principlism in general, and autonomy in particular, are becoming more common in academic circles, autonomy remains more than just first in the alphabet among Beauchamp and Childress' (2013) four principles: autonomy, beneficence, non-maleficence, and justice. Spend some time googling 'autonomy' and you will find this principle described as the 'first among equals', or 'the pillar of bioethics'. Perhaps best known in this regard is the article by Gillon (2003), entitled: 'Ethics needs principles – four can encompass the rest – and respect for autonomy should be "first among equals"':

> I personally believe that emphasis on respect for autonomy is in many circumstances morally desirable and why I personally am inclined to see respect for autonomy as *primus inter pares*—first among equals—among the four principles. Firstly, autonomy—by which in summary I simply mean deliberated self rule; the ability and tendency to think for oneself, to make decisions for oneself about the way one wishes to lead one's

life based on that thinking, and then to enact those decisions—is what makes morality—any sort of morality—possible. For that reason alone autonomy—free will—is morally very precious and ought not merely to be respected, but its development encouraged and nurtured and the character traits or 'habits of the heart' that tend to promote its exercise should indeed be regarded and extolled as virtues. Secondly, beneficence and non-maleficence to other autonomous agents both require respect for the autonomy of those agents.

(Gillon, 2003: 310)

Most important, this idea of autonomy as *primus inter pares* is an idea that guides the work of ethics committees – clinical and research. This is confirmed, interestingly enough, in the many critiques of autonomy – most of which say something to the effect of 'we know the idea is unsupportable, but it still is widely used': 'The principle of respect for autonomy, while probably lacking an adequate philosophical basis, has come to dominate medical ethics in America today and forms the basis for much of the thinking about informed consent' (Hoehner, 2003: 598).

In this same critique, Hoehner (2003: 589) points out:

> Many ethical conundrums in medical ethics are the result of specific principles coming into conflict in specific cases. The principle of respect for autonomy is sometimes taken to be *the* overriding principle in modern medical ethical deliberation. However, respect for personal autonomy does not, and should not, exhaust moral deliberation.

It is worth noting that one of the fathers of principlism pointed out, more than 20 years ago (Childress, 1990: 16, emphasis added):

> ... the principle of respect for autonomy is very important in the firmament of moral principles guiding science, medicine, and health care. *However, it is not the only principle, and it cannot be assigned unqualified preeminence.* A clear example of overconcentration on the principle of respect for autonomy and its implications can be seen in research involving human subjects, where for years the subject's voluntary, informed consent tended to overshadow all other ethical issues. As a consequence, there was neglect of other important moral considerations that must be met prior to soliciting the potential subject's consent to participate – e.g., research design, probability of success, risk benefit ratio, and selection of subjects.

And yet, just a few years ago, Karnani (2008: 4) set forth the four principles as the most useful way to approach the ethical issues physicians face:

> It is for the readers to choose which method works best for them, based on their personal philosophy and past experience. For this author, 'the

four principles approach' has stood the test of time. It is much more than a mere 'checklist' when approaching an ethical quandary.

He then gives the nod to autonomy by pointing out that beneficence and, by implication, non-maleficence are difficult to apply:

Prospective application of the principle of beneficence can, at times, be difficult, because of the inexact nature of medicine and the likelihood of predicting good or bad consequences is imprecise, at best. However, these principles will be in play long after physicians practicing now are gone.

(ibid)

It is perhaps no surprise to find a heavy emphasis on autonomy in American bioethics, but even in Europe – where solidarity is an important value and where 'care ethics' offers an alternative to principlism – autonomy informs the theory and practice of bioethics. Rendtorff begins his 'investigation of basic ethical principles in European bioethics and biolaw' by asserting, 'the basic ethical principles, *autonomy*, dignity, integrity and vulnerability, can provide a normative framework for the protection of the human person in biomedical development' (2002: 235, emphasis added). Although Rendtorff's use of the term is more nuanced than that found in the work of American bioethicists – he points out, for example, that the concept of autonomy is limited by the 'tension between the human existence as an unencumbered self and the embodied, embedded, character of human experience' (ibid: 236) – nonetheless he cannot seem to part with the idea that autonomy is essential to proper bioethical thought and practice.

As we move into the twenty-first century, however, autonomy is losing its lustre. Not only are academic critiques of the principle multiplying, but several changes in the world, and in the world of medicine, are conspiring to spell the end of autonomy as the preeminent principle of bioethics.

The move of bioethics beyond national borders in the late twentieth and early twenty-first century – into other rooms with other voices – has made the use of the concept of autonomy increasingly problematic. Autonomy and its associated moral practices *seemed* to work well in Western, individualistic societies, but when research was exported to societies outside of the West, it became clear that the autonomy-based, principlist algorithm failed to capture non-Western conceptions of ethical obligations. In these societies, decisions about one's body and one's welfare are not appropriately taken solely by the individual in question; rather, these decisions are made in consort with others, or by others. This challenge to autonomy – generated *outside* of the West – has since come back to the West, generating questions about the usefulness of the concept, even in individualistic societies. It is time for Western bioethicists to learn that when we listen to other voices and live in other rooms our academic perspectives – and the approaches to clinical and research ethics supported by those perspectives – are forced to change. It is now clear that the goal of bioethics – to prevent harm to patients and research subjects – is subverted by ignorance of the cultural variety of moral norms (Chattopadhyay and De Vries, 2013).

15.2 Culture shock: the globalization of bioethics

Change does not come easy. Confronted with another way of thinking about ethical obligations, ethicists began to seek ways to defend the Western moral tradition as the ultimate and universal arbiter of the rights and wrongs of biomedicine. Nowhere is this more visible than in the great lengths defenders of autonomy and the principlist framework have gone to in defence of their ideas. Most interesting to me is use of the tortured notion of 'second-order autonomy' in an effort to demonstrate that all peoples everywhere share the Western idea of individual autonomy. Childress explains that the 'ideal of autonomy' must be distinguished from the conditions for autonomous choice:

> It is important for the moral life that people be competent, be informed and act voluntarily. But they may choose, for example, to yield their first order decisions (that is, their decisions about the rightness and wrongness of particular modes of conduct). For example, they may yield to their physicians when medical treatment is proposed or to their religious institutions in matters of sexual ethics. Abdication of first order autonomy appears to involve heteronomy, that is, rule by others. However, if a person autonomously chooses to yield first-order decision-making to a professional or to a religious institution, that person has exercised what may be called *second-order autonomy*.
>
> (Childress, 1990: 13, emphasis added)

How has this idea found its way into practice? In 2009, Flanagan organized a course *Providing Culturally Responsive Care to Asian Immigrants* for 'continuing medical education' (courses that must be followed by health care professionals in the United States in order to keep their licences up-to-date) . She calls on Childress' notion to account for cultural differences:

> Autonomy, individualism, and self-determination are values that are highly important in Western societies, especially in the U.S. Autonomy may be organized into two categories: first-order autonomy and second-order autonomy. First-order autonomy is what Westerners espouse and value: self-determination and autonomy in decision-making. Second-order autonomy, however, is prevalent in collectivistic societies where decision-making is group-oriented and takes into account another

decision-maker who is accorded authority and respect. In many Asian cultures, particularly if the family system is based on a patriarchal authority system, a male elder or male head who is regarded as the primary decision-maker is key in this process of informed consent. Therefore, the Western ideal of autonomy will have different connotations in cultures in which paternalism is valued.

(Flanagan, 2009)

It may look different, but autonomy remains. Trust me, she seems to say, underneath all that cultural baggage these people really *do* cherish autonomy.

Why is it so important to find Western morals under the ethical ideas of others? This line of reasoning from Bracanovic offers a clue:

For Hindus and Sikhs, we are told, collective and individual decision making are equally important and we have to respect them both. However, if we take the idea of respect for cultural diversity in bioethics really seriously, it remains unclear which element should have more weight in our decision making: collective (family) decision making or individual decision making?

(Bracanovic, 2011: 230)

Bracanovic fears that if we open the door to other moral traditions we face moral confusion. Therefore we must search for the ultimate moral truth that lies under the surface of other approaches to ethics. This is a curious perversion of the Shakespearean truism, spoken by Juliet to Romeo (Act II, Scene II):

What's in a name? that which we call a rose
By any other name would smell as sweet;

In this case, the logic is reversed: 'What's in a name? A rose is a flower, so let us call *all* flowers roses'.

The effort to save autonomy as a universally held idea is part of a larger effort to champion the idea that all people share a common – sometimes referred to as a 'minimal' – morality. Childress and his colleague Beauchamp, among others, make this argument, an argument that seems to be a manifestation of intellectual culture shock. Consider these comments from Bracanovic:

Morality – as the human capacity to judge about right and wrong – is undoubtedly of social and cultural origins and it develops in each individual as he or she internalizes culturally transmitted values.

(2011: 232)

Okay, moral ideas are products of culture. But a few sentences later he asserts:

> If standards of right and wrong lie outside biology, then they lie outside culture too . . . identification of values with cultural facts and evaluation on the basis of cultural origins is . . . fallacious.
>
> (ibid)

Ten Have and Gordijn make an interesting attempt to save a common morality. They point out that just because moral ideas originate in one culture that does not mean they cannot legitimately be applied in another: 'the genesis of an activity is not identical to its validity'. They illustrate their claim with reference to mathematics: 'Our number system is inherited from the Arab culture. We are not accusing the Arabs of colonialism since they have imposed their number system on us' (2011: 2).

Their odd analogy blurs the distinction between imposition (bioethics) and gradual adoption (Arabic numbers), and it makes a precarious equation between morality and mathematics. Can a complex and rich concept like morality be compared with an abstract system of written numbers? Nearly all people would agree that the number '911' means a discrete number of things – one more than '910' and one less than '912' – but can we find the same sort of agreement about the meaning of justice? And the morality/mathematics analogy falls apart completely when you let culture in. Nine hundred eleven may be just a number, but when you say '9/11' it means much more than a discrete number to people in certain societies (Metcalf, 2012). Furthermore, the question here is not about whether the 'colonized' are accusing the 'colonizers' of the 'imposition' of *their* moral system. The question is whether the imposition of Western moral theories and methods in non-Western cultures is appropriate and ethically justifiable (Chattopadhyay and De Vries, 2013).

Lurking at the core of arguments like these from Bracanovic, Ten Have, and Gordijn is a reasonable fear that ethical relativism and particularism will result in harm and exploitation of patients and research subjects. They are members of a tribe that insists on a common morality, a tribe that fears the consequences of recognizing the value of other moral traditions. Clifford Geertz names the members of this tribe 'anti-relativists'. In his important article – 'Anti anti-relativism' – Geertz reassures the anti-relativists that they need not fear relativism, because:

> the moral and intellectual consequences that are commonly supposed to flow from relativism – subjectivism, nihilism, incoherence, Machiavellianism, ethical idiocy, esthetic blindness, and so on – do not in fact do so and the promised rewards of escaping its clutches, mostly having to do with pasteurized knowledge, are illusory.
>
> (1984: 263)

Geertz goes on to defend the value of anthropology in revealing the variation in the moral and political lives of humans:

> [We anthropologists] have been the first to insist on a number of things: that the world does not divide into the pious and the superstitious; that there are sculptures in jungles and paintings in deserts; that political order is possible without centralized power and principled justice without codified rules; that the norms of reason were not fixed in Greece, the evolution of morality not consummated in England ... Most important, we were the first to insist that we see the lives of others through lenses of our own grinding and that they look back on ours through ones of their own ... The objection to anti-relativism is not that it rejects an it's-all-how-you-look-at-it approach to knowledge or a when-in-Rome approach to morality, but that it imagines that they can only be defeated by placing morality beyond culture and knowledge beyond both ... If we wanted home truths, we should have stayed at home.
>
> (ibid; 275–276)

The desire for universal principles on the part of anti-relativists may be the result of an unsophisticated understanding of relativism, Padela et al. explain. They point out that while

> all societies have rules governing property, there is a stunning variation in those rules, such that in some places one can "take" the property of another and use it for long periods of time without permission of the "owner." In other societies this same behaviour is defined as theft. While a universalist can claim property rules exist in all cultures, that claim is of little practical value on the ground in arbitrating property disputes.
>
> (2014: 8)

Even philosophers who acknowledge the myriad ways moral 'universals' are incarnated across human cultures (Macklin, 1999) fail to see that they are using 'lenses of their own grinding' to identify 'universal' moral principles.

Perhaps the effort to defend a common morality is the last gasp of a moral algorithm that was important in establishing the authority and value of the new field of bioethics, but is now out of date. In fact, other voices in different rooms are making it apparent that autonomy is dead.

15.3 The danger of autonomy

The emphasis on autonomy in Western bioethics is understandable. But making it *the* most important among all the principles that guide bioethical decisions and bioethics policy can do real harm. This is most notable in societies where Western ideas of autonomy are not a part of the moral fabric. Examples are rife. Allow me to bring just two to your attention.

Lanre-Abass (2012) uses case studies of Islamic women from Nigeria and Ghana who were asked to participate in research to explore 'issues relating to the autonomy of women in research ethics'. Below are illustrative comments from women in Northern Ghana who were asked to volunteer for a study:

> *First female respondent*: 'I will go and tell my husband that VAST people have come to ask me to join their study and so I want to let him know about it and if he says I should go, then I will go, but if he refuses, I won't go. That is why when he agrees I always come and join them'.
>
> *Second female respondent*: 'I discussed it with my husband and he agreed for me to participate and that was why I took part in it'.
>
> *Third female respondent*: 'I make that decision and then my husband will also agree and then he will also ask'.
>
> (Lanre-Abass, 2012: 177–178)

Examining these and other comments the author concludes:

> In many African cultural settings, the authority a woman has to give consent to participate or refuse to participate in research belongs to her family especially her husband . . . against this background . . . the Western conception of autonomy . . . is too individualistic to be applied in research settings in Africa and in religions such as Islam.
>
> (Lanre-Abass, 2012: 182)

She goes on to say that her research questions 'the model of an independent, rational will that is inattentive to emotions, communal life, reciprocity and the development of persons over time'. In the context of these African countries, 'theories that focus on autonomous agents and actions seem unrealistic' (ibid). Not just unrealistic, but harmful:

> Although respect for autonomy is an important principle for subjects/ participants in research, too much stress on autonomy can lead to an isolation of the subject and even distort people's understanding of the way individual decisions are embedded in a web of relationships and familial values. Also, stressing individual autonomy to the exclusion of other values can do real harm to families.
>
> (Lanre-Abass, 2012: 175)

In their study of 'international clinical trials and bioethics discourses in contemporary Sri Lanka', Sariola and Simpson explore the problems of Western bioethics in societies where they have no connection with existing moral traditions or the life-situation of those being asked to take part in research:

> A senior doctor who has been part of several clinical trials put the issue of medical paternalism as follows:
>
> > When conducting the trial you read all the information to the patients but the reality is different and patients are likely not to understand any of this. [For example, y]ou have a 15-year-old-boy and his illiterate father who have never been to Colombo and know nothing about clinical research. Is this really informed consent?!? Patients here are complicit and medicine is paternalistic. Also, patients here will be suspicious if you give them too much information. Patients will lose their trust in the doctor if you disclose too much. They think this doctor does not know what he is doing, and he will go to someone else who will take advantage of his compliancy. This is usually overlooked because you know that your intentions are good. But it's not about you knowing that you are ethical because it is easy to overlook your own actions if you are assessing yourself. Really you should have an external person to do that. With the backdrop of ignorance and paternalism, can we really use the same standards of ethics as in the West?
> >
> > (2011: 518)

A survey of reports about the way bioethics works in non-Western societies shows that principlism is honoured in name, but not in practice (Kingori, De Vries, and Orfali, 2013). Not just autonomy, but also Western notions of beneficence, non-maleficence, and justice are ignored or modified in order to accommodate the way ethical obligations work in these societies. This strategy appeases Western sponsors of research who want access to research subjects in non-Western countries (Petryna, 2009) but it does not promote the moral treatment of research subjects and patients.

If we permit other voices in other rooms to open our eyes to the problems with autonomy, we are better able to see the same problems in our own society. More than twenty years ago, Bosk (1992) pointed out that an emphasis on autonomy allowed those doing genetic counselling to abandon patients in a sea of information: 'Hey, *you* need to choose'. Seen in this light, the rejection of paternalism and the embrace of patient autonomy allow caregivers to flee from their professional responsibility.

Defenders of the value of autonomy celebrate its triumph over paternalism, but when we look closer, we find that a non-paternalistic autonomy is impossible. The information patients use to make decisions does not come in neutral, objective, value-free packages. Consider for a moment the information that informs consent.

I have a sociological interest in evidence-based medicine, or more precisely, the way evidence is created. I have been looking at the evidence about place of birth for a number of years and have been fascinated by the different kinds of 'evidence' used by caregivers and women in making decisions about the best way to bring a baby into the world. Most interesting is the way values 'infect' science. For example, when obstetricians study place of birth, their science shows home birth to be extremely dangerous; and when midwives do the same, their science shows that home birth is preferable for healthy women because hospital birth increases the chance of unneeded and harmful interventions (De Vries et al., 2013). Add to this that women do not come to the choice of place of birth *tabula rasa*, waiting to be convinced by the evidence – they come having been subject to stories of birth seen and heard in the cinema, TV, the print media (electronic and otherwise), and from friends and relatives. Interestingly, even well-known bioethicists are part of the well of information that (paternalistically?) influences women's choices. Commenting on a story of a tragic home birth attended by an incompetent midwife, on the 'Practical Ethics' blog, Lach De Crespigny and Julian Savulescu (2012) state:

> Maternal and perinatal mortality are truly tragic outcomes. Professionals must encourage women to deliver in a safe environment and also practice safe and competent obstetrics. The professional bodies and the law must do all they can to ensure this happens.
>
> Currently the homebirth debate focuses on such disaster. It is a terrible tragedy that Claire died foreseeably and avoidably in this manner. But the silent tragedies are not the deaths, but the long term disability that results from homebirth. And it is this risk that weighs most heavily against homebirth.
>
> What disability? When a baby is obstructed in labour at home, or born with hypoxic brain injury, the delay in transferring to a tertiary hospital may result in permanent severe disability that will persist for the rest of that person's life. In some cases, that disability was avoidable if the delivery had occurred in hospital. To take an extreme example, a person might be avoidably quadriplegic.
>
> Now what risk could a parent take to have 'a really lovely spontaneous birth at home' that justifies quadriplegia? One in 1000? One in 1000000? Anything?
>
> We contend that the choice to have 'a really lovely spontaneous birth at home' is only justified if it exposes the future child to zero risk of avoidable disability. And this is just never the case.
>
> Why else would modern obstetrics have been developed?

Overlooking the absurd claim that there must be 'zero' risk of avoidable disability to justify a woman's choice of birth place (zero risk can only be achieved if a woman decides not to get pregnant), it is clear that these two ethicists are unfamiliar with the data on the safety of home birth (Olsen and Clausen, 2012) and the dangers of hospital birth. Aside from that, notice how their marshalling of their 'facts' in an effort to help women make 'good choices' about birth shapes the (autonomous?) values of those same women.

Because it appears impossible to eradicate, we must rethink our attitude towards paternalism. Is paternalism necessarily a bad thing? Okay, none of us is fond of the gendered aspect of the term, but paternalism (or, if you like, maternalism[1] or parentism) implies a relationship that goes beyond the mere transfer of information. Do we not want the connection between caregiver and patient, between researcher and subject, to be something more than a contract?

Interestingly, in its articulation of the principles of bioethics, the *Belmont Report* spoke not of autonomy, but of 'respect for persons', an attitude that requires consideration of the variety of ways people understand the moral obligations of relationships. But 'respect for persons' is a squishy concept. In the hands of research ethicists, Belmont's rich idea was narrowed to 'autonomy', the right of a research subject (or patient) to choose or refuse. This translation of respect into autonomy is practical: it allows researchers to ignore the problems that are part and parcel of clinical research. The obligation of researchers to their subjects as (culturally located) persons is reduced to plying them with information. But here again, we find paternalism creeping in. Autonomy has replaced the overweening paternalism of medicine with a new kind of 'distant paternalism' where researchers, like the classic distant father, remain aloof and detached. The helplessness of research subjects in the face of medical power is transformed into helplessness in the face of information that is incomprehensible or misleading or both. We have yet to achieve a respect for persons where professional knowledge and responsibility meet the needs of subjects for honest and simple disclosure that is tailored to the specific needs of each person.

15.4 Living in a post-autonomy world

The demise of autonomy does not mean a return to the bad old days of paternalism. On the contrary, the cold concept of autonomy is gradually being replaced by the richer concepts of *respect* and *obligation*. These concepts recognize the power differential between doctor/patient and researcher/subject and offer a way to realize the obligations inherent in each role.

Consider this recent story from the *New York Times*. The topic was the recommendation of the United States Preventive Services Task Force to discontinue screening for ovarian cancer, a process that not only has *no* effect on the death rate from the disease, but also yields many false-positive results that lead to unnecessary surgeries with high complication rates. The article explains:

> Other medical groups, including the American Cancer Society and the American Congress of Obstetricians and Gynecologists, have for years been discouraging tests to screen for ovarian cancer. But some doctors continue to recommend screening anyway, and patients request it, clinging to the mistaken belief that the tests can somehow find the disease early enough to save lives. A report published in February in *Annals of*

Internal Medicine (Baldwin et al., 2012), based on a survey of 1,088 doctors, said that about a third of them believed the screening was effective and that many routinely offered it to patients.

(Grady, 2012)

What is the appropriate response here? Should patients and doctors be allowed to continue to behave in autonomous ways that are harmful? If relationships in health care are indeed nothing more than contracts, then *caveat emptor*! The *New York Times* article continues:

> Dr. Barbara A. Goff, a gynecologic oncologist at the Fred Hutchinson Cancer Research Center in Seattle and an author of the study last year that found doctors still in favor of screening [for ovarian cancer], said: 'If patients request it, then I think a lot of times physicians feel it's just easier to order the test, particularly if it's covered by insurance, rather than taking the time to explain why it may not be good, that it could lead to inappropriate surgery, could lead to harm. I don't think they think through the consequences'.

(ibid)

A second illustration comes from Rebecca Dresser (2012), a well-known American bioethicist and attorney, who, after her own experience of illness, wrote that she wished that her doctor had been willing to move beyond mere information exchange and *argue* with her about her choices. Although she does not use the word, she was asking that her doctor be more relational – dare I say, *paternalistic*. She explains:

> The old days of medical paternalism are gone. Today we have shared decision-making, in which doctors describe treatment options and patients choose the one they prefer.
>
> It sounds simple, but it's not. I learned this when I had to decide whether to have a feeding tube during cancer treatment. Doctors explained the tube's benefits and risks, then left it to me to decide. I said no. I had my reasons – I didn't want a foreign object in my body or an overnight stay in the hospital. I wanted to prove that I was tough enough to get through treatment without extra help.
>
> But this was a bad decision. As time passed, I became too weak to continue daily radiation sessions. People kept trying to get me to change my mind, and finally a nurse succeeded. Consenting to the tube was the right thing to do, but it took a lot of persuasion for me to accept that.
>
> Argument is a legitimate part of shared decision-making, but not everyone understands this. Some clinicians think that respect for autonomy means they should never disagree with a patient. Some think that it would be cruel to question what a seriously ill person says she wants. Some don't want to devote time to the hard conversations that produce good decisions.

> Patients avoid arguments, too. Many are too intimidated to take issue with anything a doctor says. But doctors aren't always right, and patients who are afraid to argue can pay the price . . . In everyday life, arguments with family and friends help us think through the consequences of our choices and sometimes change our minds. Patients and doctors should do the same for one another.
>
> (Dresser, 2012)

We must not forget that persons are more than information processors. For better or worse – and it *is* sometimes for worse – their values are shaped by stories, images, accounts, hunches, and intuitions. It is far too facile simply to ask that a person apply one's values to a decision about health care, or about participation in research. We must ask: 'Where do those values come from?' We must push to better understand how those values have been shaped, by whom, and for what purpose. This requires more than stripped down interaction between two autonomous individuals – it requires a relationship characterized by respect and obligation. Professionals must *respect* their patients (or research subjects), listening to what they have to say – and perhaps even learning something new about themselves as a result of the relationship – but there is no escaping the fact that they also have an *obligation* to use their knowledge in the best interest of their patients.

A recent essay by Gary Gutting (2012), on 'What work is really for', highlights the necessity of doing more than simply 'giving in' to a patient's values. In thinking about the inherent value of work Gutting proposes that life could be made 'more worthwhile – by producing only what makes for better lives. In turn, workers would have the satisfaction of producing things of real value.' But immediately he notices a problem:

> . . . who decides what is of real value? The capitalist system's own answer is *consumers*, free to buy whatever they want in an open market. I call this capitalism's own answer because it is the one that keeps the system operating autonomously, a law unto itself. It especially appeals to owners, managers and others with a vested interest in the system.
>
> But the answer is disingenuous. From our infancy the market itself has worked to make us consumers, primed to buy whatever it is selling regardless of its relevance to human flourishing. True freedom requires that we take part in the market as fully formed agents, with life goals determined not by advertising campaigns but by our own experience of and reflection on the various possibilities of human fulfillment. Such freedom in turn requires a liberating education, one centered not on indoctrination, social conditioning or technical training but on developing persons capable of informed and intelligent commitments to the values that guide their lives.

Because autonomy is never autonomy and because insistence on autonomy necessarily ignores the relationships that characterize human life, a declaration that autonomy is dead is long overdue. And we have been helped to this conclusion by living in other rooms and listening to other voices.

> 'Shoot, boy, the country's just fulla folks what knows everything, and don't understand nothing, just full of em.'
> Truman Capote, *Other Voices, Other Rooms*
> (Capote, 2004: 46)

Note

1 My spellchecker suggested that I replace maternalism with paternalism, making me think about why we don't use the term maternalism. Is it because it connotes a different kind of concern for the patient/research subject, a concern that we find legitimate?

References

Baldwin, L.-M., Trivers, K.F., Matthews, B., Andrilla, C.H.A., Miller, J.W., Berry, D.L., Lishner, D.M., Goff, B.A. (2012) 'Vignette-based study of ovarian cancer screening: Do U.S. physicians report adhering to evidence-based recommendations?', *Annals of Internal Medicine*, 156: 182–194.

Beauchamp T. and Childress, J. (2013) *Principles of Biomedical Ethics*, 7th edn, New York: Oxford University Press.

Bosk, C. (1992) *All God's Mistakes: Genetic Counseling in a Pediatric Hospital*, Chicago: University of Chicago Press.

Bracanovic, T. (2011) 'Respect for cultural diversity in bioethics. Empirical, conceptual and normative constraints', *Medicine, Health Care and Philosophy*, 14: 229–236.

Capote, T. (2004 [1948]) *Other Voices, Other Rooms*, London: Penguin Books.

Chattopadhyay, S., De Vries, R. (2013) 'Respect for cultural diversity in bioethics is an ethical imperative', *Medicine, Health Care and Philosophy*, 16: 639–645.

Childress, J. (1990) 'The place of autonomy in bioethics', *Hastings Center Report*, 20: 12–17.

De Crespigny, L. and Savulescu, S. (2012) 'The Continuing Tragedies of Home Birth and the Rights of the Future Child', 6 September. Available HTTP: <http://blog.practicalethics.ox.ac.uk/2012/09/the-continuing-tragedies-of-home-birth-and-the-rights-of-the-future-child/> (accessed 13 September 2013).

De Vries, R., Parachuri, Y., Lorenz, K., and Vedam, S. (2013) 'Moral science: Ethical argument and the production of knowledge about the safety of hospital and home birth', *Journal of Clinical Ethics*, 24(3): 225–238.

Dresser, R. (2012) 'Sunday Dialogue: Conversations Between Doctor and Patient', 25 August. Available HTTP: <http://www.nytimes.com/2012/08/26/opinion/sunday/sunday-dialogue-conversations-between-doctor-and-patient.html?pagewanted=all> (accessed 13 September 2013).

Flanagan, A. (2009) *Providing Culturally Responsive Care to Asian Immigrants* © 2009 CME Resource. Available HTTP: <http://www.netcegroups.com/440/Course_5487.pdf> (accessed 13 September 2013).

Geertz, C. (1984) 'Anti anti-relativism', *American Anthropologist*, 86: 263–278.

Gillon, R. (2003) 'Bioethics: Applying the basic principles to resolve an ethical dilemma', *Journal of Medical Ethics*, 29: 307–312.

Grady, D. (2012) 'Ovarian Cancer Screenings Are Not Effective, Panel Says', *New York Times* 10 September. Available HTTP: <http://www.nytimes.com/2012/09/11/health/research/ovarian-cancer-tests-are-ineffective-medical-panel-says.html?_r=2&ref=health&> (accessed 13 September 2013).

Gutting, G. (2102) 'What Work Is Really For', 8 September. Available HTTP: <http://opinionator.blogs.nytimes.com/2012/09/08/work-good-or-bad/> (accessed 13 September 2013).

Hoehner, P. (2003) 'Ethical aspects of informed consent in obstetric anesthesia – new challenges and solutions', *Journal of Clinical Anesthesia*, 15: 587–600.

Karnani, N. (2008) 'Applying the basic principles to resolve an ethical dilemma', *Northeast Florida Medicine Supplement*, January: 3–5.

Kingori, P., De Vries, R., and Orfali, K. (2013) Introduction to the special issue on bioethics in the field. *Social Science and Medicine*, 98: 260–263.

Lanre-Abass, B. (2012) 'Autonomy and interdependence: Quandaries in research ethics', *Health*, 4: 173–184.

Macklin, R. (1999) *Against Relativism: Cultural Diversity and the Search for Ethical Universals in Medicine*, Oxford: Oxford University Press.

Metcalf, A. (2012) 'The Mystery of "9/11"', *The Chronicle of Higher Education*, 11 September. Available HTTP: <http://chronicle.com/blogs/linguafranca/2012/09/11/the-mystery-of-911/> (accessed 13 September 2013).

National Commission for the Protection of Human Subjects of Biomedical and Behavioral Research, Department of Health, Education and Welfare (DHEW) (30 September 1978). *The Belmont Report* (DHEW pub. no. (OS) 78–0012). Washington, DC: United States Government Printing Office.

Olsen, O. and Clausen, J.A. (2012) 'Planned hospital birth versus planned home birth', *Cochrane Database of Systematic Reviews*, 9: CD000352. doi: 10.1002/14651858.CD000352.pub2.

Padela, A., Malik, A., Curlin, F., and De Vries, R. (2014) '[Re]considering respect for persons in a globalizing world', *Developing World Bioethics*, doi:10.1111/dewb.12045.

Petryna, A. (2009) *When Experiments Travel: Clinical Trials and the Global Search for Human Subjects*, Princeton, NJ: Princeton University Press.

Rendtorff, J.D. (2002) 'Basic ethical principles in European bioethics and biolaw: Autonomy, dignity, integrity and vulnerability. Towards a foundation of bioethics and biolaw', *Medicine, Health Care and Philsophy*, 5: 235–244.

Rothman, D. (1992) *Strangers at the Bedside*, New York: Basic Books.

Sariola, S. and Simpson, B. (2011) 'Theorising the "human subject"' in biomedical research: International clinical trials and bioethics discourses in contemporary Sri Lanka', *Social Science & Medicine*, 73: 515–521.

Ten Have, H. and Gordijn, B. (2011) 'Travelling bioethics', *Medicine, Health Care and Philosophy*, 14: 1–3.

Index

Advance care planning (see advance decisions)
Advance decisions 3–4, 87–102, 105–119
Advance directives (see advance decisions)
American bioethics (see also principlism) 1, 2, 12, 13, 17, 18, 19, 22, 23, 25, 26, 37, 79, 193, 194
Anthropology 23, 25, 27, 29, 44, 198
Authenticity xviii, 4, 59, 112–113, 115, 116
Autonomy 2, 4, 5, 7, 13, 22, 23, 24, 27–28, 29, 44, 73, 78, 79, 81, 84, 92–93, 94, 100, 105, 106, 108, 110, 111, 113, 115, 116, 129, 148, 149, 150, 151, 153, 171, 182, 184, 187, 192–206

Beneficence (see also principlism; welfare) 2, 64, 81, 129, 150, 151, 192, 193, 194, 200
Best interests (see welfare)
Bioethics (see also medical ethics; teaching medical ethics)
  And expertise 29, 33, 35, 38–39, 137, 145
  And bioethicists 33, 34–35, 40, 77
  As a discipline 6, 12–13, 18, 32, 33–34, 37, 39, 73, 79, 82, 84, 159, 165, 166, 180, 189
  As applied xviii, 29, 35, 36, 38
  As critical xviii, 20, 45, 48, 77, 78, 82, 160, 163, 164
  As general or specialised xviii, 28–29, 34, 36
  As global 6, 12, 13–14, 21, 36, 37, 148, 195–198
  As integrated 28, 34
  As inter/multidisciplinary 12–13, 33, 34, 79, 80
Biotechnology 21, 43, 45

Capacity 88, 89, 90, 91, 92, 93, 94, 96, 98, 99, 100, 105, 106, 107, 108, 109, 115, 116, 120, 129, 132, 133, 162, 182, 195

Care ethics 1, 5, 14, 20, 24, 25, 29, 151, 153, 180–181, 182, 183, 185, 188, 190, 194
Clinical ethics support 4, 78, 79, 122, 136–147 (see also moral case deliberation)
Commercialisation 15, 26, 28 (see also commodification; economics; justice)
Commodification 15, 26
Common morality 7, 38, 197–198 (see also principlism)
Communication 44, 106, 113, 115, 116, 143, 171
Community 5, 7, 112, 114, 129
Competence (see capacity)
Confidentiality 123, 139, 160, 162, 171
Consensus 23, 27, 81, 133, 136, 138, 139, 160, 165, 166
Consent 32, 44, 81, 88–89, 93, 105, 107, 108, 121, 123, 148, 149, 150, 152, 153, 154, 162, 193, 196, 199, 200, 203
Consequentialism 15, 81

Democracy 31, 45, 48, 69, 87, 97, 99, 100
Deontology 22, 65, 67, 81
Determinism 45
Dignity 2, 22, 23, 24, 25–26, 27, 29, 77, 111, 194
Disability 24, 25, 76, 77, 121, 126, 129, 201
Diversity 2, 6, 14, 21, 36, 136, 145, 196 (see also pluralism)

Economics xvi, xviii, 2, 15, 25, 34, 46, 47, 48, 49
Emotion 26, 32, 64, 81, 109, 111, 120, 128, 129, 130, 131, 133, 139, 172, 173, 174, 175, 177, 188, 199
Empirical bioethics xvii, 4, 6, 12, 20, 28–29, 32, 34, 38, 48, 105–119, 120–135, 154, 180
End-of-life decisions 28, 74–76, 78, 79, 82, 83, 87–102, 105–119, 120–135, 140, 144

Index

Enhancement 15
Equity 14, 128, 132, 148, 153 (see also justice)
Erasmus Mundus Master of Bioethics 13, 21, 189
Ethical competence 139, 159, 160, 163, 164, 165, 169, 171, 173, 176
Ethical relativism 148, 197–198
Ethical sensitivity xvii, 14, 68, 124, 133, 144, 166, 169, 175
European Association of Centres of Medical Ethics (EACME) xvi–xix, 1, 2, 6, 13, 17–21, 148, 180
European Society for Philosophy of Medicine and Healthcare (ESPMH) 20–21
European Union/Community xvi, 13, 19, 21–22, 25, 29, 79, 88, 105
European Court of Human Rights 120
Euthanasia 28, 31, 91
Existentialism 22, 23

Family 106, 109, 111, 112, 128, 129, 132, 140, 143, 144, 150, 152, 153, 174, 175, 196, 199, 204
Feminist bioethics 5, 6, 14, 36, 181, 182
Four principles approach (see principlism)
Futility 111, 131, 140

General Medical Council 77, 110, 121, 165
Genetics 28, 31, 43–52, 95, 139, 161, 200
Genome 35, 43, 45, 48

Hermeneutics 136–147, 180, 183, 185, 188
Hidden curriculum 5, 164, 167–168, 170, 172–173, 175 (see also teaching medical ethics)
History of bioethics 11–16, 17–30, 35, 37, 150
Hope xviii, 43, 45, 68, 139, 140, 143, 144, 163
Human rights (see rights)
Humanities 3, 15, 160, 175, 176, 177
Humanity 24, 25, 28, 34, 55, 111, 130

Identity 1, 3, 27, 33, 40, 94–99, 100, 113, 139, 165, 171, 173, 174, 175, 176
Incapacity (see capacity)
Incompetence (see capacity)
Integrity 15, 23, 57, 83, 160, 161, 171, 183, 194
International Association of Bioethics (IAB) 13, 14, 17, 20, 21, 33, 34
Intimacy 80, 120, 121, 127, 128–130, 131, 133
Intuition 4, 120–121, 125, 127, 128, 130–131, 133, 134, 181, 184, 204

Justice xviii, 2, 3, 7, 13, 15, 24, 36, 48, 81, 84, 100, 137, 138, 140, 144, 160, 162, 163, 164, 173, 176, 192, 197, 198, 200

Law xvi, xviii, 3–4, 6, 7, 12, 13, 19–20, 21, 23, 24, 25, 33, 34, 44, 73–86, 87–102, 105–106, 110, 114, 115, 121, 131, 132, 133, 152, 161–162, 164, 165, 166, 168, 171, 172, 180, 189, 194, 201, 204 (see also European Union/Community; European Court of Human Rights)
Lasting power of attorney 91, 106
Libertarianism 15, 115, 116
Liberty 15, 24, 28

Market (see economics)
Mediation 136, 143, 145
Medical ethics xvi, xvii, 2, 6, 11–12, 14, 15, 23, 27, 36, 48, 65, 67, 75, 77, 148, 149, 151, 154, 159–179, 181, 185, 189, 190, 193 (see also bioethics; teaching medical ethics)
Moral case deliberation 4, 136–147
Moral character (see virtue ethics)
Moral dilemma 2, 4, 5, 6, 11, 15, 63–66, 68, 73, 77, 80, 83, 92, 115, 137, 138, 139, 141, 143, 167
Moral perspectives xvi, xvii, 12, 25, 32, 34, 35, 36, 48, 97, 107, 111, 112, 115, 132, 138, 139, 140, 143, 144, 145, 148, 149, 150, 154, 173, 181, 183, 185, 186, 188, 189, 190, 195
Moral reasoning 26, 27, 77, 79, 134, 160–161, 162, 164, 165, 166, 167, 168, 169, 173, 188, 196
Moral uncertainty 96, 130, 160, 172, 175, 181, 182, 189

Narrative and narrative ethics 5, 6, 73–74, 82–84, 125, 126, 129, 133, 141, 149, 183, 190
Neonates 76, 120–135, 139, 143, 144
Non-maleficence (see also principlism) 2, 151, 187, 192, 193, 194, 200
Nuffield Council on Bioethics 13, 79, 121, 122
Nursing ethics (see care ethics)

Objectivity 4, 121, 138, 141, 143, 182, 188, 200

Paediatrics 4, 74–76, 120–135, 169, 174, 175, 182
Palliative care 107, 108, 114, 139, 140, 144, 152, 169 (see also end-of-life decisions)

Parents 4, 57, 74–75, 98, 120–135, 139–140, 144, 175, 201, 202
Paternalism 24, 27, 89, 114, 149, 183–186, 196, 200, 201, 202, 203, 205
Patient preferences 44, 105–119, 121, 123
Persistent vegetative state 77, 90, 92, 111
Personalised medicine xvii, 3, 43–52
Personalism xviii, 22, 23
Personhood 2, 3, 22, 23, 26, 27, 29, 44–45, 87–102, 202
Pharmaceutical industry 32, 43, 45, 46, 47, 48, 49
Philosophy xvi, xvii, 3, 6, 7, 11, 12, 17, 19, 20, 22, 23, 26, 27, 33, 34, 35, 36, 38, 39, 59, 73, 80, 82, 87, 93, 94, 100, 130, 136, 137, 140–142, 143, 145, 152, 164, 166, 176, 193, 198
Pluralism xviii, 2, 6, 7, 17, 18, 19, 21, 22, 79, 81, 136, 141, 144
Power 7, 14, 36, 40, 54, 64, 68, 87, 106, 108, 128, 133, 167, 180, 181, 182, 183, 186, 192, 198, 202 (see also lasting power of attorney)
Principlism 2, 5, 7, 13, 14, 17, 19, 22, 23, 26, 27–28, 35, 36, 37, 114, 180, 182, 184, 185, 187, 188, 190, 192–206
Privacy 29, 140, 150, 187
Professional ethics 12, 23, 65, 74, 75, 77, 108, 110, 113, 143, 149, 160, 161, 162, 171, 189, 201
Psychoanalysis 3, 53–72
Public health 5, 36, 47, 48, 49, 55, 57, 66, 68, 106, 110, 153, 160, 161

Quality of life 77, 92, 93, 129

Rationality 93, 131, 134, 150, 151, 152, 154, 199
Reciprocity 73, 153, 199
Relational ethics 1, 2, 5, 22, 23, 24, 25, 27, 28, 29, 67, 80–81, 98, 110, 114, 115, 116, 149, 153, 181, 182–183, 185, 186, 188, 189, 190, 199, 202, 203, 204, 205
Relativism (see ethical relativism)
Religion xvi, xviii, 6, 12, 18, 55, 58, 59, 66, 97, 139, 140, 144, 195, 199 (see also theology)

Research ethics 15, 21, 22, 31, 32, 34, 35, 39, 43–52, 53–72, 79, 105, 107, 123, 154, 192, 193, 194, 195, 197, 199, 200, 202, 204, 205 (see also empirical bioethics)
Respect for autonomy (see autonomy)
Rights 21, 22, 25, 44, 75, 79, 81, 87, 88, 89, 94, 95, 105, 106, 111, 120, 150, 160, 162, 192 (see also European Court of Human Rights)

Self-determination (see autonomy)
Shared decision-making 111, 120–122, 128–133, 203
Social contract 24, 28, 67, 116, 151, 202, 203
Social ethics 29, 148, 153, 154
Social science (see also empirical bioethics) 4, 6, 7, 12, 15, 29, 32, 33, 34, 35, 83, 105–119, 120–135, 153, 200
Solidarity 2, 4, 5, 7, 22, 24–25, 27, 28, 29, 111, 148, 153, 194

Teaching medical ethics 5, 11, 21, 159–179, 180–191
Theology (see also religion) 2, 12, 17, 18, 19
Transparency 45, 48, 133, 140, 144, 187
Transplantation 28, 64, 95
Trust 24, 27, 144, 149, 150, 153, 162, 196, 200

Universal xviii, 26, 28, 37, 95, 141, 195, 196, 198

Virtue ethics 7, 14, 25, 81, 84, 159, 163, 164, 171, 173, 176, 180, 183, 184–185, 190, 193
Vulnerability xvii, xviii, 4, 23, 26, 27, 29, 106, 108, 112, 163, 181, 182, 194

Welfare 3, 4, 24, 25, 27, 46, 53, 67, 88, 89, 90, 91, 92, 98, 99, 100, 109, 120, 121, 124, 127, 128, 129, 130, 132, 133, 149, 150, 182, 192, 194
Well-being (see welfare)
Wisdom 17, 141, 163, 164, 171, 173, 176 (see also virtue ethics)
Withdrawing and/or withholding treatment 74, 75, 77, 92, 105, 106, 107, 108, 109, 110, 111, 115 (see also end of life decisions)

For Product Safety Concerns and Information please contact our EU representative GPSR@taylorandfrancis.com
Taylor & Francis Verlag GmbH, Kaufingerstraße 24, 80331 München, Germany

www.ingramcontent.com/pod-product-compliance
Lightning Source LLC
Chambersburg PA
CBHW070605300426
44113CB00010B/1406